REFORMATION, CONFORMITY AND DISSENT

GEOFFREY NUTTALL

REFORMATION
CONFORMITY
AND DISSENT

Essays in honour of
Geoffrey Nuttall

EDITED BY
R. BUICK KNOX

LONDON
EPWORTH PRESS

Enquiries should be addressed to
The Methodist Publishing House
Wellington Road
Wimbledon
London SW19 8EU

7162 0288 3

Printed in Great Britain by
Ebenezer Baylis and Son Ltd
The Trinity Press, Worcester, and London

CONTENTS

PREFACE

————◦◦◦◦————

THE suggestion that the work of Geoffrey Nuttall as scholar, teacher, and Christian minister should be saluted in a volume of essays arose spontaneously from many sources. In the end, the task of translating the proposal into a worthy tribute was committed to me as a colleague in the ministry of the United Reformed Church.

The readiness with which eminent and busy scholars responded to requests for contributions to the volume gave immediate proof of the high esteem in which Dr Nuttall is held. It was also clear that many other scholars would have been willing to add their tribute; indeed, a further volume could easily have been filled with worthy contributions.

Much practical assistance in the production of the volume has been received from many quarters. The United Reformed Church History Society, of which Dr Nuttall was the first President, has provided much advice and financial help and has also allowed the Society's 1977 Lecture by Dr Christopher Hill to be included in this tribute. New College, London, has shown its esteem for its distinguished member of staff by generous financial assistance, and help has also been given by the Coward Trust and from among the members of Friends Historical Society. The Methodist Publishing House, through the Chairman of its Editorial Sub-Committee, the Rev. John Stacey, has taken a deep interest in the project from the very start and the format of the volume shows the care and skill put into its production.

Dr Nuttall's many friends join the contributors to this volume in hoping that this tribute will give him pleasure and assure him of their gratitude for his indefatigable and scholarly labours.

R. BUICK KNOX

Westminster College, Cambridge

ABBREVIATIONS

BQ   *Baptist Quarterly*

CQ   *Congregational Quarterly*

DNB   *Dictionary of National Biography*

JEH   *Journal of Ecclesiastical History*

JFHS   *Journal of Friends Historical Society*

JTS   *Journal of Theological Studies*

TBHS   *Transactions of the Baptist Historical Society*

TCHS   *Transactions of the Congregational Historical Society*

In the references in footnotes, the place of publication, unless otherwise indicated, is London.

I

Geoffrey Fillingham Nuttall

JOHN HUXTABLE

GEOFFREY NUTTALL is chiefly renowned as an exact and sympathetic historian of English Puritanism. The list of weighty books and learned papers bears witness to that lasting preoccupation; but even a casual glance at the table of contents of the *Puritan Spirit* shows that the scholar who has so faithfully stuck to his last has found time and energy to become more than usually well acquainted with many other centuries and concerns; indeed in this volume 'Puritan' suggests a large umbrella of extraordinary spread. Yet if the use of the adjective is in this case loose, the spread of the umbrella well befits the author's wide interests. And has he not for years taught elementary Hebrew with more than usual success at arousing in some of his students continuing interest in the subject; has he not adequate Italian to penetrate the beauties of the *Paradiso* and write a book about it; did not the days in Marburg perfect his German and arouse a lasting interest in German culture; in fact does he not in many ways illustrate the truth of the old adage that if you have done Oxford Greats you can probably do anything else to which you care to turn your mind?

'Piety' is not a popular word nowadays; nor is 'pious' an adjective often used in praise; but you cannot understand Geoffrey Nuttall without using such words in their proper sense. In the Foreword to his *Richard Baxter* there occur these words: 'the late Dr F. J. Powicke, whose two-volume *Life* forms the last critical biography of Baxter, first invited me to read Baxter, indeed urged me so solemnly that I could not but feel he looked on me as his Elisha.' That sense of being entrusted with a task, so marked in this prolonged study of all that belongs to Baxter and his works, is characteristic of Geoffrey Nuttall in so many other ways. Whether it were lecturing to students, preaching to a village congregation or a university, lecturing to some specialist audience or attending to a librarian's chores, the task once undertaken had to be discharged to the best of his ability; 'once undertaken' also fills in a detail of the picture, for he sometimes needs a good deal of persuasion that a suggested task really is on his plate. Nevertheless, once accepted, it will be done.

> A charge to keep I have,
> A God to glorify . . .

For that attention to duty arises, I judge, from more than an academic's proper sense of responsibility, though in part, of course, it is just that. It springs without doubt from a deep Christian conviction and faith which is principally understood in the light of the Puritans whom he knows so well. To read *Visible Saints* is to observe an understanding of the Gospel and the Church and to breathe an atmosphere of devotion in which Geoffrey Nuttall is entirely at home. To be rooted in the Bible, to be open to the leading of the Holy Spirit, to be in convenant fellowship with some local group of Congregational folk is sufficient. He shares their dislike of read prayers, distrusts the use of symbols in worship, regards the Church of England as too 'royalist' not to mention too episcopal for a Puritan, and would find it, at least initially, difficult to like anyone whose Christian names were Charles Stewart.

To some extent this means that he looks at modern Church life from an unusual angle. As one deeply committed to reconciliation, he welcomes the removal of obstacles to understanding, but is not much interested in and rather suspicious of anything that could be called 'organic unity'. No doubt the formation of the United Reformed Church in 1972 brought his churchmanship too near to Presbyterianism, about which his researches had made him antipathetic; but no doubt after much heart-search he did not hold back from exercising his ministry within the newly-formed Church. What elements there were in that judgement none can tell; I am convinced that at least one element in it was his readiness to see that change there is bound to be, nor should it necessarily be resisted, provided that those proposing changes and those accepting them are clear what they are doing and why. The historian's involvement with a beloved past does not and must not inhibit living in the present.

Geoffrey Nuttall was born at Colwyn Bay on 8th October, 1911. His father was a general practitioner. Among his forbears on either side he could number several who had been Congregational ministers. After schooldays at Bootham's, he entered Balliol College, Oxford, and read Greats. At a very early stage he had set his heart on the ministry, and he entered Mansfield College as soon as his Balliol course was completed. After a year at Marburg, he was ordained to the ministry at Warminster Congregational Church in 1938. Then followed two years 1943-5 at Woodbrooke, successively as Research fellow and Lecturer. It was during these years that the research was done which resulted in *The Holy Spirit in Puritan Faith and Experience*, for which the Oxford D.D. was awarded.

Ever since 1945 Geoffrey Nuttall has been Lecturer in Church History at New College, London; this college is an institution associated with London University, and Geoffrey Nuttall has been for many years a recognized teacher in the Faculty of Theology. His reputation as a scholar and his care for academic standards has made him a valued and occasionally formidable member of the Board of Studies in Theology. A. M. Fairbairn, first Principal of Mansfield College, Oxford, used to claim that one advantage of having a theological college associated with a university faculty of theology was that the influence of the faculty would be to maintain academic standards, which theological colleges, if left to themselves, might be tempted to allow to decline to meet the average ability of candidates for the ministry. It has been no small part of Geoffrey Nuttall's very distinguished service to New College that he has himself been a witness to that combination of scholarship and devotion which are the marks of the best ministers. He has taught by example as well as precept. To the less able, provided he be willing, he could be as encouraging as he could be wrathful in his rebuke to the more able who slacked. Within the college both on corporate occasions and in personal dealings with students, he has had an incalculable influence on several generations of men and women now in the ministry. His anxiety to maintain proper academic standards and a rather traditional pattern of ministerial training makes him at least cautious about, if not openly critical of, a good many new ways of ministerial and theological training; but in a day when a minister is apt to be trained to be a jack of all trades and master of none, who shall say that such influence was misplaced? Certainly during this quarter century, Geoffrey Nuttall has supervised and examined a great deal of research work. Many universities, in addition to London, have invited him to be an examiner and the University of Wales in 1969 made him an honorary D.D. When he was Chairman of the Board of Studies in Theology and Dean of the Faculty of Theology in London University, he displayed an administrative flair which few had suspected. He was also honoured by a wider circle of scholars when he was elected as President of the Ecclesiastical History Society in 1972.

For many years he has been the Librarian of New College, London, and his knowledge of and care for old books, of which the College has a number of great value, prompted a zeal for the library's good order. The large collection of funeral sermons are often combed through to cull this or that precious detail of some long-forgotten divine of whose importance he was aware. The Doddridge manuscripts are alike carefully preserved and closely studied. Dr Williams' Library has a special place in his interest and to its concern he has given a great deal of thought and time; and it is one of his regrets that he has had less than he wished to do with the Congregational Library in Farringdon Street, London.

It was once said of Robert F. Horton, the once famous minister of Lyndhurst Road Church, Hampstead, that when he preached he sounded like a combination of an Oxford don and a Salvation Army Officer; I have often recalled that remark when I have heard Geoffrey Nuttall preaching, whether in college chapel or elsewhere. The two university sermons in the *Puritan Spirit* are evidence of his capacity to state a case, of his insight into Scripture and of a certain fearlessness in applying its meaning to the condition of his hearers. Sermons in college chapel, however, are more intimate and the preacher may speak even more directly to those whom he knows well; and it was in this context that colleagues and students alike heard sermons that stretched the mind, reached the heart and stirred the spirit. The Bible was interpreted with an originality that arose from loving and diligent study, *always* studied in the Hebrew and Greek, and for preference read from the Authorized Version, the theme developed with an artist's clarity and illustrated often from some little known poem or some homely incident, and the message driven home with a controlled passion which inevitably moved the heart. Geoffrey would approve that phrase 'moved the heart', for academic as he is, he knows that religion is as much of the heart as of the head and that emotion and will as much as intellect are involved in lively faith. There is surely something of Baxter here. Those who have not sampled these sermons may catch something of their quality by reading *The Life of Heaven* and *Better than Life*.

If in many ways Geoffrey Nuttall seems to be conservative, looking with affection and loyalty to a period three hundred years or so past, that should not disguise a basic radicalism in outlook. In an earlier book, *The Holy Spirit in Puritan Faith and Experience*, it seemed to some readers at least as if the more radical the group the more he sympathized with it. Whether that be a sound judgement or not, it is clear that a good deal of Puritan radicalism rubbed off on him. His sympathy with the Society of Friends and his advocacy of Christian pacifism and total abstinence, his concern about liberty and his hatred of slavery all derive no doubt from his basic Christian discipleship; but here as elsewhere that is understood in the light of the Puritan ideal. Not that he is an uncritical admirer or advocate of anything! He can discomfit pacifists by illustrating on what different grounds Christians have held pacifist convictions; and the less wise ecumenist will be plainly reminded of those real obstacles which enthusiasm is apt to discount. That spirit betokens an honesty which will allow no trifling with truth.

It is said you have to live or to work with someone really to know him. For the eleven years of my Principalship of New College, London, Geoffrey Nuttall was a colleague. From him I received much loyalty and affection and still do. A mere recitation of the titles of his published works or a bald description of his interests and activities would miss the unusual mixture of qualities that comprise his character: gentleness with children and old folk, openness in dealing with all, sensitiveness to beauty and friendship, costly determination to oppose evil, stern discipline with himself and, where necessary, with others, and withal the simplicity that is in Jesus Christ.

'I have tried to combine honesty and frankness with the glow of conviction': so Geoffrey Nuttall *wrote* in the Preface to *The Reality of Heaven*. That ambition covered much more than the writing of one book; and as well as any other phrase I know it describes the man.

II

Johannes Sleidan and Reformation History

A. G. DICKENS

APART from being the fullest, broadest and most famous contemporary narrative of the Protestant Reformation, the *Commentaries*[1] of Johannes Sleidan have a long-term interest, since they foreshadow the problems of later historians working in the classical-humanist tradition. The present essay will accord special attention to Sleidan's relationship with that tradition. What limitations were imposed by pagan mentors when he came to depict the religious movements of his day? And given his remarkably international range, what complications arose from his vernacular culture, which happened to be French rather than German or Italian? Again, how should we regard his protestations concerning the 'truth and candour' of his own work? Did he really achieve his obviously sincere ambition to relate events impartially, 'as they had really happened'? What view of the historian's task and what scheme of world-history underlay his view of his own times; and whence did he derive these concepts? Why did he stress so heavily the political aspects of the Reformation while paying so little attention to the interior life? What is his usefulness as a historian of mass-movements? Did he significantly transcend the social prejudices of his class and his patrons? Which successors did he influence, and why was he able to set some durable patterns of historiography stretching into our own day?

Though Sleidan's life-story (1506–56) is not our main

---

[1] *J. Sleidani de statu religionis et reipublicae Carolo Quinto Caesare commentarii*, Strasbourg 1555.

concern, his writings cannot be understood in isolation from a career as rich in political contacts as in literary influences.[2] His very name Sleidanus betrays the modish humanism of the period, since he was born with the surname Philippson or Philippi, but restyled himself by reference to his birthplace: Schleiden in the northern Eifel. From the beginning his fellow townsman and school-companion Johann Sturm, destined to an equal eminence in German cultural history, exercised no little influence upon his career. In 1519 Sleidan went on to Liège, whither he was followed a couple of years later by Sturm. There they both entered into a fine heritage of humanism at the school of St Jerome, founded in 1496 by the Brethren of the Common Life in the fine tradition of Agricola and Hegius. Thence the two young scholars proceeded in 1524 to a more advanced classical academy, the Trilingual College recently (1517) established by Jerome Busleiden at Louvain. Sturm remained there almost until he left for France in 1529, but some years earlier Sleidan had been sent by his parents to study in Cologne. Around this time, the dating of his movements remains imprecise, but he is known to have tutored the son of the local overlord of Schleiden – and Sturm's early benefactor – Count Dietrich of Manderscheid. We also know for certain that Sleidan was back at Liège in the spring of 1530, when he wrote the first of his letters still extant.[3] Its recipient was Rutgerus Rescius, his former pro-

---

[2] The standard biography is still W. Friedensburg, *Johannes, Sleidanus. Der Geschichtsschreiber und die Schicksalsmächte der Reformationszeit (Schriften des Vereins für Reformationsgeschichte)*, Jahrgang 52, nr. 157, Leipzig 1935, which improved upon the thesis by P. Welz, *Etude sur Sleidan, historien de la Réformation*, Strasbourg 1862. H. Baumgarten in *Allgemeine deutsche Biographie* xxxiv, 454–61 remains useful, but his major contribution was to edit *Sleidans Briefwechsel*, Strasbourg and London 1881, cited below as *Briefwechsel*. His earlier volume *Uber Sleidans Leben und Briefwechsel*, Strasbourg and London 1878, was in effect a preparatory compilation for this latter. Other indispensable aids are A. Hasenclever (n. 5 below) and E. Menke-Glückert (n. 3 below), the latter being of especial value for the Melanchthon-Sleidan relationship. Modern textual criticism of the *Commentaries* may be said to have begun in 1824 with Ranke's *Zur Kritik neuerer Geschichtsschreiber*, 2 edn. Leipzig 1874, 65–70, and it was greatly extended in 1843 by the still useful work of Theodor Paur, cited in n. 35 below. For the historiographical background see H. Ritter von Srbik, *Geist und Geschichte vom deutschen Humanismus bis zur Gegenwart*, 3 edn. Munich and Salzburg 1964, i. ch. 3; and for general background, C. Schmidt, *La vie et les travaux de Jean Sturm*, Strasbourg 1855 photo-reprinted by de Graaf at Nieuwkoop 1970. For further items see K. Schottenloher, *Bibliographie zur deutschen Geschichte* 6 vols., Leipzig 1933–9, ii, nos. 20133–20179.

[3] *Briefwechsel*, 1–3. Cf. E. Menke-Glückert *Die Geschichtsschreibung der Reformation und Gegen-Reformation*, Leipzig 1912, 71.

fessor of Greek at Louvain, and it significantly shows the young man as a devout admirer of Melanchthon's all-conquering scholarship.

Three years later he followed Sturm to France, and at Paris and Orleans he continued to the Licentiate those legal studies through which many a young humanist raised himself to courtly, diplomatic or municipal office. Though Sleidan called himself *homo Germanus*,[4] his career and writings represented an early phase in the colonization of western Germany by French culture. Recommended by Sturm to Cardinal Jean du Bellay, bishop of Paris, he became in 1537 that prelate's secretary, and thus an agent of the anti-Habsburg group led by the Cardinal and his able brothers, Guillaume and Martin. Accomplished statesmen, the du Bellays had served French interests by promoting the divorce-suit of Henry VIII and by exploring the possibilities of alliance between the French crown and the Lutheran states. And though by 1537 King Francis I had decisively turned against Lutheranism, the du Bellays remained something more than a political faction, for they were culti-vated Erasmian reformists who at once patronized Rabelais and maintained contact with Melanchthon and Bucer. In short, the young German scholar achieved intellectual maturity in the same adventurous atmosphere as that breathed a few years earlier by Calvin. Incidentally, the surviving correspondence of Sleidan – doubtless a small remnant of the whole – includes several letters to Calvin: one in 1539 and others in 1553-5.[5] Some of them show that Sleidan joined the great network which kept the Genevan leader so supremely well informed on European affairs.

---

[4] In his preface to Comines (1548; see below n. 8) he asks *Quaerat aliquis unde haec de Cominaeo tibi, homini Germano?* He then describes his friendship with a former associate of Comines, Matthew of Arras, who had told him much about the historian, and had also read Sleidan's own manuscript.

[5] On Sleidan's French connections see V. L. Bourrilly, 'Jean Sleidan et le Cardinal du Bellay' in *Société de l'histoire du Protestantisme français*, I (1901), 225–42; and A. Hasenklever, *Sleidan-Studien. Die Entwicklung der politischen Ideen Johann Sleidans bis zum Jahre 1545*, Bonn 1905. On the du Bellays see especially *Mémoires de Martin et Guillaume du Bellay*, ed. V.-L. Bourrilly and F. Vindry, 4 vols. Paris 1908–19. The most interesting of Sleidan's letters to Calvin is that of 2 April 1554 (*Briefwechsel*, 266–9), in which he includes a report on England and his English friends. All this does not make him a Calvinist or even cause him to stress Calvinism in his *Commentaries*. Cf. Friedensburg, op. cit., 60.

Meanwhile Guillaume du Bellay had assembled voluminous materials for a large-scale history of France to be arranged on the pattern of Livy, but his influence upon Sleidan can hardly have been more than confirmatory, since Sleidan's letter to Rescius shows him already a student of earlier French historians and an enthusiastic observer of recent and contemporary affairs. At the end of 1536, just before the German humanist joined the du Bellays, Johann Sturm had left France for Strassburg, there to become internationally famous as a teacher and educational theorist. Sleidan preserved contact with him, as also in numerous letters with his unrelated namesake Jacob Sturm, the distinguished leader of the Strassburg city council. Having in 1540–1 personally witnessed the breakdown of the Catholic-Protestant conferences at Hagenau and Regensburg, Sleidan seems to have become disillusioned by the withdrawal from the French alliance of the Landgrave Philip of Hesse, who, scared by the legal consequences of his bigamy, was seeking peace with the Emperor Charles. Sleidan now settled permanently at Strassburg, the most liberal and intellectual of the German cities. Under the rather transparent pseudonym 'Baptista Lasdenus' he published two widely-read orations (1541, 1544) addressed respectively to the Diet and to the Emperor in person.[6] Here he sought to reunite the Emperor and the Protestant powers on the basis of a breach with Rome, thus committing himself openly and finally to the Lutheran cause. Amid his political reflections, he greeted the Reformation as a miraculous work of God; and apparently without attaining any deep understanding of Luther's spiritual experiences, he steadfastly maintained this verdict throughout the rest of his career.

Already in 1537 Sleidan's historical interests had extended to the publication of Latin translations from Froissart,[7] and this apprentice-work he followed in 1545 and 1548 by two

---

[6] *Oration an alle Churfürsten, Fürsten und Stende des Reichs* (1541) and *Oration an Keiserliche Majestät* (1544). In 1544 he republished both these under his own name, also at Strasbourg but in Latin: *Joannis Sleidani orationes duae*. These are reprinted and edited by E. Böhmer, *Zwei Reden an Kaiser und Reich* (*Bibliothek des litterarischen Vereins in Stuttgart*, cxlv, Tübingen 1879).

[7] *Frossardi . . . historiarum opus breviter collectum et Latino sermone redditum*, Paris 1537.

volumes containing a free Latin version of Comines.[8] Again, in the latter year he published a Latin translation of Claude de Seyssel's *La grande monarchie de France*.[9] Originally issued in 1519, this treatise had perhaps attracted his aristocratic French patrons, since it had sought to institutionalize an apparently absolute monarchy. Perhaps Seyssel also appealed to the constitutional instincts of a German. In dedicating the book to Edward VI of England, Sleidan commended its message to all godly princes, whose duty to protect true religion Seyssel had stressed.

As for Froissart and Comines, both attracted him as realistic writers on their own times, and his prefaces display an ambition to follow their examples, especially that of Comines. In his own age he saw everything to attract a historian. He had already asked in 1537:

> Has there ever been a century in which such varied and wonderful occurrences have been compressed into the shortest space of time? What mighty changes have we experienced, as well in political as in ecclesiastical affairs![10]

In 1545 he proclaims the ideal of absolute truthfulness in the writing of history, and he urges the leaders of the Schmalkaldic League to ensure that, just as Comines had created a true picture of his age, so now a worthy memorial to their own far greater age should be created.

> For you it is to provide that all men should experience what has been transacted through you, and that they should learn to honour therein the unspeakable wisdom and power of God.

[8] *De rebus gestis Ludovici. . . . Galliarum regis, & Caroli, Burgundiae ducis . . . commentarii. . . . Ex Gallico facti Latini, a Joanne Sleidano*, Strasbourg 1545; and *Cominaei equitis de Carolo octavo, Galliae et bello Neapolitano commentarii. Joanne Sleidano, interprete*, Strasbourg 1548. The former of these includes a description of France, the latter a brief life of Comines.

[9] *Claudii Sesellii viri patricii de republica Galliae et regum officiis, libri duo*. It is printed along with a summary of Plato's *Republic* and *Laws*, dedicated to Sleidan's friend, the councillor and diplomat William Paget. Roger Ascham, who was among Sleidan's correspondents in 1552 (*Briefwechsel*, 234–6), owned the copy of the 1562 edn. in British Library, C.45 d.7. On Claude de Seyssel see J. H. Hexter, *The Vision of Politics on the Eve of the Reformation*, London 1972, ch. 5.

[10] Preface to Froissart (n. 7 above); cf. *Allgemeine deutsche Biographie*, xxxiv, 456, which also summarizes the Comines Preface of 1545 cited below.

He then soberly observes that such a memorial could not be built upon the archival resources available to any private citizen. When the Strassburg leaders Jacob Sturm and Martin Bucer persuaded the League to employ Sleidan as historiographer and interpreter, he wrote to the former proudly insisting that he should be commissioned to write histories and not mere chronicles.[11] Yet while the League granted him special access to its archives, it stipulated that he should submit his text for correction and should refrain from publishing without its express allowance. In our terminology the *Commentaries* would thus be called both 'contemporary history' and 'official history'. And do they not clearly bear the familiar marks of each? When he took up his appointment in 1545 Sleidan had already for six years been collecting materials reaching back to Luther's revolt, and he now approached his task in a spirit of joyful dedication. In contrast with that restraint which marks his actual writing, a letter to Jacob Sturm written on 24 June 1545 shows how deeply the task attracted him.

> You would not believe how much this work delights me; it demands great industry and diligence, but since I have a natural leaning in this direction, I find in it a wonderful pleasure.[12]

Nevertheless from the first there occurred interruptions, such as the English mission on which he and the Hessian diplomat Baumbach were sent in the autumn of 1545. In our Public Record Office there remain several informative letters by Sleidan and others describing this visit,[13] through which the Germans sought to reconcile Henry VIII with Francis I, and thereby to deprive the Emperor of his freedom to attack the Schmalkaldic League. In his first missive to Henry, written in French when he was already at Windsor, he styles himself 'Licentiate of Laws and Historiographer to the Protestants'.[14]

---

[11] *Briefwechsel*, 75; 3 July 1545: *in quo nihil est quod mutari velim, nisi, ut loco Chronic' ponatur Historie.*

[12] *Non credas quantopere me delectet hic labor, qui tametsi magnam requirat industriam et diligentiam, mihi tamen, quoniam naturae quadam propensione huc inclino, mirifice dulcescit* (Letter of 24 June 1545 to Jacob Sturm in *Briefwechsel*, 72–3).

[13] *Briefwechsel*, 90–101.

[14] Ibid., 90.

On his return to Strassburg the *Commentaries* went rapidly ahead. By October 1547 he had completed the first four books, covering the years 1517–25.[15] Nevertheless in the previous April a sensational – though in the event by no means fatal – disaster had overtaken the Protestant cause. For Sleidan the Emperor's victory at Mühlberg over the Elector John Frederick of Saxony was bound to present a series of obstacles and interruptions. Before he could exploit the Saxon and Hessian archives, their princely owners were prisoners, while for a time even the city of Strassburg hesitated to expose its recent documents to publication. Through the influence of Bucer, newly exiled to England, the young King Edward VI promised financial support to Sleidan, who dedicated his second volume of Comines to Protector Somerset in a flattering preface to which we shall presently revert.[16] Even so, no substantial English money came his way. Then in 1551 Strassburg sent him to the Council of Trent, where the motley concourse of ecclesiastics and statesmen greatly enlarged those first-hand political contacts which Sleidan deemed essential to any historian. The gathering at Trent had not yet become rigidly Tridentine, and it may have helped him a little to see ecclesiastical history in terms of dialogue rather than in terms of mere polemic.

Whatever the case, on his return home, the worst of the Habsburg threat was over, and he resumed work on the *Commentaries*, invaluably aided by Jacob Sturm, whose experience of Reformation politics rivalled that of any living statesman. The materials must already have been arranged in good order, since the last stages of writing were accomplished with great expedition. In March 1553 Sleidan wrote to Sir John Cheke and Sir William Cecil that he had reached the year 1536, and in the following September he told Calvin, 'I have carried the thing through from the year 1517 to the year 1546 and I am already engaged upon the Emperor's war against our people'.[17] By April 1554 he had finished the narrative up to that present time: a year later the first edition, a folio volume

---

[15] Menke-Glückert, op. cit., 71.
[16] In addition he dedicated his translation of Seyssel (above n. 9) to Edward VI.
[17] *Briefwechsel*, 259, 263.

of some 940 pages arranged in 25 books, was being distributed. A second edition followed before the end of 1555; two German editions, one French and one Italian in 1557; a third Latin edition with a twenty-sixth book in 1558; then two more in 1559, both published in Geneva. The English translation by John Daus called *A famous cronicle of oure time* appeared in 1560, two further issues being made within the same year.[18] From the first, the sales proved immense and international, while the many editions and copies in old libraries throughout Europe indicate that the stylish Latin version continued to attract countless educated Europeans for nearly three centuries.[19]

These particulars might suggest a period of quiet composition followed by immediate literary fame, yet in truth, as his career attained its climax, Sleidan was contending with personal difficulties and sorrows. In 1553 after seven years of happy married life came the loss of his wife Iola von Niedbruck, and the cares of raising a family of three young daughters. In a letter of that year he sadly signs himself *Joan[nes] Sleidanus lugens uxorem suavissimam*.[20] At the end of October there died his close friend and helper Jacob Sturm: *Scis quantum virum amisimus*, he writes to Calvin in the December.[21] In addition he was obstructed and attacked both before and after publication, but less by Catholic adversaries than by influential Protestants, who resented his disclosures or felt irritated by his moderation. Even Melanchthon thought he had revealed many things best left in eternal silence.[22] One Job's comforter warned him that he could henceforth expect no employment from princes, and that it might be unsafe for him to leave the shelter of tolerant Strassburg. Saddened by these dismal rewards, the historian had not long to taste fame or notoriety,

[18] Pollard, A. W. and Redgrave, G. R., *Short Title Catalogue*, London 1926, nos. 19848, 19848a, 19848b.

[19] On the early sales see Friedensburg, op. cit., 72–3. About 80 editions culminated in the elaborately annotated version published at Frankfurt in 1785–6. This latter has been photo-reprinted by Otto Zeller in 3 vols., Osnabrück 1968.

[20] *Briefwechsel*, 263.

[21] Ibid., 265.

[22] *Multa narrat quae malim obruta esse aeterna silentio* (*Corpus Reformatorum*, viii, 483, no. 5784). On the reception of the *Commentaries*, see especially Friedensburg, op. cit., 72ff., and K. Schottenloher, 'Johann Sleidanus und Markgraf Albrecht Alcibiades' in *Archiv für Reformationsgeschichte*, Jahrgang 35, 1938, 193–202.

since in October 1556 he died after a long 'fever' of uncertain character. Among his friends he left attractive memories. Johann Sturm remarked on his musical gifts and agreeable singing voice. The humanist Martin Crusius recalled him as tall, fresh-complexioned and manly, though blind in his left eye. 'Since he combined dignity with cordiality and friendliness, he was in every respect an honoured figure.' The same writer also describes a dinner held in October 1550 along with the Strassburg Protestant leader Kaspar Hedio and the martyrologist Ludwig Rabus, at which Sleidan dominated a discussion concerning the events and personalities of the day. As a young lecturer in law, the political theorist François Hotman also associated with Sleidan during the last year in Strassburg, and later paid tribute to his easy, unassuming character, a thing rarely found in a man so learned.[23]

In the event Sleidan's posthumous renown owed much to a factor he cannot fully have foreseen. Only four months before his death he had published a little book destined to rival in fame the massive *Commentaries*. This was an outline of world history called *De quatuor summis imperiis*[24] and specifically directed at young students. It followed the 'Four Empires' scheme arising from the Book of Daniel, a scheme already accepted by Melanchthon in 1532 for the so-called Carion chronicle. In course of time Sleidan's textbook won widespread acceptance: it was used even by Jesuit schoolmasters, and expanded by later tormentors of the young, it grew into a stout volume of more than a thousand pages. Thus through Sleidan, Melanchthon imposed upon western historiography a cyclical scheme of history, which made 'modern' times an appendage to the story of Rome; a scheme which differed most radically from the thin red line of historic faith offered to Christians by the eleventh chapter of Hebrews.

Sleidan's most familiar accounts of his professional ideal are contained in his Preface to the *Commentaries* and in his *Apologia*,

[23] Friedensburg, op. cit., 79–81 describes the last years. For the evidence regarding his illness see *Briefwechsel*, pp. xxviii–xxix.

[24] *De quatuor summis imperiis lib. iii*, Strasbourg 1556. Ultimately it was to achieve over 70 editions, becoming available in German and French 1557; in English 1563 (Pollard and Redgrave, op. cit., no. 19849). The Four Empires, based on Daniel vii–xi, were the Assyrian or Babylonian, the Persian, the Greek and the Roman, the last being treated by Sleidan down to 1520.

a vigorous riposte to his critics written shortly before his death, and added to the successive editions from 1558 onwards.[25] The former of these two pieces he begins with a short reference to the 'Four Empires', the last of which, that of Rome, had been reduced to Germany, but had now been restored to something like world-status through the huge inheritance of Charles V. Here stood an Emperor more powerful than any since Charlemagne; yet by far the most extraordinary event of his reign has been the 'alteration of religion', that dangerous theme upon which Sleidan had embarked and at last, after the interruptions of war, had during the last three years brought to completion. He then proclaims:

> Nothing adorns the writing of history more than truth and candour. Indeed, I have taken the utmost care that neither of these may here be wanting. To that end I have assumed nothing upon surmise or light report, but I have studiously collected what I have written from the public records and papers, the faithfulness of which can be questioned by no man.

At this stage he acknowledges the counsels of Jacob Sturm, based upon Sturm's thirty years of arduous public affairs. So far as concerns France, Sleidan has gathered the information personally during his nine years' residence in that kingdom. Throughout he has sought to attain impartiality by refusing to be drawn away from the truth by personal affections, and by a close adherence to the record sources. He has followed the public acts – in many cases already printed – the orations, petitions, answers and the like.

> *Haec omnia, nude, simpliciter, et bonafide, prout quaeque res acta fuit, recito.* I do not add anything of my own, nor do I make any judgment on them, but willingly and freely leave it to my reader. I make no rhetorical flourishes, nor do I write anything out of favour or envy toward any man. No, I only furnish the style, and use my own words, so that the tenor of my language may be harmonious; I digest everything and put it in its proper place, as it came to be done in order and time.

[25] I use below pp. 4–21 in the 1785–6 edn., i, with some regard to Edward Bohun's translation, *The General History of the Reformation of the Church*, London 1689.

As might be expected, in the *Apologia* Sleidan defends his values in more militant terms. He insists on the unique character of the Reformation and its central position in his own work. Though he rejoices in his membership of the reformed Church, he calls God to witness that he has never intended to hurt any man's reputation falsely, since it would have been madness to misrepresent transactions which still remained fresh in everyone's memory. Starting from religious affairs, he could not isolate these from their secular context.

> In this history of religion, I could not omit what concerned civil government, because . . . they are interwoven one with the other, especially in our own times, so that it was impossible to separate them.[26] This union of the sacred and the civil state is sufficiently revealed in the Scriptures, and is the reason why the change of religion in any nation is always immediately accompanied by offences, contentions, strikes, tumults, factions and warfare. For this cause, says Christ, the son shall be against the father and the daughter against the mother; his teaching would not bring peace but a sword, and raise burning contention between the nearest relatives.

Significantly, it is in terms of its secular consequences that Sleidan then proceeds to summarize the Reformation. No sooner, he says, had the Gospel been preached against papal Indulgences and human traditions than the whole of society, and especially the clergy, fell into tumult and so ensured that the matter would be brought before the Imperial Diet. Thereupon some princes and cities embraced the reformed doctrine and the fire spread which was ultimately to break out in a war.

At this point he reverts to those rare gifts of impartiality and restraint. But how can any truthful historian write history without some frank admissions, or without reference to facts and opinions which may displease somebody or other? Platina spoke critically of the popes: Comines did not hesitate to blame certain policies of his own sovereign, while Pietro Bembo, though employed by the Senate of Venice, reported

---

[26] *In describendo autem religionis negocio, politicas causas omittere non mihi licuit, nam ut antea dixi, concurrunt fere semper, et nostra cumprimis aetate minime potuerunt separari* (1785–6 edn., i, 15).

in full the violent attack made by a French spokesman upon Venetian land-snatching. Sleidan also cites the example of Paulus Jovius, whose insults against the Germans have never obstructed the publication of his works. Indeed, Comines and other historians had constantly turned aside to deliver their personal judgements on the actions of history. Yet despite such instances, Sleidan himself has avoided following them. *Et licet hoc ego minime faciam, tamen usitatum est plaerisque.* Cochlaeus published six years ago rival commentaries full of 'horrible, unheard-of and invented slanders'. Likewise Cardinal Pole in a recent work has slandered the Protestant religion lately established in Germany as 'a Turkish seed'. Renouncing all such bitter exchanges, Sleidan has resolved to write 'the story of that wonderful blessing God has been pleased to bestow upon the men of this age'. He has made no undue haste, but during sixteen years has collected and arranged his materials: he now feels sure that the impulse came from God, whose cause he will uphold, however ill men may requite his labours. He even concludes by acknowledging the Emperor and King Ferdinand as supreme and divinely appointed magistrates, to whom he owes all obedience, 'in all things which are not against God'.

The Preface and the *Apologia* form the testament of Sleidan's last years, yet almost equally revealing if far less noticed is that earlier Preface which he had addressed in May 1548 to Protector Somerset, when dedicating to him the second volume of the Latin Comines.[27] Here he sees Somerset as charged by God to carry out a holy Reformation in England; but coming to the immediate issue, he then urges the Protector to bring up young Edward VI on a diet of Comines, as a sure method to foster wisdom and teach a statecraft which shall prove at once moral and profitable. Comines is the model for the writer who seeks to depict his own times. Such a historian must not only eschew actual falsehoods; he must avoid being biased by any particular interest or passion. So armed, he must depict with the utmost clarity the designs of those who manage affairs. Ideally the historian should have been a participant in the great transactions he depicts; failing this, he needs direct

[27] Cf. above, n. 8.

information from persons who were present. Even so, it is fatally easy to sink from the task of the historian to that of the mere orator or special pleader. Successful generals and politicians who try to write history will make themselves ridiculous unless they can fairly depict their opponents. Sleidan here approvingly quotes Cicero on the high merits of Caesar's plain unaffected commentaries, 'because they are bare, direct and plain, divested of all oratorical ornament'.[28] Again, Sallust is known to have been Cicero's personal enemy, yet one would never guess it from his generous account of Cicero's vigilance in suppressing Catiline's conspiracy. So if he aspires to exert a deep moral influence on his readers, the historian must free himself of passion and subordinate ambition to truth. Among the few who have realized these aims, a high place must be given to Comines, a man not very well versed in the Latin tongue, but having great dexterity of mind. Is not this last sentence of Sleidan the most significant of all? Historiography is now freed from at least some of the trammels of fifteenth-century Florentine oratorical humanism; substance is exalted over literary elegance. Here in a word is the great advance of the sixteenth century, an advance which Machiavelli had already in some degree exemplified. Yet at this point we need to remark that Sleidan owed very little to his older Italian contemporaries. He died too early to have read Guicciardini.[29] From those Italians whom he cites in detail[30] he could not have derived his methods and ideals. Jovius in particular might be regarded as the Horace Walpole, rather than the Polybius or even the Comines, of the High Renaissance.

A historian of historiography has recently remarked that 'Sleidan set out to be the Polybius of the Reformation'.[31] We have not observed that he ever expressed this ambition, yet would agree that his attitudes and methods often appear strikingly Polybian. Like Sleidan, the renowned Greek proclaims that historical knowledge contributes to the right conduct of life, yet only if its practitioners shun fables and marvels, only if they avoid the emotional excitement which

---

[28] . . . *quod sint nudi, recti et venusti, omni ornatu orationis tanquam veste detracta.*
[29] The *Storia d'Italia*, though finished before 1540, was not published until 1561-7.
[30] I.e. Platina, Bembo and Paulus Jovius; above, pp. 27-8.
[31] Burke, P., *The Renaissance Sense of the Past*, London 1969, 124.

characterizes the dramatists. The good historian, adds Polybius, needs personal experience of great events and knowledge of historical topography, yet he must also conduct painful researches, collecting, sifting and weighing all the available evidence. Above all, he needs to be inspired by a calm impartiality and a love of truth.[32] Similarly, Polybius anticipated Sleidan in disliking the fictitious speeches put by rhetoric-loving historians into the mouths of their protagonists. Again, both so admire comprehensiveness and chronological tidiness that they will interrupt particular narratives, however enthralling, in order to bring the broader picture up-to-date. Both admire a plain, bald style appropriate to such sober designs. Even so, we have already observed that it was Caesar whom Sleidan selected as his stylistic model. These striking comparisons made, it remains hard to gauge how consciously or directly Sleidan may have studied Polybius, printed editions of whose work stood readily available: in Latin since 1473 and in Greek since 1530. Like his mentor Melanchthon[33] Sleidan certainly knew Polybius at first hand. In the preface to *De quatuor summis imperiis,* he places Polybius alongside Herodotus, Thucydides and Xenophon as one of the four supreme historians among the Greeks.

Turning from precept to practice, we naturally ask how far the *Commentaries* can be held to justify the idealism and complacency of their author. No one would dispute that he has indeed striven hard to tell everything *prout quaeque res acta fuit,*[34] a precise anticipation of Ranke's famous phrase *wie es eigentlich gewesen.* In contrast with the muck-raking Centuriators of Magdeburg or with the dishonest calumnies of Cochlaeus, he provides a model of balance and good manners. Moreover,

---

[32] The relevant passages are in Polybius, *Histories,* i, 4, 35; ii, 16, 35, 56; iii, 36, 48; xii, 25, 28; xvi, 14.

[33] Melanchthon cites Polybius for the adage *oculus historiae est veritas;* and again for the necessity of historical knowledge as a basis of political action and moral principle. He also probably drew from Polybius the idea that geographical study was a leading ancillary to historical studies. Cf. Menke-Glückert, op. cit., 20, 42, 57; and compare Polybius op. cit., ii, 16; iii, 36.

[34] Preface to the Commentaries (1785–6 edn., i, 10). Some later historians have been accorded excessive praise for their objectivity. For example, La Popelinière's reflections on this theme are little more than a repetition of Sleidan's, which he must have observed. Cf. G. W. Sypher, 'La Popelinière's Histoire de France' in *Journal of the History of Ideas,* xxiv (1963).

like Beatus Rhenanus and a few other superior contemporaries, he has progressed not merely beyond the superstitious medieval chronicler but also beyond the romantic, legend-loving humanists who continued to distort early German history. When unsure about a fact he uses qualifying verbs like *creditur, fertur, ut putatur*; or expressions such as *sunt qui putant, qua nescio de causa; nolim istud pro vero ponere, et solent ejusmodi consilia tegi.*[35] Archival texts he most often presents indirectly, but sometimes he breaks into direct quotation. He does not allow the occasional stylistic 'improvement' to become the misleading excrescence. Even Luther's hymn *Ein' feste Burg* he introduces merely as sober documentary proof of its author's steadfast courage, and he reduces it to Latin prose.[36] His own statements might be taken to imply that he seldom used other than archival sources, but this was far from being the case: indeed, many transactions would have remained unfamiliar to him without such narrative sources as were by then available. Concerning the excesses of the Anabaptists at Münster he was indebted to the eyewitness-account by Heinrich Dorpius, though he prudishly omitted certain of its lurid details. For the war between Charles V and the Protestant princes he drew upon the *Commentaries* of Luis de Avila y Zuniga, by 1550 accessible in a Latin edition. When looking back to the beginning of the Emperor's reign, he used the *De Electione et coronatione* by Georg Sabinus, published at Mainz in 1544.[37] Needless to add, the industrious and versatile reading of Sleidan could not ensure factual infallibility, and nineteenth-century scholarship was able to convict him of occasional minor errors.[38] For example, in relation to Swiss affairs – including the Marburg Conference – he could at last be put alongside the more intimate witness of Bullinger. The errors nevertheless remain honourable, and one might well have anticipated many more, in the face of difficulties greater

---

[35] Paur, T., *Johann Sleidans Commentare über die Regierungszeit Karls V historisch-kritisch betrachtet*, Leipzig 1843, 76.

[36] *Commentaries* 1785–6 edn., ii, 433. The first lines run: *firma nobis est arx et propugnaculum, Deus: ille vetus humani generis hostis, rem totis nunc viribus agit, et omnis generis machinas adhibet.*

[37] On this and related issues see also R. Fester, 'Sleidan, Sabinus, Melanchthon' in *Historische Zeitschrift*, lxxxix (1902).

[38] Paur, op. cit., 96–9.

than those which beset modern 'contemporary' historians.

At the same time his pretensions to impartiality remain a very different matter, and must obviously be regarded with reserve. His selections and rejections create a strongly anti-papal and anti-prelatical atmosphere throughout the book. For example, in the *Apologia* of 1556, he cites only Catholic examples of slanderous history, and while he details the sins of the Farnese family, he has nothing to say of reforming influences at Rome during the pontificate of Paul III. In Book IX he summarizes at length a very bitter anonymous French pamphlet setting forth the superstitions and barbarities characterizing Parisian Catholicism. He loses no opportunity to report the inhumanity of German bishops against rebels and heretics. In lighter vein, he relates how the Catholic Henry duke of Brunswick faked the death of his mistress Eva von Trott ('Eva Trottina'), and then spirited her away to a remote castle where he could visit her in privacy. Granted the probable truth of this story, it seems not unfair to remark that Sleidan, official historian of the League, does not regale his readers upon the sexual sins of its leader, Philip of Hesse. As one might anticipate, he has little or nothing good to say of any rebel, and he takes the excesses at Münster as typifying Anabaptist behaviour. The list of prejudices could be extended, but to little profit, since it is clear that no man of his time could have achieved anything approaching either angelic impartiality or even modern liberalism. Both in principle and in practice Sleidan overstresses the superficial virtues of urbane language and factual correctness, as opposed to that deeper impartiality which selects with fairness and steadfastly seeks to understand the viewpoint of a religious or political opponent. To this day, in Reformation studies such virtues remain rather precarious!

This obvious theme does not, however, exhaust the interest of the *Commentaries*. In re-reading them, the present writer saw certain graces which in earlier years he tended to take for granted. One of these is the international range of the work, a feature which can hardly be paralleled in any other history of that period. It constantly breaks out from Germany to keep abreast of religious and political affairs in France, England, the

Netherlands, the Swiss Confederation, on the Turkish front, at the Council of Trent. With increasing fullness as he reached recent years, Sleidan was clearly making excellent use of his personal experience and friendships all over Europe: as one of the best Europeans of his day, he did not need to fear comparison with men like Erasmus and Vives – and certainly not with the Italians, who tended to equate their own peninsular microcosm with the civilized world. By the same token, he is by no means so unmindful of the medieval background as one might at first suppose. He mentions for example the introduction of Peter's Pence in England, the impact of the Teutonic Order, the sequence of Turkish conquests from the early fourteenth century, the particulars of John Huss's attendance at the Council of Constance. Again, as befits the work of a fine humanist, the *Commentaries* display urbane values and a dimension which can without anachronism be called 'cultural history'. A man's literacy and learning very largely determine Sleidan's overall estimate of his character. Praise is accorded to the writings of Erasmus, Hutten, Lefèvre, Marot, Guillaume du Bellay and Budé; also to enlightened patronage by Francis I and Edward VI.[39] In Luther Sleidan admires two attributes: his steadfastness and the fact that he was a very great writer.

By modern (and Polybian) standards we should all complain that the *Commentaries* contain too little searching causal analysis and too much scissors-and-paste rendering of pamphlets and official documents. Yet despite his half-concealed prejudices, Sleidan does fulfil his promise to avoid the moralizing and partisan judgements which disfigure the writing of so many contemporary historians. Quite often we strongly sense the presence of the trained jurist:[40] we hear the advocates for plaintiff and defendant, but then the author deliberately renounces the office of judge as contrary to the function of the historian. In his own way he rivals the austerity of the impassive Guicciardini himself, since while he lacks the Italian's tireless and intelligent search for motive, he avoids the risk of attributing to politicians imaginatively-conceived but

[39] Menke-Glückert, op. cit., 83.
[40] Ibid., 79.

C

undocumented aims. Considering the sources available to Guicciardini, it is hard to avoid the suspicion that he often (like Sarpi in later days) presents his own shrewd conjectures as if they were the diarized intentions of his anti-heroes. So much can be said in favour of Sleidan's inhibited caution and scruple, even though these qualities diminish his readability and human interest.

Both in Guicciardini and in Sleidan, attention now seems far too exclusively devoted to princes and rulers. Even had Guicciardini attempted a full-scale treatment of the Reformation, would he have troubled to analyse that medley of religious and secular reactions which marked common townsmen and peasants, the sort of 'grass-roots' which interest us, but which interested neither him nor Sleidan? A straightforward distrust and contempt for that 'foolish animal' the people could easily lead to the cavalier treatment of real if complex mass-movements. Such a contempt, such sins of omission, may have mattered little when Guicciardini described the nine-days wonder of the tumult in Genoa suppressed by Louis XII,[41] yet it mattered everything in regard to the German and Swiss Reformations, which – as modern research shows ever more clearly – cut deep down into the middle and lower social strata. Regarding the Peasants' War of 1524–5, Sleidan for once does provide a sustained account[42] without Polybian interruptions. Like any member of the governing class, he rejects the right to rebel and he does not fail to recall atrocities by the peasants. Nevertheless he also mentions cruel acts of repression and he emits a note of pity when describing the ghastly slaughter of barely-resisting peasants at Frankenhausen. Faced by the grim spectre of a causal relationship between Protestantism and popular sedition, he takes refuge in the personal adventures of Thomas Müntzer. As already suggested, the elaborate narrative concerning the horrors of Anabaptist Münster[43] is not accompanied by any serious analysis of religious radicalism or spiritualism in any of their widely varying forms.

[41] *Storia d'Italia,* lib. vii, cap. 2. Compare his *Ricordi,* no. 140.
[42] *Commentaries,* lib. iv–v.
[43] Ibid., lib. x.

Restrictions of outlook akin to these have been charged against scholars of later periods, including Ranke himself. Even in our own age, many historians of the Reformation have failed to extricate themselves from the simplifying tyranny of high politics, from aristocratic or hero-seeking predilections, from the love of mere external events, from a classic 'dignity' of themes. In other words, we have only just begun to explore with adequate attention and industry those pre-existent social and intellectual forces which enabled Luther to enlist the support of the German nation. Yet narrow politicizing did not merely arise amid the fears of social chaos besetting the sixteenth century; from the start it lay inherent in the very fabric of humanism. As long before as 1405 Lionardo Bruni had expressed the view that history, however elegantly phrased, should form just a straightforward factual sequence.

> For, after all, history is an easy subject; there is nothing in its study subtle or complex. It consists in the narration of the simplest matters of fact which, once grasped, are readily retained in the memory.[44]

Closely related was that externalizing habit, which doubtless sprang in part from the models set by the admired ancient historians such as Livy and Caesar, writers who never had to cope with any theme remotely resembling the Protestant Reformation. In the mid-sixteenth century it would have needed an original genius to have plumbed either the individual psychology or the mass-psychology of these religious or part-religious movements. Nevertheless, we are not quite guilty of asking for the moon when we complain that Sleidan devoted so little effort and ingenuity to the theological and religious impulses of the Reformation within the actual society of his day. With all their faults, the Protestant martyrologists Jean Crespin,[45] Adriaen van Haemstede[46] and John Foxe were

[44] Bruni d'Arezzo, L., *De studiis et literis,* trans. W. H. Woodward in his *Vittorino da Feltre and other Humanist Educators,* Cambridge 1897, 128. In the same passage Bruni praises the style of Caesar's *Commentaries* in Ciceronian terms strikingly similar to those of Sleidan.

[45] Crespin, J., *Le livre des martyrs . . . depuis Jean Hus . . .* Geneva 1554: best edn. by D. Benoit, 3 vols., Toulouse 1885–9.

[46] On Haemstede's martyrology (1559) see J. F. Gilmont, 'La genèse du Martyrologe

making more progress on this particular front. And again, not long afterwards Jesuit historians like Ribadeneyra,[47] powerfully aided by the techniques of Loyola's *Spiritual Exercises* and *Autobiography*, were exploring the interior as well as the exterior lives of their heroes. The Lutheran revolution beginning in 1517 was after all Sleidan's chosen theme: as observed, his Preface and *Apologia* make it clear enough that he became deeply involved with the actual movement, that he did not merely aspire to write a *deutsche Geschichte im Zeitalter der Reformation*. And by 1550 there stood available to him a vast literature on the religious and theological aspects, a literature just as relevant as the archives of Strassburg or the Schmalkaldic League. A closer study of the available works of Luther – some of which he does baldly summarize – would surely have sufficed to focus these aspects far more sharply. Equally accessible tracts by lesser authors such as those reprinted in the nineteenth century collections by Schade,[48] Clemen[49] and others could also have provided myriad insights at all social levels. We may praise Sleidan for rising above the polemical hurly burly of Luther and Cochlaeus, yet may not our approval come dangerously near to praising a modern historian of socialism for recoiling with an expression of pained gentility from the writings of Marx, Engels and their epigoni? We may well ask whether any historian can afford this cloistered virginity. To fish in the troubled waters of popular, even of semi-educated polemics, has become a routine task for the modern historian of religious and social movements; yet this was hardly a task in the classical tradition as understood by scholars of the Renaissance. To Sleidan's calm, legalist, aristocratic eye, state papers and official confessions remained acceptable in the raw, while popular, passionate, self-revealing sources were neglected or toned down in accordance with a Roman *gravitas*.

---

d'Adriaen van Haemstede' in *Revue d'histoire ecclésiastique*, lxiii (1968). He compares it with Crespin and with Ludwig Rabus, *Historien der...Bekennern und Martyren*, Strasbourg 1554-8.

[47] Pedro de Ribadeneyra (1527-1611) based his biography of Loyola (Madrid 1594) on a Latin version published at Naples as early as 1572. *New Catholic Encyclopedia*, xii, 466 gives references.

[48] Schade, O., *Satiren und Pasquille aus der Reformationszeit*, 3 vols., Hanover 1856-8.

[49] Clemen, O. C., *Flugschriften aus den ersten Jahren der Reformation*, 4 vols., Leipzig and New York 1907-11.

The legitimate (and explicitly grateful) descendants of Sleidan were political and pragmatic authors like Sarpi, de Thou and Camden.[50] And to illustrate how this attitude has dominated Reformation historiography almost to our own day we British readers need go no further than our own Victorians. Some of these were avowed Tractarians, anxious to defame the English Reformation by pretending it was a secular product, made in Parliament. Others, however, were natural if unconscious Sleidanians, staunch islanders who accepted the constitution of England as the very frame of the cosmos, but who did not very passionately believe that God was an Anglican, either High or Low. Whatever the case, a century ago Canon Dixon began the first chapter of his six-volume work on the English Reformation[51] with the opening of the Reformation Parliament in 1529, just as if Tyndale had not been at work for several years, just as if Wyclif and Lollardy had never existed or any religious unrest seeped through from the Continent. A little later Gee and Hardy filled their standard documentary collection[52] with parliamentary statutes, with royal and episcopal injunctions, to the almost complete exclusion of material on religion and its dissemination in society. We have all heard of Reformation without tarrying for theology, but here was Reformation without tarrying for religion; and it has owed not a little to the humanist tradition as developed by Sleidan and his disciples. Rather oddly at first sight, pre-Enlightment historiography in northern Europe did not reconstruct the Reformation in terms of cultural or philosophical humanism, but rather as an emanation of princes, diets, parliaments and councils. This trend was not merely political but institutional, the emphasis of men whose public and literary *personae* were those of jurists and officials first, humanists second and men of religion third. Religious debate and emotion they allowed to escape from the noble hall of history and take up residence in the noisome cellars of polemics. If you would witness this externalizing, read the

[50] Burke, P., op. cit., 124–30.

[51] Dixon, R. W., *History of the Church of England from the Abolition of the Roman Jurisdiction*, 6 vols., Oxford 1878–1902.

[52] Gee, H. and Hardy, W. J., *Documents Illustrative of English Church History*, London 1896.

early pages of the *Commentaries*, where Sleidan, having failed to describe Luther's earlier life, imagines he is displaying the origins of Luther's Reformation. You will find little beyond a Victorian textbook account – innocent alike of theology and of psychology – rehearsing Luther's public protest against Indulgences. While Sleidan's Reformation is initiated by Luther, this hero has not much more depth than, say, Guicciardini's cardboard figure Martino Lutero in Book XII of the *Storia d'Italia*. And when Zwingli appears, he is an even simpler phenomenon. Meanwhile this Luther-without-tears is soon pushed from the centre of the stage by the politicians; though it is fair to add that the later references to Luther's best-known writings do add something to the picture of an otherwise enigmatic titan. Men with Sleidan's training understood Melanchthon far better than Luther, and their values must owe more to classical convention than to mere ignorance. Sleidan may indeed have missed the few passages wherein Luther describes his experiential and exegetical crises, yet he cannot have remained wholly oblivious to their solution in Luther's central doctrine of Justification by Faith Alone. For one thing, few laymen grasped this message of Luther better than did Jacob Sturm, and Sturm was not merely intimate with Sleidan, but carefully advised him concerning his history. Again, Sleidan must have experienced the religious and theological dimension through his close friendship with Martin Bucer, who was by any reckoning one of the half-dozen great religious leaders of the Reformation. In the last resort this situation cannot be elucidated with great precision, yet there exists one more or less pertinent factor: the historiographical concepts of Philip Melanchthon, *praeceptor Germaniae*.

Too easily we tend to think of the classical tradition as a more or less homogeneous complex of ideas; as a decalogue that Renaissance men encountered in solitude, perusing the stone tables of Antiquity on the summit of Olympus, face to face with the gods. On the contrary, did they not always meet the classical tradition within some localized context created not only by their fellow-humanists but also by what we call 'medieval' scholarship and social ideas? This was especially true in Germany from the years around 1530, when Sleidan first acquired his methodology. As shown in E. C. Scherer's investigation of historical studies within the German universities,[53] humanist history had penetrated deeply into these institutions. So many of them, especially those within the Protestant lands, were recent foundations which had never experienced the pre-humanist world. On the other hand, German humanism had long since cast off the laurel-crowned romanticism of Celtis and his rebellious *demi-monde*. Its studies, and in particular its historical studies, now lay safely in the headmasterly hands of the prim little *praeceptor Germaniae*. Sleidan's discipleship to Melanchthon – paralleled by the discipleship in pedagogy of his friend Johann Sturm – cannot be claimed as a recent discovery. As long ago as 1912 it was worked out by Emil Menke-Glückert of Leipzig[54] in his able little book on Reformation and Counter Reformation historiography. Already we have seen the neat-minded Melanchthon teaching world history by developing the scheme of the Four Monarchies, long beforehand conceived on the basis of that humble forerunner of Arnold Toynbee, the Book of Daniel. Here was a cyclical scheme matching early Lutheran distaste for any notion of human progress in this dark terrestrial life.[55] As for the *Commentaries*, their debts to Melanchthon are less overt, yet they remain impressive.

Melanchthon publicly despised the ill-informed, withdrawn, monkish historians of past centuries.[56] So did Sleidan, who from the first consorted with lay historians like Froissart and Comines. In 1532, long before Sleidan started writing, Melanchthon had already demonstrated the use of original sources by organizing materials sent him by Johann Carion and in effect producing the *Chronica Carionis*.[57] Again, Melanchthon anticipated Sleidan by identifying states with their political rulers, and he parted company with the all-too-human Italians by teaching Protestants to regard every historical event as divinely engineered. *Deus transfert et stabilit*

---

[53] Scherer, E. C., *Geschichte und Kirchengeschichte an den deutschen Universitäten*, Freiburg im Breisgau 1927.
[54] Cf. n. 3, above.
[55] Menke-Glückert, op. cit., 46ff.
[56] E.g. in *Corpus Reformatorum*, iii, 217.
[57] Menke-Glückert, op. cit., 21–39.

imperia.[58] Luther's God, that truly omnipotent yet notoriously masked God, alone knew the reasons why things happened. Thence opened an arcadia for the worried historian, who could now literally cast his care upon the Lord. In this comfortable belief, duly echoed by Sleidan, we doubtless find the basis of the latter's conviction that a wise historian will narrate the deeds and reprint the documents, but modestly shrink from assessing the ultimate causes and merits. Sleidan would have applauded Melanchthon's scorn for the undisciplined, subjective historical writing of the sectarian humanist Sebastian Franck. And one may scarcely doubt that the cautious man also shared Melanchthon's as well as Guicciardini's distrust of that wild beast, unredeemed humanity, represented by its unprivileged classes.

> Take but degree away, untune that string,
> And, hark! what discord follows; each thing meets
> In mere oppugnancy.

On the other hand, Sleidan evidently admired Melanchthon's bright-eyed search for heroes, those exceptions fashioned by heaven who could make history a safe subject for the young, could make it into a philosophy-teaching-by-examples. All the world's a stage, says Melanchthon, on which God produces morality-plays. *Totus hic mundus velut proscenium quoddam est Dei, in quo omnium officiorum exempla quotidie exhibet.*[59] And one need only read his famous funeral oration on Luther to see the marble effigy of the hero emerging from the ambivalent, disturbing man of flesh and blood.

> To that splendid list of most illustrious men raised up by God to gather and establish the Church, and recognized as the chief glory of the human race, must be added the name of Martin Luther. Solon, Themistocles, Scipio, Augustus, and others who established or ruled over vast empires were great men indeed; but far inferior were they to our leaders, Isaiah, John the Baptist, Paul, Augustine and Luther.[60]

[58] *Corpus Reformatorum,* xii, 777. Elsewhere in the Carion chronicle (ibid., xii, 870' 1023) Melanchthon replaces 'imperia' by 'regna'.

[59] Ibid., xi, 166.

[60] From Melanchthon's *Funeral Oration over Luther,* translated in L. W. Spitz *The Protestant Reformation,* Englewood Cliffs, N.J. 1966, pp. 69–70; cf. *Corpus Reformation,* xi, 728.

Here we may recognize a noble tribute and yet suspect a
sigh of relief. For orderly moralists, to live close to genius is
hard; to live alongside religious genius, with all its fluctuations
of humility and arrogance, must be a recurrent crucifixion.
Philip Melanchthon revered Luther and sought his strength
so long as it was available, yet who can blame him for burying
his friend at last among the cold monuments of the heroic
dead?

Armed with this set of convictions, neither Sleidan nor
Melanchthon could find a genuinely social dimension in
history; they were all too inclined to depopularize as well as
to dehumanize the Reformation. As compared with the
secularist Italians, they added a theological reason for averting
their eyes not merely from the human quirks of genius but
from the distasteful spectacle of mankind in general. For this
mass of perdition in the world's twilight they saw a short
future, and certainly not a future of human freedom or 'progress'. All in all, we can understand Sleidan not merely
through the official character of his work, not merely through
his French and classical literary models, but by reference to
the sententious teutonic world of ethical teachers like
Melanchthon and Bucer. Close behind the licensed historian
of princes and cities, behind the Strassburg ambassador, there
stands a senior assistant in the school of the all-German
preceptor from Wittenberg. If Sleidan became an ancestor of
the pragmatic Sarpi, was he not also an ancestor of Samuel
Pufendorf, over a century later still anxious to apply what he
called 'the useful science' of history to the 'youth of high rank'
who would one day hold 'offices of state'?

Sleidan's *Commentaries* continued invaluable into the late
eighteenth century or even longer. Without them, one can
hardly imagine, for example, the Reformation passages of
William Robertson,[61] the best historian of that movement to
arise from the Enlightenment. But as the nineteenth century
reprinted, reconsidered and amplified Sleidan's documenta-
tion, his work rapidly lost this indispensable character.

---

[61] Robertson's writing on the Reformation greatly excels that of the Continental
Enlightenment. See especially his *History of the Reign of Charles V*, London 1769, bk. ii;
and his *History of Scotland*, London 1759.

Confessional and polemical history took two heavy hammerings: the one from Lutheran pietists like Gottfried Arnold, the other from the secular Enlightenment which so closely followed. The latter movement introduced the idea that the Reformers – despite their now detested intolerance – had willy-nilly contributed much to the liberation of the human mind, a half-truth constantly rediscovered or rejected by naive thinkers ever since. Meanwhile, if nineteenth-century historians achieved an immeasurably fuller knowledge of the facts, a more sensitive feel for the contours, they did not revise the traditional attitudes so radically as might have been expected. Nowadays, as I have already hinted, even Ranke's deservedly famous book on the German Reformation also seems defective in terms of causal analysis. Ranke – also in Döllinger's words *praeceptor Germaniae* – had not fully detached himself from the God-given 'ages' and he made no very sustained departure from the Sleidanian political structure of history. His deeper and more original insights into the German mind and German society are brief, though sometimes precious and prophetic. Was it not the religious partisan Janssen, rather than the virtuous Ranke, who recovered for the common man a place in religious history? Even scholars of our own day have felt happier in turning out books called *The Age of the Reformation, Die Neugestaltung Europas,* and so forth; books which 'cover the period' but are scarcely histories of the movement.

Apart from such books, the enterprises of the twentieth century have tended to be narrowly based, even monothematic. Today the cloudlands of Weber and Tawney remain little more than the playground for undergraduates fledging their wings,[62] though by contrast Troeltsch[63] did at least point the way toward a firmer sociological analysis of the Reformation. Karl Holl and the theologians of the so-called Luther Renaissance added more intellectual subtlety to Luther – some of it their own subtlety rather than his.[64] Naturally,

[62] Kitch, M. J., *Capitalism and the Reformation,* London 1967 summarizes these controversies.

[63] *Sociallehren der christlichen Kirchen und Gruppen,* Tübingen 1912, translated by O. Wyon as *The Social Teaching of the Christian Churches,* London 1931.

[64] A perceptive introduction to the movement is E. G. Rupp, *The Righteousness of God: Luther Studies,* London 1953.

their work contributes very little towards our grasp of the social origins and impacts of religious change, for history can receive little help from disembodied ideas. To more catastrophic effect, a few psychiatrists intervened, certain of them inspired by the concept of a Reformation welling up from the subconscious mind of young man Luther. Their misadventures only convince one that a capacity for assessing historical evidence is not after all inborn: we must all acquire it the hard way, through detailed comparative studies. If Reformation historiography still continues to make progress, it is perhaps because historians are emancipating themselves not merely from the Sleidenian political tradition but also from the pathetic illusion that there must exist some one magic formula, some one golden key which will open the way into the heart of this great historical episode. If general historians are to advance beyond Ranke they must surely follow his rejection of simplifications, slogans, doctrinairism; and though they would be wise to love the people, the streets, the seas and the soil, they should reject insularity and nationalism, for they are dealing with an essentially supranational movement. But unlike Ranke, they will also need to attack at all the social and all the intellectual levels, while at the same time reaching back deeply into those ancient and medieval worlds where lie the roots of both Renaissance and Reformation.

III

The Making of a Reforming Prince:
Frederick III, Elector Palatine

———⊰∘⊙∘⊱———

OWEN CHADWICK

FREDERICK of Pfalz-Simmern was born on 14 February 1515, child of an impecunious branch of one of the historic houses of Germany, the Wittelsbach. He was the eldest son and fourth child of a prince with not much property and little to rule, the Duke of Pfalz-Simmern. The 'duchy' extended to a few villages round the castle of Simmern, in the hills of the Hunsbrück ridge lying between the Rhine and the Mosel.

As the family could not exist merely by governing an exiguous territory, its head needed employment. Through the Wittelsbach connexion, they found employment easy to get. They were servants of the Emperor, and as imperial officials often received the respect which lands and poverty failed to win. The Emperor Charles V made Frederick's father, John II, one of the presidents of the imperial court of justice which sat at nearby Speyer. John II was a humane and widely respected man. He ran a printing works, and prepared the illustrations with his own hand. His wife, Frederick's mother, was Beatrix, daughter of the Margrave of Baden, a good-looking lady who went out among the poor of Simmern.

The household of such a princeling was simple. When seeking a fiancée they did not think it unfitting to consider whether the woman could manage a kitchen or was capable of sewing and embroidery. They were even more likely to consider whether she could bring a dowry.

The Simmern parents educated the children at home with

tutors. We do not know how Frederick was educated, except that he became fluent in French and Latin as well as German. But we know how a prince from Pomerania was educated in the neighbouring Palatinate at much the same period.[1] In summer he must get up at 6 a.m., in winter at 7 a.m. After his ablutions and private prayers, there was a grammar lesson, then mass with sermon, and then breakfast. About noon there was a lesson in poetry, no doubt Latin poetry, followed by a snack. Afterwards, at 2 p.m., there was an hour at philosophy, rhetoric, or history; from 3 p.m. to 4 p.m. recreation; at 4 p.m. supper then Latin. Nightcap drink in winter at 7 p.m., in summer at 8 p.m., and an hour afterwards bed.

The manly exercise was still the old tournament of chivalry; and as the young man grew he would take part in jousts which were rough and dangerous and far from ceremonial. We hear of public duels which resembled the old gladiatorial combats of the Romans. Frederick learnt to hunt. Hunting was the universal sport of German princes; fox, wild boar, deer, aurochs, bear in the mountains in the east, herds of wild horses though they were disappearing during the sixteenth century. The east was the breeding land of good horses, and they preferred to fetch hounds from the east if they could not get them from England, which German princes regarded as the country of the best hounds but also the most expensive. They enjoyed falconry, and even an archbishop did not think it wrong to have an expert falconer.[2] For shooting they had begun to use guns, of which the expert manufacturers lived in Augsburg. But whether it was the guns or the marksmen which could not yet shoot accurately, most hunters still preferred the crossbow, of which the best were manufactured in Nuremberg. Antlers were regarded as fair ornaments on the walls of the living-room. But they had no feeling that they must shoot the beast before they affixed the antlers. They received them as presents, or even bought them from traders. Frederick hunted, but never became master of a horse. Indeed

---

[1] Häusser, L., *Geschichte der rheinischen Pfalz nach ihren politischen, kirchlichen und literarischen Verhältnissen*, 2nd ed. (Heidelberg, 1856) i, 587.

[2] Voigt, Johannes, *Deutsches Hofleben im Zeitalter der Reformation* ed. E. Schaeffer, Dresden 1927, 66ff.

good horses were difficult to find. If they found a good horse they must compete against the prices being offered by military quartermasters.

Though Protestant princes began to send their princelings to university it was more customary to send youths travelling to the houses of other princes, if possible greater princes, to become familiar with the ways of the world and to make acquaintance which might later be of service. Sometimes they were sent young, even at twelve years. Frederick was sent first to stay at Nancy with the house of Lorraine, then to Liège to live with the prince-bishop and finally to the court of the Emperor Charles himself at Brussels. At the age of eighteen he joined the Emperor's army which marched to throw the invading Turks out of Austria, and the lance which he carried there was hung on a pillar of the church of Simmern.[3] At the age of twenty he was regent of Simmern while his father was away serving as a judge of the imperial court. At the age of twenty-two he was married to Maria, the daughter of another and slightly more important prince, the Count of Brandenburg-Anspach. This territory lay in Franconia between the land ruled by the free city of Nuremberg and the territories of the prince-bishops of Bamberg and Würzburg. Its chief place and district was Anspach, its chief fortress Plassenburg.

Though the Counts of Anspach were more important than the Dukes of Simmern, they were no richer. Some years after the death of Maria's father the land was divided between her uncle and her younger brother, who became known as the Count of Brandenburg-Culmbach. This Count was a lad of fifteen, Albert, who showed signs of devotion to drinking; and he inherited a territory burdened with debt. The various expedients of Anspach for keeping the creditors from the door were comic and extraordinary. The regents made promises, borrowed, pawned goods, sold jewels, and at a moment of desperation in 1530 sold the silver of the land including chalices and furniture from the churches. Ten years before the wedding of Frederick, the debts amounted to 473,519 gulden, and the annual expenditure still exceeded

[3] Kluckhohn, A., *Friedrich der Fromme 1559–76*, Nördlingen 1876, 5.

income by nearly 6,000 gulden a year;[4] and during the succeeding ten years the debts continued to grow alarmingly. Maria brought no large money with her by way of a dowry.

Penniless though she might be, she came of a powerful family. She was a minor member of the great house of Brandenburg. Her father, who died so young, was the eldest of eight brothers. Several of the brothers were provided with stipends in the Church, one of them being elected prince-bishop of Würzburg. But the most important of Maria's uncles was Albert, who for his ecclesiastical post was elected Grand Master of the Teutonic Order, which ruled broad lands out upon the Polish border; and in 1525 the Grand Master converted his ecclesiastical office into a secular office and became Duke of Prussia. The history of Prussia tempted posterity to imagine the first Duke of Prussia as eminent and powerful. In reality his position was more modest. Maria, when in need for herself, her husband or her children in their impoverishment, constantly turned for help to Duke Albert of Prussia. She did not mention, perhaps she did not know, that at times Duke Albert himself hardly knew where to turn for money.

Frederick and Maria first met at Krailsheim, by arrangement of the parents, on 20 June 1537, and were then betrothed, amid scenes of such drunken dancing in the heat, that three guests died. Frederick's new brother-in-law, the Count of Brandenburg-Culmbach, aged only fifteen, drank and danced so that for months afterwards he was dangerously ill; and one of the guests who died was the young count's tutor.[5] Evidently Frederick was not remarkable for piety. The wedding was celebrated at Kneuznach on 21 October 1537. Ancient German custom demanded, after the wedding breakfast, a torch-light dance, according to a rhythm and ritual

---

[4] Voigt, Johannes, *Albrecht Alcibiades von Brandenburg-Kulmbach*, Berlin 1852, i, 19, 24. For the development of the Reformation in that area, see J. B. Götz, *Die Glaubenspaltung im Gebiete der Markgrafsschaft Ansbach-Kulmbach in den Jahren 1520–1535*, (Erläuterungen und Ergänzungen zu Janssens Geschichte des deutschen Volkes, ed. L. Pastor, V, 3–4) Freiburg-im-Breisgau, 1907. The expenses of Albert Alcibiades when young were partly met from monastic revenues, Götz, ibid, 143, n. 6. For Church furniture, cf. Götz, ibid, 152. Albert Alcibiades certainly had some education for he possessed an official praeceptor, by name Christoph Beck; Götz 196.

[5] Voigt, *Albrecht Alcibiades*, i, 43.

somewhat resembling the older quadrillion, with a solemn conducting of bride and groom to the bridal bed. He brought her to live at Simmern, and they began to be happy.

Personally Maria was a suitable match. She introduced, however, a problem into Frederick's life. She was a devout Protestant, and the ward, since her father's death, of a devout Protestant uncle.

The difference of his wife's religion confronted Frederick for the first time with the Reformation. He had been brought up, as his admirer Daniel Paerus afterwards put it, like Moses in the house of the Pharaohs, later to become their chief enemy.[6]

In the political struggle over religion which raged through Germany since Frederick was an infant, the west and south-west of the country was open to strong influence from both sides. The Rhine carried down from Switzerland the Protestant doctrines. Protestant Strasbourg had ties of trade and culture with the Palatinate and its subordinate territories. Further to the north lay Protestant Hesse under the Landgrave Philip, and not far to the north-east lay Saxony. Melanchthon was a child of the Palatinate. Everywhere in Germany Protestantism was still a popular movement, advancing except only in those unusual territories where the ruler felt strong enough, and convinced enough, to contain its impetus. It commanded the best of the printing trade and the most widely read writers. Printers who published books against Luther could hardly find a market. The universities found difficulty in filling their chairs with adequate scholars unless they elected Protestants; and where they refused to elect Protestants, it showed that the curriculum and the administration were running out of date. *Test the Church by the word of God* – this was a cry accepted throughout Germany, and not only in the states already labelled evangelical, adherents of that Protest which was issued at Speyer eight years before Frederick's marriage.

The division into Catholic and Protestant was not yet clear. Many German clergymen and laymen, perhaps most, could not have told an enquirer in 1537 whether they were Catholic or Protestant. The lines were drawn less firmly than twenty

[6] Pareus, *Historia Bavarico-Palatina* ed. G. C. Joannis, Frankfurt 1717, VI, 2, 260.

years later. When Frederick's parents, by later standards Roman Catholics, negotiated with Maria's family about the wedding of the children, they cannot have been unaware of difference in the religion of the parties. But they did not think it necessary to mention the matter of religion in the discussions before the betrothal.[7] Neither side found it an obstacle to so suitable a marriage. This optimism, however, ran a risk. Ten years earlier the marriage of the Elector of Brandenburg ended in calamity, ostensibly by reason of religious disagreement with his wife.[8] We cannot quite tell, however, how far the religious argument was the cause of the separation and how far the pretext for other forms of incompatibility.

Frederick's father was an official of the Emperor Charles V, who was the mainstay of old Catholicism in Germany. He got both Frederick's younger brothers into ecclesiastical prebends, and put five of his eight daughters into nunneries while they were still young; a course normal among the impecunious noblemen of Germany when seeking to assure the future for their younger children.

The marriage turned Frederick into a Protestant. His wife persuaded him that religion was worth his attention, familiarized him with the doctrines of Luther, and persuaded him to read the Bible regularly. This did not happen quickly. While he remained at Simmern he conformed to his father's wishes. He became an open Protestant only when, nine years after marriage, he became the custodian of Bayreuth on behalf of his wife's only brother Albert Alcibiades, Count of Brandenburg-Culmbach, and therefore went to live away from home, at the castle of Plassenburg.[9]

Albert Alcibiades became a landmark in, and a trial to, Frederick's life. He was christened only Albert, but acquired the Alcibiades as a nickname while a young man, because he resembled the Greek in enterprise and in rakishness. Since he was fourteen, when complaints first began about the amount of drink which he consumed, he had troubled his family. With no father, he had to struggle for his Franconian territory,

---

[7] Kluckhohn, 7–9.
[8] Voigt, *Hofleben*, 249–50.
[9] But the castle of Plassenburg which the visitor now sees was mostly built 1560–70.

never experienced home life, and suffered from a restless and unpredictable spirit. Not at all interested in books – so we read in lamentations from his uncles – and coming from a long line of *condottieri* and cavalry-leaders, he turned instinctively to hunting and drinking by way of leisure and to military adventures by way of an occupation. He took service as one of the leading commanders of cavalry in the imperial army and rendered distinguished service when in the war of 1544 the Emperor beat the French.

In the year 1546 the Emperor Charles V determined to crush the Protestant princes and enforce imperial power in the Holy Roman Empire.

To serve under the imperial standard Albert Alcibiades raised a formidable little force in Franconia. This force in central Germany frightened everyone, including Albert of Prussia, who begged Albert Alcibiades, however he served the Emperor, not to allow himself to be used in an onslaught on God's truth. Albert Alcibiades replied that he owed his military service to the Emperor; and that the Emperor intended not to fight men for their religion, but to suppress men who rebelled against the just law of empire under the pretext of religion. This was just what the Emperor told the public, though not what he said in private to his friends.[10]

On 2 July 1546 Albert Alcibiades moved his force out of Bayreuth to join the Emperor's army at Ratisbon. He left his brother-in-law Frederick of Simmern as governor of his Anspach territory while he was away.

In the Schmalkaldic war which followed, Albert Alcibiades is found at one time riding shoulder to shoulder with the commander of the Emperor's Spanish troops; at another, kept out of the campaign for several weeks by grievous illness; then found under orders from the Emperor to round up and execute imperial troops, especially Spanish and Italian, who robbed and plundered the civilian population. As commander of a separate force he invaded the domains of the Elector of Saxony, occupied the fortress of Rochlitz, and was there surrounded in the night by the Elector's forces and captured after a short and messy fight (2 March 1547). He was conveyed

[10] Voigt, *Albrecht Alcibiades*, i, 102–11.

via Wittenberg to a secret prison in the castle at Gotha. Eight weeks later the Emperor met the Elector at the Battle of Mühlberg and won so devastating a victory that most of Germany lay at his feet. One clause in the conditions of the treaty of Wittenberg (19 May 1547) required the release of Albert Alcibiades and the restoration of his lands, money, and goods.

During the winter war Frederick of Simmern held the castle of Plassenburg, and whatever lands the enemy did not over-run, for Albert Alcibiades. Frederick, being a convinced Protestant, anxiously protested that this war was not a war of Catholic versus Protestant, but of constitutional government versus rebels, and that his brother-in-law did only his loyal duty by his liege master the Emperor. He ordered prayer for a right outcome in all the churches of the domain, and busily strengthened Plassenburg further with men-at-arms, privately not confident that he could hold it against attack in force. He tried to get King Ferdinand of Austria to send him two hundred Bohemians to help man the walls. Suspecting that some of the citizens were more likely to side with the Protestant princes than with the Emperor, and hearing of Protestant preachers who sermonized to that end, and who even assailed the Emperor from their pulpits, or in pamphlets, he ordered such utterances to cease, and that nothing might be published against the Emperor under pain of severe punishment.[11]

The capture of Albert Alcibiades left Frederick isolated and threatened. Enemy troops occupied the surrounding country. His wife was inconsolable at the fate of her brother. A letter has survived from Frederick in Plassenburg to Duke Albert of Prussia, seven days after the castle at Rochlitz fell and Albert Alcibiades was captured, pleading that Duke Albert may do all that he can to get the prisoner released.[12]

Everything was changed by the Emperor's triumph. Albert Alcibiades stood at the peak of his fortunes, to be rewarded

[11] Voigt, *Albrecht Alcibiades*, i, 120–9.
[12] Frederick to Albert of Prussia, Plassenburg, 10 March 1547; part printed in W. Hubatsch, *Europäische Briefe im Reformationszeitalter: zweihundert Briefe am Markgraf Albrecht von Brandenburg-Anspach, Herzog Preussen*, Kitzingen 1949, 112. Another letter of 3 June reports the release.

as one of the Emperor's famous captains. He had a European reputation. Men talked of his marrying Mary Tudor and becoming King of England.[13] It looked as though the fortunes of the family were established, and Frederick of Simmern could share in the spoils of victory.

Frederick and Maria, however, could be less comfortable than Albert Alcibiades. Frederick, like his brother-in-law, fought on the Emperor's side with the plea that the war was not a religious war. But after victory Charles V showed that it was a religious war. At the armed Diet of Augsburg in 1548, he ordered the Interim, as a religious settlement of Germany until the ultimate settlement by some recognized General Council of all the Church.

This near-Catholic church order meant nothing to Albert Alcibiades. 'What has the Interim got to do with me?' he told a questioner. 'I'll believe whatever the Emperor says.' Though educated in a formally Protestant family, his religion was vague. Under pressure from the Emperor he was willing to declare himself a Catholic and to pooh-pooh the Protestant church order of the territories of Anspach. He at once began to introduce the Interim into his land, restoring an abbot and monks to the great monastery of Heilbronn which his uncle had dissolved, and seeking the advice of the papal nuncio and his visitors to recreate Catholic order in the churches. He wrote the Pope a letter that he was a good Catholic and would long ago have expelled 'the Lutheran faction' from his lands if he had not feared a rebellion;[14] though the object of the letter was to get papal sanction for his dealings in monastic property. He found the Interim difficult to introduce into his churches. The preachers refused, and then the knights, parents refused to send children to school where the master accepted the Interim, and Albert Alcibiades (who did not care) was forced to give way.[15]

Still, he stood high in favour of the Emperor. The predica-

---

[13] Strype, *Ecclesiastical Memorials*, 2, 250, 517.
[14] Lang, K. H., *Neuere Geschichte des Fürstenthums Baireuth*, 2, Göttingen 1827, 206.
[15] For his troubles over the Interim, K. H. Lang, *Neuere Geschichte des Fürstenthums Baireuth*, 2, 207ff; Voigt, *Albrecht Alcibiades*, i, 189–93; F. Pietsch, *Geschichte der gelehrten Bildung in Kulmbach* (Die Plassenburg Schriften für Heimatforschung und Kulturpflege in Ostfranken), 1974, 53.

ment of his brother-in-law Frederick was less enviable. His Protestant conscience was too strong to allow him to accept the Interim. He had forfeited whatever respect he might have won from Protestant princes by taking the Emperor's side in the war. Now he must forfeit the Emperor's respect by being unwilling to accept the religious settlement. He went back to his obscurity at Simmern. Albert Alcibiades, who happened to be in economizing mood, carefully inspected all his accounts after he went.[16]

Frederick dallied with idea of exile in England or the Netherlands, but remained at Simmern and kept his conscience in order and tried to do what he could for preachers who suffered under the Interim. His father was much displeased at this Protestant behaviour and cut his allowance. The eight years after the Interim were in outer circumstances the most miserable of Frederick's life.

His wife, who was now responsible for eight children (four sons and four daughters living) had powerful relatives and begged. How much she needed money was shown when she begged even for clothes and travelling expenses. Like her brother, and like her younger sisters, she thought that her mainstay must be her uncle, Duke Albert of Prussia. The Duke, who received begging letters from other women besides Maria, helped her with occasional gifts of money but the begging letters continued passionate in their suppliant cries. To pay debts the pair sold for 2,000 florins a ring given to them by the Emperor.

The cares of Frederick's life were multiplied by the next activities of his brother-in-law, Albert Alcibiades.

To enforce the religious settlement and his political power, the Emperor ordered Maurice of Saxony to besiege and take the Protestant city of Magdeburg, and Albert Aleibiades joined Maurice in the siege. But soon the princes conspired with the French to overthrow the Emperor, whom they accused not only of trampling on true religion but of attempting to destroy German freedom. Albert Alcibiades went in disguise to the French court to confirm a treaty with the king, whereby the princes handed over to the French the imperial

[16] Voigt, *Albrecht Alcibiades,* i, 225.

cities of Metz, Toul, Verdun and Cambrai in return for military support. In the ensuing war which broke the power of the Emperor and secured the safety of the Protestant states for seventy years, Albert Alcibiades tasted plunder. With the virtue and vice of a buccaneer, he found himself in command of an army in Central Germany. Claiming to stand for freedom and justice and the defence of the Christian religion, he mercilessly ravaged the territory of Nuremberg, annexed two-thirds of the prince-bishopric of Bamberg, plundered the prince-bishopric of Würzburg, and in two months of 1552 forced the city and the two bishops to pay him 870,000 gulden. The occupation of Catholic bishoprics became a habit. He moved over into the Rhineland, occupied Mainz, from which the Archbishop fled, extracted 100,000 gulden from the clergy and when they could not pay sacked the archbishop's palace and the canons' houses and five churches in the city. Then he moved up the Rhine, bishops fleeing before him, extracted money from the cities, plundered the churches in Speier; then down again, into the archbishopric of Trier, where the inhabitants were so frightened that they refused entry to an imperial garrison which tried to protect them, and where Albert Alcibiades only plundered the houses of the canons who fled.

In 1553 he turned back to engage in 'the Bishops' War' – another attack on Würzburg and Bamberg because they failed to carry out the treaties which he enforced upon them in the previous year. Popular with his troops and worshipped by his lieutenants, he frightened everyone who now cared for peace and law; for there were ominous suggestions of a new peasants' war, in which the old hatred of peasants against clergy and monasteries would rise again and be centred in a veteran army under the most formidable commander in Germany. He occupied Halberstadt and compelled the chapter to elect a Protestant bishop. In 1553 he was beaten at Sievershausen near Hanover by his old comrade-in-arms Maurice of Saxony, who was mortally wounded in the battle. Driven southward by Henry of Brunswick, he finally fled as a refugee to France, his fortress of Plassenburg falling on 22 June 1554. The Emperor confirmed the loss of all his territories; and the ensuing lawsuit, which friends conducted on behalf of Albert Alcibiades, lasted until he died aged thirty-four on 8 January 1557.

The rise and fall of Albert Alcibiades astounded and shocked Europe. The English agents in Germany never failed to report what he was doing, sometimes with excited expectation of some new adventure.[17] Even when he was destitute, and could hardly pay a groom, governments liked to know where he was and what he might be planning.

The curious thing about Albert Alcibiades – spendthrift, swashbuckling, piratical – was his capacity to elicit admiration from a few respectable men. His brother-in-law Frederick believed in him absolutely. Frederick was not unique; for the chaplain to Albert Alcibiades, who reconstructed the reformation of Culmbach after its destruction in the wars, shared the same unwavering regard.[18] Frederick saw his brother-in-law as a warrior for truth who was grossly injured by two corrupt bishops and an untrustworthy Emperor. His language was pitying: 'this poor prince', 'this good religious prince'. He would hear no ill of him, in every controversy he stood at his side. When from the walls of Königshofen hidden guns fired at Albert Alcibiades as he rode privately on a journey, one side said that it was attempted murder and the other that it was a warning shot at an unknown traveller – Frederick had no doubt that the shot was aimed to kill. He argued for his brother-in-law at the Diet, wrote letters to the Brandenburg princes, tried to persuade Duke Albert of Prussia to do more for his nephew. In the last refugee years of Albert Alcibiades, Simmern was one of the harbours safe from the hunt. In Frederick's house, Albert Alcibiades met his chief agent Grumbach, and planned new armies. But even Simmern cannot have been comfortable. For there Frederick did not yet rule. 'I . . . would gladly help him but it is not in my

---

[17] *Calendar of State Papers, Foreign, Eliz.* I, *1553–8*, frequently; cf Sir John Mason from Brussels to Queen Mary, 26 June 1554 (ibid., 100): So often down and so often up again; thinks there was never none; but now there is nothing to fear at his hand, since the only poor castle belonging to him, Plassenburg, cannot longer hold out.

[18] Georg Thiel; cf. Pietsch, *Geschichte der gelehrten Bildung in Kulmbach*, 53ff.

power because I am still under my dear father's rule and have nothing of my own.'[19]

Albert Alcibiades died not at Simmern but at the house in Pforzheim of his other brother-in-law, Charles of Baden. He accepted the ministrations of a Lutheran chaplain, and Frederick was with him when he died.[20]

The fate of Albert Alcibiades probably made a subtle difference to Frederick's Protestant outlook. It led him even more to distrust Catholic prince-bishops and a Catholic Emperor. But, more important, it led him to eye the chief Lutheran princes critically. Albert Alcibiades, who claimed to stand for Protestantism and the liberties of Germany, was overthrown not by prince-bishops but by Protestants: Maurice of Saxony, the burghers of Nuremberg. In his flight he found more kindness in the Cardinal of Augsburg than the Protestant Duke Christopher of Württemberg. In Frederick's later attitudes to the German Reformation these memories must have lasted.

In 1556 Frederick's circumstances took a turn for the better. The Elector Palatine, Frederick II, died and was succeeded by Otto Henry, who was an old widower and childless. If Otto Henry died childless, most assumed (it was not uncontested) that the Simmern line stood next in succession to rule the Palatinate.[21] Frederick suddenly became heir presumptive to one of the principal states of Germany; whose ruler was one of the seven electors to the imperial crown, and who had the right to preside over the empire at an interregnum and to bear the imperial orb. The Elector Palatine had his seat at Heidelberg and his domains in the Rhineland. He ruled also the Upper Palatinate, a small territory on the borders of Bavaria, separated from the Palatinate proper by many miles, with its capital at Amberg. Otto Henry at once made his heir-presumptive the governor of the Upper Palatinate. Frederick

[19] Frederick to Duke Albert of Prussia, Stuttgart, 3 July 1554; in Voigt, *Albrecht Alcibiades*, 2, 214–5.

[20] Kluckhohn, 20: the chaplain was Jakob Heerbrand, afterwards professor at Tübingen and a distinguished writer.

[21] The Simmern line descended from the younger brother of the Elector Palatine Ludwig III, who succeeded in 1410.

and Maria took up residence at Amberg. A year later Frederick's father died, strong Roman Catholic to the end, and he succeeded to Simmern.

He owed a lot of money. His creditors still pressed, and less hopelessly, for the heir to a great princedom might be expected to borrow on better credit. He was so badly off that at one moment he considered a secret bargain with Bavaria to sell his right to the succession to the Palatinate. Now he must begin to maintain princely style. His daughters were sought after, pawns in a system of political and social alliance. On 12 June 1558 he carried off an apparent coup when his eldest daughter, Elizabeth, married none other than the Duke of Saxony, John Frederick, son of the Elector who lost the title of Elector and part of his domains after the battle of Mühlberg. This good alliance brought him into a deeper pit of debt. A dowry suitable for a princess must contain not merely an annual allowance in gulden, but suitable 'furniture' appropriate to her station – and this furniture always included an extravagant amount of jewellery, which princes regarded not only as an ornament but as a way of saving and of investment during the inflation.

The Elector, Otto Henry, was a reformer. It was easy and agreeable for Frederick to conform in the Upper Palatinate.[22] He was free to reform Simmern where, unlike the Palatinate, nothing Protestant had happened. Only two months after his father's death he ordered the mass to cease, and began to close monasteries, abolish relics, and introduce the new church order of the Palatinate.

The Elector, Otto Henry, made the Palatinate Protestant. The land was already unsatisfactory to Catholics. Its geography meant that to keep out Protestant ideas had been impossible for three decades. Ludwig V (Elector 1508–44) made no attempt to hold the line. He was a Catholic of the modern type, with a humanist education which inclined him to liberality and made him see the faults of the old Church. He

---

[22] For what little is known of the Reformation in the Upper Palatinate during his short period as governor, see J. B. Götz, *Die religiöse Bewegung in der Oberpfalz von 1520 bis 1560* (Erläuterungen und Ergänzungen zu Janssens Geschichte des deutschen Volkes, ed. L. von Pastor, X, 1–2) Freiburg-im-Breisgau 1914: Sehling, *Die evangelischen Kirchenordnungen des XVI Jahrhunderts*, xiii, 262–3.

was willing for change, provided the change was faithful to Catholicism and not accompanied by disorder. His successor Frederick II (1544–56) was another moderate. But if Ludwig was a moderate who inclined to Catholicism, Frederick was a moderate who inclined to Protestantism. If change was to come, it could hardly mean less change than: (1) a more prominent place for the Bible; (2) services and sermons which the people could, at least in part, understand; (3) communion in both kinds, and (4) allowing the clergy to marry. But to allow these things in the Germany of 1544 was to look like a public Protestant. At Easter 1546 for the first time the Elector received communion in both kinds. In January 1546 the first German mass was celebrated in Heidelberg. But everything was very conservative. A lot of the services, especially the singing, was still in Latin. The new services stopped masses without communicants and forbad the devotion or reservation of the sacrament.[23] But priests still wore vestments. The Elector tried to persuade Melanchthon to accept a post at the university of Heidelberg. But Melanchthon, pleading health and the situation at Wittenberg – for Martin Luther had just died – would not come.

Then the Emperor Charles V won the Schmalkaldic War, and ordered the Augsburg Interim. The Elector Palatine comfortably submitted. The government of the Palatinate conformed, and all the Catholic rites came back (officially, at least), though the sacrament might be in two kinds and clergy kept their wives. Frederick II the moderate was regarded with suspicion by Catholics as a Protestant, and by stouter Protestants as Iscariot. Meanwhile the churches of the Palatinate stood in a state of indescribable confusion, every priest doing what was right in his own eyes, or what his congregation would suffer him to do.

The extent of Protestant success, under an outwardly Catholic government, can be judged by the number of monasteries which already stood empty because the monks secularized themselves. Between 1549 and 1551 there were long negotiations between the Elector and the Pope, seeking that these empty houses might be applied to the university of

[23] Successive church orders in Sehling, xiv, 90ff.

Heidelberg or to found a college of higher education for poor students. Even at this time the Elector tried to win Melanchthon for his university, and still without success. In 1551-2 the Emperor was defeated, and no longer a threat; and so from 1553 Protestant services, where men wanted to hold Protestant services, began again to be celebrated. The Elector received communion after the Protestant liturgy on the Sunday before he died, and was buried with Protestant rites.[24]

Otto Henry had been a convinced and active, but powerless, Protestant since his 'conversion' (for so it could be described) fourteen years before. He was only fifty-four years old, but already ill, perhaps of the stone, must take the waters regularly, was too crippled to travel except in a mule-cart. During his uncle's rule he lived either in a private house on the Cornmarket in Heidelberg, or, when Charles V objected to his presence, in a country estate, and made his house the centre of the Protestant groups in the Palatinate. He corresponded with Melanchthon and Bucer and with the princely leaders of the Reformation. When he became Elector, men all over Germany could see now that the Palatinate was going to be Protestant. A decree at once abolished the mass and the Catholic ceremonies.

The orders were stronger than their execution. The new Elector Palatine could command the mass to cease, but in the country a priest went on saying mass if his congregation let him, and government was seldom quick to interfere. Visitors were appointed, and went round making inventories of church property, and altering what needed to be altered in the churches. Many pictures and statues vanished from churches, where possible at night so that the population would not be disturbed without necessity. Monks and nuns were not ejected from houses where they wished to remain, but were ordered to have Protestant services instead of Catholic, and to read Protestant books instead of Catholic, and to live virtuously. One of the male houses, that of the Holy Ghost in

---

[24] Sehling, xiv, 22. For Frederick II's position 1554-6 see now the nuncio's reports in H. Goetz (ed.), *Nuntiaturberichte aus Deutschland 1553-9, nebst ergänzenden Aktenstücken*, Band XVII, Tübingen 1970.

Heidelberg, was taken over to be a College of Wisdom for higher education. The surviving archives do not determine how far these instructions were executed. It looks as though they were not carried through systematically; perhaps because the Elector was ill and dying, perhaps because opinion in the land was divided. It looks as though the order to avoid disturbance was not always observed, and that local crowds occasionally rushed into churches to destroy pictures or statues.[25]

Otto Henry ruled for a short time and left his successor to tidy. Though a devout Protestant, he was not puritan. He loved art, spared no expense on the magnificence of his buildings, and created a lovely monument of Renaissance architecture. He made his library one of the two or three best libraries in Europe. The music in his chapel was renowned. He paid good stipends to his servants, and attracted scholars to make his university one of the leading universities of Europe. But to do all these excellent things he had no money. Books, pictures, buildings, stipends, scholars, music were paid for on credit.

He was a Lutheran. Caring far more for scholarship than for orthodoxy, he filled the chairs at his university with the best men that he could find – Xylander the first Byzantinist of Germany to the chair of Greek, Ehem in the faculty of law, the ex-Carmelite Frenchman Pierre Boquin as professor of theology, and above all Thomas Erastus to head the faculty of medicine. The incoming scholars all looked towards Switzerland as the way of Reformation. Before he died Otto Henry began to realize that he had brewed trouble, with a Lutheran church and a university going Reformed. He decided to dismiss his French theologian Boquin, but died.[26] Frederick of Simmern, now Frederick III of the Palatinate, came to Heidelberg to find vast debts and radical disagreement among the religious leaders of his new land: especially a deepening antipathy between church and university.

[25] Kurze, Barbara, *Kurfürst Ott Heinrich: Politik und Religion in der Pfalz 1556–9* (Schr. d. Verein f. Reformationsgeschichte, 174) Gütersloh 1956, 70.
[26] Wolfgang of Zweibrücken to Frederick, Neuburg 21 June 1560; in *Briefe Friedrichs des Frommen*, ed. A. Kluckhohn, Brunswick 1868–72, i, 140. It would be pleasant to have evidence from a less partial source than Duke Wolfgang.

Frederick had a Lutheran wife who converted him to the evangelical faith. German Protestants were satisfied to see him reign. The agent of the English government reported to London as though he had never heard of him before ('a Duke of Symmern'), but that he did well by religion in Simmern and all good men have a good hope of him. Another English agent reported him as a lover of true religion, who might be of much service to Queen Elizabeth.[27] For months afterwards the English agents assumed that this was a Protestant prince like other German Protestants, and had no inkling that Frederick's mind moved.

Frederick could lessen the inherited troubles at once by stopping the buildings, dismissing architects, letting the music decline, and doing less for the library. But he could not so simply manage the conflict between church and university, just then moving into a climax.

The leader of the church in the Palatinate was Tilemann Hesshusen, a learned young pastor (aged thirty-two) sent there on the recommendation of Melanchthon. Historians have competed in denouncing him as the most rigid or fanatical of Lutherans. It has been shown that he was a true disciple of Melanchthon, and thus far moderate, until the moment when he became convinced that Melanchthon departed from Luther's doctrine of the Eucharist.[28] Any disciple of Luther who was determined to preserve the faith would look rigid in a city where professors like Boquin or Ehem or Xylander or Erastus educated young men. Nevertheless, Hesshusen was in no circumstances an easy colleague. The new Elector, though he did not yet know it, and irrespective of his personal attitude in religion, was confronted with a forced choice, either to destroy a flourishing university or to dismiss his chief pastor.

In his first months he discovered that the senate of the University refused any longer to invite Hesshusen to its meetings, though he was dean of the faculty of theology. The

[27] Mundt to Cecil, 27 February 1559; Polantus to Sir Henry Killigrew, 15 February 1559; *Calendar of State Papers, Foreign, Eliz. I, 1558–9*, nos. 329, 357.

[28] Barton, P. F., *Um Luthers Erbe: Studien und Texte zur Spätreformation; Tilemann Heshusius* (1527–59) (Untersuchungen zur Kirchengeschichte, 6) Witten 1972; with literature. For a fuller biography see meanwhile Karl von Helmolt, *Tilemann Hesshus und seine sieben Exilia*, Leipzig 1859.

trouble arose over the granting of degrees in theology to persons whom Hesshusen believed to be Zwinglians: one a visiting Frisian, the other (by a misfortune) a deacon at Hesshusen's own Church of the Holy Ghost, by name Wilhelm Klebitz.[29] While Hesshusen was away from Heidelberg, the university approved Klebitz for a degree on a thesis which Hesshusen believed to be heretical. When he came back he denounced Klebitz from the pulpit as a Zwinglian and a sacramentary, and attacked the university as sectarian. On 6 September 1559 Hesshusen publicly excommunicated Klebitz. Things were difficult in church services when the chief pastor insisted on the words *in the bread* and his deacon on the words *with the bread*.

On 9 September the Elector summoned all the City pastors to the Chancellery, and explained his attitude. On the following day the pastor Diller, not with wisdom but probably at Frederick's wish, told the decision to the people. No one was to use the words *under the bread* or *in the bread*. No one was to refuse communion with Klebitz. All must keep silence on the controversy.

On the same day at noon another pastor Pantaleon demanded the ejection of Klebitz. On 13 September Hesshusen used all the phrases in church, *in the bread, under the bread, with the bread*. He denounced the order to keep silence, and called the Augsburg Confession in its Variata form (which contained *with the bread* only) as 'a boot that would fit either foot' and 'so broad a cloak' that the Lord and the devil could live comfortably. Hesshusen was not afraid of his sovereign.

On 16 September Frederick dismissed both Hesshusen and Klebitz from office. He allowed Hesshusen to remain for six months on full pay.

Frederick ended the employment of Hesshusen not because he was Lutheran but because he disobeyed. Only a month

[29] The chief authority for the ensuing events is Klebitz's own later apology, *Victoria Veritatis, ac ruina papatus Saxonici: responsio ad argumenta Tilemanni Heshusii* (Freiburg 1561). P. F. Barton, in his wish that justice be done to Hesshusen, pointed out how one-sided is the evidence (*Um Luthers Erbe*). But the factual information in *Victoria Veritatis* rings true. For the earliest account by a historian see Alting, *De Ecclesiis Palatinis*, xxxiii, in *Mensonis Altingii Vita*, ed. A. M. Isinck, Groningen 1728. Modern account in Sehling (J. F. G. Goeters), xiv, 38; cf. Kluckhohn, 52ff.

after the dismissal a schoolmaster was hired to teach the young in accordance with the Augsburg Confession and the catechism of Dr Luther.[30] That same October Frederick sent his secretary Stephen Cirler to Wittenberg, to ask Melanchthon's advice.

Melanchthon, in the last months of his life, wrote in reply the most anti-Lutheran letter that he ever wrote;[31] or at least a letter that was more outspoken than might be expected of his prudent spirit, especially since Hesshusen was his old pupil and his choice for Heidelberg. Some suspect, though without evidence, that Cirler gave a one-sided story of what happened in Heidelberg. Melanchthon approved wholeheartedly of the Elector's conduct; praised the order to keep silence; advocated the formula *with the bread;* and urged an end to controversy by the use of the words on which all men may agree.

The Elector had this letter printed and distributed.

The argument did not cease, nor the frictions of the Palatinate. Amid the cares of state and administration Frederick found, like the Emperor Justinian before him and King James of England and Scotland after him, that he must study divinity. His subjects were divided, and his rule hampered, and his brain troubled, by a conflict in theology where both sides claimed truth. For the first time in his life he set out systematically to understand arguments for and against an expression of Christian doctrine. His method was not to attempt the folios of eminent theologians. He read not a word of Zwingli or Calvin. That autumn he spent nights and days poring over his Bible. He studied so hard that the palace staff were anxious about his health.

Historians have sometimes blamed the princes of the Reformation for intruding into divinity. They seldom recognize sufficiently that statecraft forced them into divinity.

These studies did not bring a clear answer. But they helped to move him in one direction. For in the family circle, though not yet in the wide public, the letters of wife and son-in-law show growing worry – worry that Frederick was in danger of departing from the truth – worry first for his soul, in the

[30] Häusser, ii, 13 note.
[31] *Corpus Ref.* ix, 961ff.

presence of God, but soon worry also for the politics of the Holy Roman Empire and the safety of the Palatinate.

He was bound in loyalty to the evangelical faith by affection for a devout Lutheran wife, to whom he owed his Protestant convictions. The politics of the Palatinate did not push him away from her religion, for although the leaders of the university and half his cabinet wanted change, the people were conservative – one disciple of Calvin, who arrived in Heidelberg during 1560 and was later celebrated as Caspar Olevianus, was refused a bride because he was a Calvinist.[32] Anyone more worldly, or more diplomatic, or more experienced in government, might have felt bound to the same side by reluctance to sever links with the Protestant powers of Germany, or a fear of what the Emperor could do if he made no part of the Protestant alliance. No evidence exists that this matter of the public interest affected Frederick's judgement on his Bible. He was intent on truth.

Yet a question of policy may have affected his mind. That winter the Protestants of Germany became ever more concerned over what was happening in France. The Huguenots were persecuted, and the country evidently moved towards civil war. All the German princes thought what they could do; and if they were not disturbed enough for themselves, English agents did whatever could be done to disturb them further, as Queen Elizabeth sought to protect England from a French threat in Scotland. It is probably a mere accident, but nevertheless a symbol, that the first Englishman on the Continent to report division between Frederick and the other Germans, was none of the Englishmen in Germany, but the ambassador to the French at Orleans.[33]

The dismissal of Hesshusen gave the world no cause to suppose that the Elector Palatine fell away from Luther. The Englishman at Strasbourg was hardly aware what had happened until over a year had passed.[34] The papal nuncio in

[32] Calvin, *Epistolae*, lx, no. 3250 (*CR*. xlvi, 195) 'Who', asked Olevianus bitterly, 'would give his daughter in marriage to a Calvinist, at the risk of her soul?'

[33] Throckmorton to Cecil, 18 January 1561; *Calendar of State Papers, Foreign*, Eliz. I, 1560–1, no. 891. On 12 July 1560 Melville reported to Killigrew from Marburg on the differences on the 'cene' between Palatinate theologians and Saxon theologians, ibid, no. 328.

[34] Mundt to Cecil, 8 October 1560; ibid, 615.

Germany failed to report anything to Rome until another six months later. Perhaps the expulsion of a strictly Lutheran chief pastor might be expected to have private consequence in the psyche. But Frederick acted in a way which Luther's lieutenant then approved.

In Heidelberg Frederick was surrounded by counsellors of various opinions. We cannot at this range tell whether any of them gained such influence as to pull him in one direction. His Chancellor von Minckwitz was a stiff Lutheran. The chief justice was a Lutheran. His wife was nervous that two of his relatives who lived in Heidelberg would draw him towards the Zwinglians.[35] But one of the Zwinglians in Heidelberg began to exercise a growing influence – paradoxically, in the hindsight of what happened later – the big bearded Erastus, with his nodding head and oddities like wearing a large hat on top of a small hat.[36] Erastus was the only man in Heidelberg to be intimate with the Zwinglian leaders in Zurich. He was also the Elector's physician. He contrasted markedly with Hesshusen in one important matter which was political as well as religious. Hesshusen the strict Lutheran flagrantly disobeyed the orders of his godly prince because he thought them ungodly. Erastus the Reformed from Switzerland held a high opinion of the sovereign's power in religion. That Frederick respected his judgement is proved by the minutes of the Heidelberg disputation of 3–7 June 1560.

This meeting was caused by the perturbations in the family. Maria saw her husband and her son-in-law, Duke John Frederick of Saxony, drawing apart in religion. Wife and duke together believed that all might be well if they met. In the presence of the two princes the theologians of John Frederick held public debate of four days with Peter Boquin – is *This is*

[35] Maria to John Frederick II, 7 April 1559; Kluckhohn, 49. She meant chiefly Count Eberhard of Erbach, who as court chamberlain had the advantage of access – the court chamberlain, despite his title, was the chief officer of state. Frederick's sister Elizabeth married Eberhard's brother George. For the influence of George, cf. Calvin, *Ep.* ix, no. 3249 (*CR.* xlvi, 189), cf. ibid., no. 3250; Volker Press, *Calvinismus und Territorialstaat, Regierung und Zentralbehörden der Kurpfalz 1559–1619* (Kieler Historische Studien, 17) Stuttgart 1970, 225–6.

[36] Barton, 198 n. 19; for the part of Erastus at this time, see R. Wesel-Roth, *Thomas Erastus, Ein Beitrag zur Geschichte der reformierten Kirche und zur Lehre von der Staatsoveranität* 1954. For the probable influence of Ehem in the same direction, though it is only discernible later, see Volker Press, 232–3.

my body literal or metaphysical? Is the sacrament received by faith or also with the mouth? If these are metaphors, is reason intruding where reason has no place? . . . Erastus sometimes intervened – to the resentment of the Saxons, one of whom said that the Palatinate theologians must be weak if they needed a doctor of medicine to defend their case.

The Heidelberg disputation has been claimed to mark the turning-point in Frederick's mind. The oldest historian of the Palatinate, Alting[37] testified that Frederick expressed his opinion of the debate thus: the Lutherans won in force and repartee, the Reformed in simplicity and modest defence of the truth.

In the later months of 1560 and in 1561 the expulsions of Lutheran preachers came faster.

The last stage appears to have been reached when Frederick, who refused to read the works of Zwingli or Calvin, was forced to read Luther.

In the winter of 1560–1 the Protestant princes agreed to meet at Naumburg to bring Frederick back from his errors. They were concerned what would happen if Frederick became a public heretic and put himself outside the terms of the peace of Augsburg which was the guarantee of everyone's safety and of German prosperity. Any politician could see that the event brought nearer a risk of civil war over religion. The meeting at Naumburg in January 1561 had the demerit of drawing European attention to the Protestant dispute. The English agents started to send reports, even the papal nuncios, quick to be informed on these matters, at last reported to Rome.[38]

---

[37] xxxix, ed. cit., 73. Olevianus, who was wholly on Boquin's side, reported to Calvin that Boquin was not easily understood because of his French accent – Olevianus to Calvin, Frankfurt, 22 September 1560, *CR* xlvi, 192 (Calvin, *Epistolae*, ix, no. 3250).

[38] Mundt arrived in Naumburg on 6 February but sent no report till 4 March, *Calendar of State Papers, Foreign, Eliz. I*, 1561–2, no. 9; cf. ibid., 1560–1, no. 935, Mansfield to the Queen, 26 January 1561. Hosius to Borromeo 7 April 1561, in *Nuntiaturberichte aus Deutschland nebst ergänzenden Actenstücken* Vienna 1897, I, 240: the Elector Palatine 'qui tamen Augustae confessionis subscripsit nihilominus, sed manu non corde'. The nuncios Commendone and Delfino were received at Naumburg in connexion with the invitation to the renewed sessions of the Council of Trent. Their speeches had less than supreme tact, emphasizing the radical divisions which they found; cf. Ludwig von Pastor, *History of the Popes*, Eng. trans., xv, 220ff; E. Reimann, *Die Sendung des Nunzius Commendone nach Deutschland im Jahre 1561*, in *Forschungen zur deutschen Geschichte*, vii, Göttingen 1867, 235ff; see also Delfino to Borromeo, Speier 20 April 1561, ibid., I, 350, saying that Frederick is in effect a Sacramentary. Before

The meeting at Naumburg discovered to Frederick more of his mind.

The princes had the plan that they should display their unity by signing again the Augsburg Confession. But even before they met at Naumburg they found themselves in confusion over what text to sign. No one could find the original Latin of 1530, or a reliable copy (we know, but they did not, that the original Latin lay at this time in the imperial archives at Brussels, to be destroyed by Philip II of Spain eighteen years later). No one could find the original German text, which no one can find today. They began to talk of signing the original edition printed by Melanchthon in quarto at Wittenberg. But a comparison with the second (octavo) edition of 1531 showed that the Apology attached to the quarto edition was acceptable to the Roman Catholics in the doctrine of transubstantiation. Henceforth the princes talked of signing the 1531 edition.

This discovery perturbed Frederick. That men like Luther and Melanchthon should have written or approved such language showed that they were not always reliable divines. This perturbed him the more because until now he had not known these first and second editions, which we know as the Invariata. All his Protestant life he had used the 1540 edition, known as the Variata, which avoided using phrases like *in the bread*. Melanchthon never treated the words of the Augsburg Confession as a sacred text that no man might alter, but regarded it as a book which he had written and which he could improve in successive editions. The Variata had been presented to the imperial envoys, and was used in other public documents of the Empire. Therefore it could be regarded as a text legal under the Peace of Augsburg (1555) which gave protection to those who signed the Augsburg Confession.

Frederick could not sign the Invariata, unexplained. His son-in-law of Saxony could not sign the Variata lest it be a cloak for heresy. For a moment the meeting at Naumburg looked as though it might end in disaster. But the Elector Augustus of Saxony proposed an intelligent compromise. They

Naumburg the real state of opinion was not at all clear to the world. For special treatment of Naumburg, R. Calinich, *Der Naumburger Fürstentag, 1561* (Gotha 1870), especially 110ff, 159ff.

should sign the 1531 edition with the proviso that it was further explained in the 1540 edition.

Frederick signed; though his son-in-law could not, and hurriedly left the conference. The meeting at Naumburg was regarded afterwards as a failure. But it helped to save Germany from civil war for half a century, by showing that a state need not be strictly Lutheran to receive the protection of the imperial law. It also opened to Frederick the legal possibility of turning the Palatinate into a Reformed instead of a Lutheran state.

Frederick returned from Naumburg with the conviction that Luther and Melanchthon had not seen all truth. Someone – evidently his son-in-law John Frederick – persuaded him, by way of an antidote, to read Luther's last confession of faith written in 1544 against Schwenckfeld and Zwingli, *Kurzes Bekenntnis vom heiligen Sakrament*.[39] Immediately he came back to Heidelberg he was hard at the book. He did not like what he found. Anyone who thought the book a likely antidote to his state of mind wildly misjudged what he needed. A man whose father was a judge in the imperial high court might prefer a judicial attitude of mind. The old Luther, especially when he thought about Zwingli, was anything but calm. Frederick blamed the book for vague abuse without any precise definition of what the author found blameworthy.[40]

So Heidelberg became a new capital of the Reformed faith, third only to Zurich and Geneva. The Heidelberg catechism, still the best and most widely used of all documents of Reformed faith, was not published till 1563, but something like it was inevitable from the moment that Frederick returned from Naumburg. A deeply religious man followed the path

[39] Weimar ed., 54, 119ff; Eng. trans. by M. E. Lehmann in *Luther's Works*, vol. 38, Philadelphia 1971.

[40] Frederick to Duke John Frederick, 10 March 1561, Heidelberg, *Briefe*, 1, 166ff: Wiewohl ich das gedruckt büchlin zuvor in den tomis Luteri seligen auch gelesen, so hab ich doch bey andern gescheften sovil weyl genohmen, das ichs denselbigen tag wider durchlesen, befind aber wenig darin, das zu bawung [= Bauung] der Kirchen Christi dienlich, . . . etc. Walter Hollweg, who staunchly defended Frederick against a row of critical historians, showed also that we should not exaggerate the lowering of Luther's reputation in Frederick's mind – see his *Neue Untersuchungen zur Geschichte und Lehre des Heidelberger Katechismus* (Beiträge zur Geschichte und Lehre der Reformierten Kirche) Neukirchen 1961, 40; cf. Frederick's learned letter of 15 February 1565 on the subject of Luther, in *Briefe*, I, 557–8.

along which he believed that his Bible led him,[41] took no account of the political risk, did not care or notice that he made others run an equal risk, and made a radical difference to the future of Germany.

---

[41] For a fine defence of his personal religion, Frederick to Duke John Frederick, Heidelberg, 10th June 1562, *Briefe,* i, 308–13.

IV

Magistracy and Ministry: A Suffolk Miniature

PATRICK COLLINSON

'OH THE heavenly harmony and sweet amitie that then was amongst you from the highest to the lowest! The magistrates and the ministers imbracing and seconding one another, and the common people affording due reverence and obedience to them both.'[1] Our text is provided by William Burton, a Norwich minister forced into a kind of exile as the price of an intemperate sermon,[2] looking back on the halcyon Elizabethan days when Norwich was as kind to its preachers as it was famous for its government. This essay is about not Norwich but a small corner of Suffolk, although a certain reciprocity links Burton's 'religious and famous citie' to what Bishop Hall called 'that sweet and civil county of Suffolk, near to St Edmunds Bury'.[3] For if Elizabethan Norwich provides the paradigm of urban puritanism, Suffolk was the pattern of rural England under puritan government. And the subject is not 'the common people' either. Burton's faith in the willing subordination of their kind was no more than a rhetorical convention, a *topos* which can be contradicted with more rhetoric from the same mouth.[4] On this occasion we shall look no further than 'magistracy and ministry', the 'imbracing and seconding'.

The intention will be modestly descriptive, but descriptive

[1] Burton, William, *Seven dialogues both pithie and profitable*, 1606, Sig. A2.
[2] Burton, William, *A sermon preched in the cathedrall church in Norwich the xxi day of September 1589 . . . and published to the satisfying of some which took offence thereat*, n.d.
[3] *Works of Joseph Hall*, ed. Wynter, P., 1863, I, xxv.
[4] In his 1589 *Sermon* (Sig. D4v) Burton complained of the 'discourteous dealing' of the Norwich citizenry, 'whose hearts runne after covetousnes', and who hear the preacher 'for a fashion' but go home to jest their 'bellyesfull'.

of particular circumstances which have almost never been described, as an offering to a scholar who delights in particularities, especially those of place. The miniature is composed of fragments, restored to a frame which itself has to be reassembled from a variety of fugitive sources. Puritan Suffolk is one of those worlds we have lost, together with almost all record of its civil administration, many important ecclesiastical sources, especially those relating to the two archdeaconries, and all but a few materials of a more intimate character: that is to say, letters and diaries.[5]

If a world of understanding is to be discovered in a grain of sand it will be found to consist in our *leitmotiv* of 'magistracy and ministry'. The equal and reciprocal value of civil office and ecclesiastical office was a matter on which John Calvin was insistent, and the magistrates and ministers of Elizabethan and Jacobean Suffolk were never more Calvinist than in their understanding that these roles stood in equal need of each other, and the christian commonwealth of both. Historians have seemed reluctant to admit even the possibility of such a working mutuality, perhaps because the topic of 'church and state' has trained us to look for instability and ceaseless competition for the upper hand. Thus what Eugène Choisy identified as the 'double régime' of Calvin's Geneva[6] has been depicted as not only a theocracy but a one-sided clerical dictatorship to which an equally extreme 'Erastianism' has been seen as a realizable, even inevitable alternative. As for the English Reformation, it is fashionable to interpret it as a process of assertion of the laity against the clergy. Elizabethan puritanism is represented as a clerical backlash, its ideology, according to Professor Michael Walzer, entirely a clerical creation. 'The ministers were forced to act on their own.' Then in the early seventeenth century, as Walzer would have it, their alienation was alleviated, thanks to some improvement in the social standing of the more celebrated puritan clergy.[7]

[5] In gathering the fragments that remain, mostly in national collections, the essential tool is W. A. Copinger's remarkable publication *The County of Suffolk. Its History as Disclosed by Existing Records and other Documents, being Materials for the History of Suffolk*, 5 vols., 1904–6.

[6] *La théocratie à Génève au temps de Calvin*, Geneva 1897.

[7] *The Revolution of the Saints: A Study in the Origins of Radical Politics*, 1966, esp. 114–17, 135–40.

It is questionable whether these oscillations were as clearly visible in actuality as they appear in Walzer's model. It may be that the perfect mutuality of Calvinist theory was unattainable in any real world, but so were the stark alternatives of pure Presbyterianism or unadulterated Erastianism. To understand the relationships which in fact obtained between the puritan ministry and the governing class it may be the beginning of wisdom to recollect the principles to which lip service, at least, was paid.

We begin with what was said in Suffolk about this matter. In 1618 the famous Samuel Ward of Ipswich delivered an assize sermon at Bury St Edmunds which went through at least four editions as *Jethros justice of peace*.[8] In the dedication to Francis Bacon, a lord chancellor of Suffolk stock, Ward noted that the ills of the body politic were likely to arise from faults in 'magistracy and ministery', which he calls its principal lights, 'these two opticke peeces'.[9] The biblical figure of Jethro, prince and priest, was the archetype of both. The 'principall scope of magistracy in God's intention' was to promote his glory and to countenance the gospel and its professors. And 'what is our office that are ministers, but as God's trumpets and drummers to encourage, hearten and put life in these that fight his battles and doe his work' It is interesting that Ward should underline these reflections by referring to the advice given to Edward VI by the reformer Martin Bucer in a book by then all but forgotten, *De Regno Christi*. For, as had been noted in Elizabeth's reign, 'he that concludes that to have the Church governed by meet pastors and ministers taketh away the authority of christian magistrates is by Bucer sufficiently confuted'.[10]

Walzer would regard Ward as representative of a less isolated and alienated generation of preachers. So compare *Jethros Justice of Peace* with *The doctrine of superioritie and subiection,* a catechism on the fifth commandment[11] based on

---

[8] *STC* (revised) numbers, 25046–25048, 5.
[9] *Jethros justice of peace*, 1618, Sig. A3, pp. 1, 27, 34.
[10] Ibid., pp. 1, 7; Brit. Libr., MS. Lansdowne 18, fols. 55–6.
[11] *STC* 20337; edited (in 1609) by Robert Allen, a Suffolk minister and prolific author who moved to London after deprivation of his living. The book bears a further commendation from the leading London puritan minister, Stephen Egerton.

sermons preached by Robert Pricke, minister of the Suffolk village of Denham for more than thirty years until his death in 1608, one of the figures who will compose this miniature. The fifth commandment was the foundation of all subordination, private and public. Public superiority was exercised by both magistrates and ministers. The office of magistrate concerned principally religion and godliness and only secondarily the civil estate. He was to 'call and cause to be chosen learned and fit ministers' and to 'inforce and compell' the faithful performance of their duties, defending the worthy and if need be deposing the unworthy. Clerical immunity from such procedures was held to be 'a cursed devise of Antichrist'. As for the people, they were to be constrained by the magistrate to attend and submit themselves to the ministry of the word. 'Take away the magistrate and there would remain no outward worship of God.' But the minister was possessed not only of a ministry but also of his own ecclesiastical government, which included the power to excommunicate. No practical limits were placed on the obedience owed to magistrates and ministers. The subject was to pay willingly 'all such taxes, customes, subsidies and other such paiments as are levied, commanded and imposed' (not freely voted!). And the ministers were to be loved, 'not coldly nor feebly but most fervently and aboundantly'. 'Whosoever doth despise the minister (which is the Ambassador of God) despiseth and contemneth God himself and Jesus Christ, which is a fearful and execrable thing.'[12] We will look in vain within these commonplaces for any suspicion that the two 'optic pieces' could fail to see eye to eye (set in the same head they must have looked out at the world together) except in a negative form of the *topos* already heard from William Burton: 'If magistrates and ministers agree not and the people reverence and love them both, what can come of it?'[13] A tradition of radical dissent and non-conformity was the most unintended of consequences to follow from such a doctrine.

At this point we may put away the mirror or, as we have to

---

[12] *The doctrine of superioritie,* Sigs. B8, C7–8, D1, 5v–6, E2, 6v, F1, 3v.

[13] George Estey, preacher of Bury St Edmunds, to an unnamed correspondent, 14th April 1599; Brit. Libr., MS. Add. 24191, fols. 40–1.

say nowadays, the model, and turn to reality, for the preachers were dealing not with some unattainable ideal but with what was actually the case within local experience. In Elizabethan and Jacobean Suffolk there may have been a closer approximation to the type of a godly commonwealth than in any part of England at any time: closer than anything achieved in the years of ostensible puritan triumph, which was also a time of confusion and division. The mutually supportive alliance of magistracy and ministry was first consolidated in Suffolk in the 1570s, when a generation of ministers who would make their names as preachers, writers and contenders in the cause of reformation began to settle in the rural parishes where many would spend the rest of their days, extending into the first, second and even third decades of the following century. Robert Walsh was at Little Waldingfield from no later than 1573 until his death and notable funeral[14] in 1605. Boxford was the home of Henry Sandes from the early eighties until 1626. John Carter ministered at Bramford for thirty-four years, from 1583 until 1617, and then for a further eighteen years at Belsted. These were famous names, in their time and place. John Knewstub, the most famous and the acknowledged president of the Suffolk preachers, was rector of Cockfield for as many years as Elizabeth was queen of England, from 1579 until 1624. And at Denham, the setting for our miniature, the succession of father and son in the ministry ensured a pastoral continuity of sixty years. These vital details provide the rough confining dates of what might be called the primitive puritan commonwealth in Suffolk, from about 1580 to about 1630.

Also arising from the 1570s, a fervent and public-spirited Calvinist piety begins to appear as the most conspicuous attribute of a number of gentlemen entering upon their inheritances and starting careers on the Commission of the Peace. To name the two who were among the magistrates as Knewstub was among the ministers: Sir John Higham inherited Barrow from his popish father, Sir Clement, in 1570, and his ally Sir Robert Jermyn of Rushbrooke succeeded his father Sir Ambrose Jermyn in 1577. The two shared office

[14] *Winthrop Papers,* I. *1498–1628,* Massachusetts Historical Society, 1929, 89, 153.

as deputy lieutenants in 1585 and as knights of the shire in the parliament of the following year, and they shared the disgrace of being temporarily put out of the Commission of the Peace as the penalty of their puritanism.[15] In the reign of James I their pre-eminence was inherited by the 'eminently religious'[16] Sir Nathaniel Barnardiston of Kedington, reputedly the richest man in Suffolk.[17] Without fuller evidence we are left with the problem of the chicken and the egg. Should the conversion of Suffolk be attributed to the gentlemen who brought in the preachers and were their patrons, Jermyn in no less than ten livings,[18] or to the preachers who won over the gentry? Or should we look to various fundamental characteristics of the county with its 'exceptionally advanced' economy?[19] The preaching ministers were not settled on the light soils of the eastern parts of Suffolk, nor in Ipswich, where the parochial tithes were alienated and the churches served by curates on starvation wages. Their employment was in the affluent townships, on the intensively-farmed corn and dairy lands around Bury St Edmunds, and in the clothing belt which ran down the valley of the Stour, along the Essex border.[20] It was not a new thing for religion to benefit from the prosperity of this region: witness many famous churches of cathedral-like proportions.

When Robert Reyce composed his 'Breviary of Suffolk' in 1618 he listed 'a learned ministry' first among the 'commodities' of his native country, before 'clothing', 'the aire', 'the evenness of the country', 'the soyle'. The then bishop of Norwich was quoted as saying that no bishop in Europe had so grave, learned and judicious a ministry, 'especially in this county'.[21]

---

[15] Collinson, P., 'The Puritan Classical Movement in the Reign of Elizabeth I', unpublished London Ph.D. thesis, 1957, ch. 9.

[16] Clarke, Samuel, Lives of sundry eminent persons, 1683, 106.

[17] Everitt, Alan, Suffolk and the Great Rebellion 1640–1660, Suffolk Record Society, III. 1960, 16 and passim.

[18] Brit. Libr., MS. Harley 4626, fols. 324–46; Seckford Library Woodbridge, V.B. Redstone's transcript of 'Inductionum Liber Redivivus', an eighteenth-century copy of Induction Registers for the Archdeaconry of Sudbury, 1537–1641.

[19] Everitt, op. cit., 17.

[20] The distribution is indicated on one of the maps and in the accompanying list appended to my 'Puritan Classical Movement'.

[21] Suffolk in the XVIIth Century: the Breviary of Suffolk by Robert Reyce 1618, ed. Hervey, Lord Francis, 1902, 21f.

The Suffolk clergy were indeed a remarkable society, one of the first groups of English clergy to have realized the reformed ideal of the pastoral ministry, and to have achieved it in concert, as 'brethren and fellow ministers', 'the reverend, wise and godly learned fathers and brethren'.[22] Most of the first generation had been contemporaries at Cambridge, no less than thirty at St Johns,[23] where Knewstub was twice a candidate for the mastership.[24] (Their sons favoured Emmanuel.) They were inveterate attenders of one another's sermons, especially at the administrative centre of Bury St Edmunds, with its regular Monday combination lecture [25] and its 'then famous school', from which Knewstub sent the young Richard Sibbes to Cambridge – to St Johns, not Emmanuel.[26] Many of them were comfortably off and died possessed of silver and pewter, four-poster beds and feather bedding, and sizeable libraries.[27] They bred large families and baptized their children with biblical names, the inevitable Sarahs and Susans, the more occasional (and surprising) 'Rabshakeh'.[28] But Knewstub was a bachelor, admired for his 'contentation in a sol life'.[29] Many wrote books, in which there is sometimes evidence of familiarity with recent theological literature from the Continent, as well as with the Tremellius Bible, the most scholarly of the Reformation

[22] Phrases from the dedicatory epistles to works by Nicholas Bownd: *The holy exercise of fasting*, 1604, Sig. ¶3; *The doctrine of the sabbath*, 1595, Sig. A3.

[23] Evidence summarized in my 'Puritan Classical Movement', 123–6 and Appendix B.

[24] Thomas Ithel to Lord Burghley, 3 June 1577, P.R.O., S.P. 12/114/5; twenty-two fellows of St John's to Burghley, 15 December 1595, Brit. Libr., MS. Lansdowne 79, fol. 156.

[25] Collinson, P., 'Lectures by Combination: Structures and Characteristics of Church Life in 17th-Century England', *Bulletin of the Institute of Historical Research*, XLVIII. November 1975, 191–5.

[26] Bedell, William, 'Life and Death of William Bedell', *Two Biographies of William Bedell*, ed. Shuckburgh, E. S., Cambridge 1902, 15; *DNB.*, art. Sibbes.

[27] Among a number of Suffolk clerical wills consulted particular reference is intended to those of William Browne of Culford (ob. 1607) and Reginald Whitfield of Barrow (ob. 1608); P.R.O., P.C.C. wills 23 Huddlestone, 79 Dorset.

[28] These remarks are based on the examination of parish register transcripts in the Ipswich Public Library. Thomas Jeffray of Depden fathered fourteen children: Sarah, Elizabeth, Lydia, Ann, Priscilla, two Thomases, Martha, Josias, Dionisius, Rabshakeh, Samuel, Phoebe and Esther; Richard Dow of Stratford St Mary ten: Dameris, Daniel, Mary, Elizabeth, Susan, Barjonah, Amy, Robashry, Sarah and Abijah.

[29] By Richard Rogers of Wethersfield in his diary in a passage bearing the marginal, note 'the example of mr knew [stubs]': *Two Elizabethan Puritan Diaries*, ed. Knappen M. M., American Society of Church History, 1933, 95.

versions.[30] Learning like the cloth industry was widely dispersed in this countryside. One Suffolk author explained that it was life in a small village which provided the leisure to study and write, and he published a 1,000-page book on *The doctrine of the gospel* so that the world should know 'what those things are which the faithful ministers of Jesus Christ doe beate their wittes about, and wherein they spend themselves among their severall flockes and charges'.[31]

Original ways were found of expressing appreciation of the ministers. When Nicholas Chaplin of Chelsworth made his will he provided for pairs of winter gloves to be given to ten preachers, Knewstub being named first. Sir Robert Jermyn's sister left copies of the Tremellius Bible, again to ten ministers, Knewstub on this occcasion ranking second. The godly among the minor gentry and rising clothiers seem almost as a matter of course to have left sums of £5 or 40s. to groups of preachers, headed by Knewstub: as Thomas Gale, clothier of Edwardstone, puts it, 'for that I have receyved manye spirituall benefits to the singuler comforte of my soule by the prechinge of certaine godlie prechers hereafter named'.[32]

The major gentry, such of them as Knewstub addressed as 'those gentlemen in Suffolke whom the true worship of God hath made right worshipful',[33] provided a more political support, standing shoulder to shoulder with the ministers as occasion required, against a hostile bishops and his officers, or even against the assize judges.[34] There was a set piece at the summer assize of 1582 when 'fourteen of the principal men out of Suffolk', seven of them knights, waited on the judges at their lodging to ask for greater forbearance to be

[30] Collinson, P., 'The Beginners of English Sabbatarianism', *Studies in Church History*, I. ed. Dugmore, C. W. and Duggan, C., 1964, 212–15.

[31] Allen, Robert, *The doctrine of the gospel by a plaine and familiar interpretation of the particular points or articles thereof*, 1606, Sig. *4–5.

[32] Muskett, J. J., *Suffolk Manorial Families*, III. iii. Exeter 1911, 82; Suffolk Record Office (Bury St Edmunds), Register of Sudbury Wills, vol. 34, fol. 284v; ibid., vol. 37, fol. 125. Cf. the wills of Martha Higham (see p. 81 below), Joan Barflet of Boxford (Register of Sudbury Wills, vol. 39, fol. 166), Robert Gurdon, Esq., of Assington (Muskett, *Suffolk Manorial Families*, I. Exeter 1900, 278–9), Edward Appleton, gentleman of Edwardstone (ibid., 324).

[33] *An aunsweare unto certayne assertions tending to maintaine the church of Rome to be the true and catholique church*, 1579, dedicatory epistle to the gentlemen of Suffolk.

[34] Cockburn, J. S., *A History of English Assizes 1558–1714*, Cambridge 1972, 199–206, following pp. 881–929 of my 'Puritan Classical Movement'.

shown to non-conformist ministers 'for our sakes'.[35] Such stray records of administration as survive suggest that it was permeated with religion. An act of bigamy was described by Jermyn and Higham and other justices as 'quite contrary unto the worde of God and the lawes of the realme', a matter 'offensyve unto all good men who with sorrowful hart lament the lyke precedent in a christian commonwealth'.[36]

Towards 1580 the solidarity of godly magistracy and ministry in Suffolk was already well enough established to be satirized. The preacher's sermon must on no account touch on the social sins of the gentry, rack-renting, enclosure, oppression of the poor, but must be confined to attacks on the constitution of the Church. The sermon ended, 'the chief gentleman in the place begynnynge with a gronynge, but yet with a lowde voyce crieth most religiously, *Amen*. And then the whole companye of that sect followe. *Amen. Amen.*' This was from the future Archbishop Bancroft's poison pen.[37] But forty years later a preacher of the country was denounced as a 'turbulent spirit' after a sermon at the Clare lecture in which he castigated hypocrisy even among 'our greatest professors', some of whom said Amen to every petition but once out of the church took their own highway to Hell as usurers, 'extreme landlords' and reluctant tithers. The preacher wished to defend property, but not an absolute property. 'Though thy goods be thine, yet are they not so thine, but that the poore have a letter of attorny from God to have to their use as well as thy selfe.' Was it the preacher's 'Christian Socialism' or his scandalous aspersions which went down so badly at the lecture which Sir Nathaniel Barnardiston regularly frequented?[38]

According to Professor Alan Everitt, the Suffolk gentry were surprisingly uncultured, 'absolutely impervious to new ideas', comparing in this respect unfavourably with their Kentish counterparts.[39] Perhaps so. Calvinism may have had a progressively narrowing effect on some. Yet the earliest

---

[35] Lord North to Lord Burghley, 13 February 1583, Brit. Libr., MS. Harley 6993, no. 33, fol. 61.
[36] Brit. Libr., MS. Harley 286, fol. 22.
[37] *Tracts Ascribed to Richard Bancroft*, ed. Peel, Albert, Cambridge 1953, 71–3.
[38] Carter, Bezaleel, *Christ his last will and John his legacy*, 1621, 71–3, 86.
[39] Op. cit., 19.

madrigals to be printed in England were first performed in Rushbrooke Hall and were dedicated to Sir Robert Jermyn's daughters by the composer, George Kirbye, who was Jermyn's music master.[40]

Within this setting we come to our miniature, set in the village of Denham, not far from Bury St Edmunds, the home of the Lewkenor family and of their ministers, Robert Pricke alias Oldmayne and his son Timothy.[41] A more celebrated partnership was that of Sir Natheniel Barnardiston, 'top-branch of the Suffolk cedars' in the days of James I, and his minister Samuel Fairclough, which came to fruition in the Long Parliament. Of this alliance it was noted, in a variant of our now familiar *leitmotiv*, 'that the magistracy and ministry joined both together, and concurred in all things for promoting of true piety and godliness'.[42] Sir Nathaniel was thirteenth in succession in a Suffolk pedigree which runs from the reign of Richard I to modern times. But the Lewkenors of Denham came and went in three generations, their time in Suffolk coinciding exactly with our primitive puritan commonwealth, from the early seventies when Edward Lewkenor took up his residence in the county to 1634, when his grandson died without a male heir at the age of twenty-one.

To visit Denham[43] is to be given the doubtless deceptive impression that the sixty years of the Lewkenors were the only eventful years in its history. Certainly this was the only period when it knew a seigneurial presence. The small, cheaply-built manor house is still there, close to a tiny church, reconstructed and given a tower in the nineteenth century but otherwise the same modest chapel which the Lewkenors knew, not one of Suffolk's village cathedrals. The parish was

[40] Kirbye, George, *The first set of English madrigalls to 4.5. and 6. voyces,* 1597.

[41] A principal source for what follows is an (unnumbered) volume in the series of 'Suffolk Green Books' edited by the Suffolk antiquary S. H. A. Hervey: *Denham Parish Registers 1539–1850, with Historical Notes and Notices,* Bury St Edmunds 1904.

[42] Lives of Fairclough and Barnardiston in Clarke, op. cit. This alliance is a centre-piece of the Yale doctoral dissertation by Mr Kenneth W. Shipps, 'Lay Patronage of East Anglian Puritan Clerics in Pre-Revolutionary England', 1971. I am grateful to Mr Shipps for allowing me to read a revised version of this work, intended for publication.

[43] I am greatly indebted to Mr Paul Stannard of the Parochial Church Council of Denham who in August 1976, in the vacancy of the cure, introduced me to the church and its monuments, and allowed me to consult the documents in the church safe.

scarcely a parish, its tithes being appropriated in the past to St Osyth Priory and later to the lay landlords who succeeded the monks in ownership of the manor of Abbots Denham. The chaplains and curates who served the place before the time of the Lewkenors and Prickes are mostly unknown, even by name. In 1591 a gentlewoman living in the village willed twenty shillings for the repair of the stools in the church, which gives some impression of the accommodation which it provided.[44] At the north-east corner there is a mortuary chapel, containing two very immodest tombs, the only objects in view to have cost a lot of money. The older of the two bears a fulsome Latin inscription which announces that Sir Edward Lewkenor, who had served at Court and in almost every parliament for thirty years, was to be praised 'chiefly' for bringing the preaching of the gospel into this tiny community: *Inter caeteras autem justi praeconii causas, haec maxime duxit et sempiterna memoria digna quod ejus opera in perexiguam hanc villam obscuramque evangelii praedicatio est introducta, cujus luce et beneficio ad extremum vitae terminum fruebatur.*[45] We may suspect that it was not so much the 'town' as his family and household and indeed his own personal life which Lewkenor sought to enrich by sustaining a godly ministry on his doorstep. The place was and is too small to support much of a congregational life. What we confront at Denham is an example of the very personal values and priorities to which that famous East Anglian worthy John Stubbs gave expression when in middle life he resolved to settle down and 'give continually some time to an ordinary and standing exercise of the word'.[46]

The Denham ministry was provided by Robert Pricke, from no later than 1577 and perhaps earlier, until 1608, and then for a further thirty years by his son Timothy. The older Pricke is described by the younger as 'a right grave devine and learned clerke', but there is no record of him at either university and he was probably of very local origin, Robert and John Pricke, carpenters, being assessed in the nearby village of Barrow in the subsidy of 1568. Still preserved in

[44] Hervey, 114–15.
[45] Ibid., 74–5.
[46] John Stubbs to Michael Hicks, 22 July 1581, Strype, John, *Annals of the Reformation*, Oxford, II. ii, 305.

Denham church is the parish register which Pricke began to keep and to make up retrospectively in 1599. Under the record of his son's baptism in 1577 he entered a curious antiquarian fable in explanation of the alias of Oldmayne. Oldmayne was said to have been the original family name, traceable to the twelfth century. The name of Pricke was acquired from a Suffolk man of that name who had reared an orphaned ancestor in Henry VII's days. Much of this entry has been erased, perhaps by Timothy, who used the name of Oldmayne and may have objected to this inventive piece of family history. Professor Everitt has commented on the indifference of even the greatest in Suffolk to such trifles. In his later years Timothy was well-connected among the spiritual brotherhood of East Anglia. His sister married the famous Richard Blackerby who had ministered to the Lewkenors for a time and whose own daughter later married Samuel Fairclough. In the account of Blackerby published in Clarke's *Lives* it is said that the alias 'Oldman' was assumed by Robert Pricke to escape the Marian persecution. Perhaps neither tale contains the true explanation for this curious alias, the only one known to me among the Elizabethan clergy. In his sixty-first year, the last of his life, it was a matter of wonder to Timothy that he had spent almost all his days in the obscurity of Denham: 'This towne, which now affordeth me my being, formerly afforded mee my first breath.'[47]

The principal credit for making this little corner a place of evangelical enlightenment may belong to neither Prickes nor Lewkenors but to Lewkenor's mother-in-law, Martha Higham. Martha was a Jermyn, married to Thomas Higham of Higham, so that she was an aunt of Sir Robert Jermyn and a cousin by marriage of Sir John Higham, to whom she bequeathed her husband's ring. The last thirty-five years of her life were spent in widowhood, mostly at Denham, where she acquired the formerly monastic property of Abbots Denham, apparently from the Howards, joined it to her husband's manor of Denham, and built a house. Her religious persuasion is left in no doubt by her will, proved in 1593. Apart from the almost

---

[47] Hervey, pp. 53, 116–19, 268–78, 246; *Suffolk in 1568: Being the Return for a Subsidy Granted in 1566*, Suffolk Green Books XII. Bury St Edmunds 1909, 257.

customary legacies to eleven preachers, headed by Knewstub, there are some very personal features, suggestive of concern for the religious future of Denham. Her Geneva Bible was left to the church, for the use of the parishioners. She endowed a scholarship at Emmanuel on condition that in due course it should be awarded to Timothy Pricke: which came to pass. And in place of an annuity of forty shillings, previously allowed to his father, she left the sum of £40 to provide a parsonage: a house which still exists. Presumably Pricke had previously lived in the manor house, and we may suspect a relationship of spiritual intimacy between Pricke and Mrs Higham of the kind which so often grew between a pious gentlewoman and her chaplain.[48]

Edward Lewkenor was not a native. He belonged to a large and ramified Sussex family with a persistent talent for marrying its sons to heiresses.[49] It was through such a match, with Susan, one of the two daughters and co-heirs of the Highams, that he came to Suffolk, round about 1570. In his lifetime he built up an estate of middling size, through his marriage, by subsequent conveyance from Martha Higham, and by purchases from his sister-in-law Ann Higham and her husband, Thomas Clere of Norfolk, and from Thomas Howard, Earl of Suffolk. In addition he held the manor of Kingston Bowsey in Sussex which was inherited from his father, Edward Lewkenor, groom porter in the court of Edward VI and in the following reign a conspirator who died in the Tower. Lewkenor was to fill one of the Sussex livings in his gift with Samuel Norden, who became the most militant of the puritan ministers in that county, and another with the no less radical Christopher Goldsmith. With lands valued (in the artificial terms of an inquisition post mortem) at a little less than £100 at the time of his death Lewkenor was not the richest of the Suffolk gentry. The house which Mrs Higham had built on a moated site beside Denham church was an unpretentious structure of lath and plaster of only four bays, which found no difficulty in becoming a

48 Hervey, 93–100, 192–5.
49 Mousley, Joyce E., 'Sussex Country Gentry in the Reign of Elizabeth', unpublished London Ph.D. thesis 1955, 575, 578.

simple farmhouse after the passing of the Lewkenors, and which owes its present brick façade to the nineteenth century.[50]

Lewkenor's distinction arose from what the sixteenth century knew as 'virtue', learning, public-spiritedness – and religion. He entered St John's College late in Mary's reign, matriculated after the lifting of his father's attainder, and took his degree in 1561. He was then a fellow of the college for two years before going on to the Middle Temple, surely one of very few eldest sons of the gentry to have held a fellowship. (A cousin and namesake, a minor Latin poet, was a fellow of St Johns at the same time and went on to an academic career in Oxford.[51]) Lewkenor was perhaps not active in Suffolk affairs until his later years and may not have been a J.P. until 1592. It was as a 'parliament man of mark', John Chamberlain's description,[52] that he was somewhat famous, sitting for every parliament from 1571 until his death in 1605, with the exception of the session of 1601.[53]

In the parliaments of 1584, 1586 and 1589, when the campaign to reform the Church and the ministry reached a crescendo, and again in 1593, Lewkenor sat for the Essex borough of Maldon, a town under strong puritan influence,[54] where the recorder was an old room-mate from the Inner Temple, James Morice, himself an outspoken puritan M.P. There can be no doubt that Lewkenor's regular presence in the House of Commons was the result of inner motives and external persuasion of the kind to which Peter Wentworth referred elusively in one of his speeches.[55] He was there as a puritan, to advance the cause, and although he was a committee man rather than an orator, much of his recorded activity was in matters of religion. In 1587 he was one of a select group

[50] Wills, inquisitions post mortem and other information in Hervey, pp. 86–93, 101–7, 128–38, 198–258, 298–300; Loades, D. M., *Two Tudor Conspiracies,* Cambridge 1963, 232–3. For Norden and Goldsmith, see Manning, R. B., *Religion and Society in Elizabethan Sussex,* Leicester 1969, pp. 212–13, 215–16 and Babbage, S. B., *Puritanism and Richard Bancroft,* 1962, 192–6.

[51] Venn, J. and J. A., *Alumni Cantabrigienses,* I. iii, Cambridge 1924, 82; Cooper, C. H. and T., *Athenae Cantabrigienses,* I. 1858, 251.

[52] Winwood, Ralph, *Memorials,* 1725, II. 141.

[53] I am indebted to the History of Parliament Trust for making available information on Lewkenor's parliamentary career.

[54] See many references in my *The Elizabethan Puritan Movement,* 1967.

[55] Neale, J. E., *Elizabeth I and her Parliaments, 1559–1581,* 1953, 181–4.

REFORMATION, CONFORMITY AND DISSENT

of puritans who spoke in support of the extreme measures contained in Anthony Cope's presbyterian 'bill and book', and he was among those sent to the Tower, where his father had died thirty years before, apparently for his part in quasi-conspiratorial meetings associated with this initiative. In one parliamentary speech he referred bitterly to the bishops as 'rather deformers than reformers'.[56]

In 1910 the British Museum acquired among the Townshend MSS. a collection of Lewkenor's papers preserved through the marriage of his great-granddaughter to the first Viscount Townshend. This is now MS. Additional 38492 and comprises a unique file of the working parliamentary papers of an Elizabethan and Jacobean puritan M.P. All sixty-five items relate in one way or another to religion; and all but thirteen are connected with the national campaign for further reformation. No less than forty belong to the first two years of James's reign: to the Hampton Court Conference and (the vast majority) to the issues of conformity and subscription as they impinged on James's first parliament, where Lewkenor, now knighted, once again represented Maldon. This was a replay of the struggle waged twenty years earlier at the time of the subscription crisis provoked by Archbishop Whitgift, and a few papers of major interest relate to 1584. They include a survey of the state of the ministry in the home country of Sussex, addressed from there by a relation to 'his verie good cousin Mr Edward Lewkenor', which Lewkenor is known to have tabled in the House of Commons,[57] and an account of the troubles of the godly people of the Suffolk village of Lawshall, the kind of propaganda which may have circulated from hand to hand in the House.[58] A brief account of the second day of the Hampton Court Conference is addressed: 'To mi veri loveing and wel beloved husband sur Edward Lewkenor att mistres quarles in rumforde geve thes with spede.'[59]

[56] Neale, J. E., *Elizabeth I and her Parliaments, 1584–1601*, 1957, 145–65, 66.

[57] Brit. Libr., MS. Add. 38492, no. 50, fol. 91; D'Ewes, Simonds, *The Journals of all the Parliaments During the Reign of Queen Elizabeth*, 1682, 349.

[58] MS. Add. 38492, no. 63, fols. 107–8. See Neale, *Elizabeth I and her Parliaments, 1584–1601*, 229–30.

[59] MS. Add. 38492, no. 44, fol. 81. The Lewkenors' daughter Hester was married to Robert Quarles Esq. of Romford, Essex.

In the relations between Lewkenor and his minister, Robert Pricke, we encounter an institution subtly different from 'magistracy and ministry' and one with which historians of early modern society are more conversant: the nexus of gentleman and chaplain, patron and protegée. Whereas magistracy and ministry may imply formal parity, this was an intrinsically unequal relationship. And since Denham was a wholly impropriate parish, a 'donative' cure, Pricke lacked even the financial independence of a rector or vicar. He was said to have been the first curate of the parish for two hundred years to have enjoyed the tithes in full,[60] and we know that he received an additional annuity from Mrs Higham, but all this was of mere grace and favour. Yet there is no reason to suppose that Pricke's bearing towards his patron was servile or excessively deferential, and every indication that each acknowledged the integrity of the other in his proper sphere.

The evidence is in MS. Additional 38492. Among the contents is the draft of a petition to the bishop's chancellor, perhaps in the name of several gentlemen, asking for the restoration of Pricke's preaching licence, probably to be dated in 1584, the 'woeful year of subscription'.[61] Scribbled on the back of another document is a list of nine 'books borrowed of Mr Lewkn[or]', doubtless by Pricke. All the titles are theological, and they include William Fulke's sermons on the Apocalypse and works by Beza, Danaeus and Pierre du Moulin.[62] There is a letter from Pricke to Lewkenor, written on 22 February 1585, in the midst of a parliament which was critical for the puritan cause:

> Sir, although it was not so necessarie for mee to write to you at this tyme, considering the abundance of meanes where you nowe remayne, your owne sufficiencie without mee, and my smale skill in anything which in that honorable assemblie where dailie you are might anything availe you. Yet for the dutie which in many respectes I owe unto your w[orship] I could not staie but write a fewe lines.

[60] Noted in the parish register in the entry relating to Timothy Oldmayne's funeral: Hervey, 53.
[61] No. 38, fol. 70.
[62] No. 39, fol. 101v.

Fervent exhortation follows, sharpened by fear that 'sin' may frustrate the godly endeavours of Lewkenor and other godly members:

> We cease not here in our smale measure to lift up our unworthie eies and handes toward the god of heaven both in confessing of our sinnes and striving with his majestie by humble requestes for all necessarie blessing upon you and the rest of your worthie yokefellowes in the service of Jesus Christ. . . . Ah sir that I could further you any waies, I wold by the grace of God be willing to the uttermost of my power.[63]

Another 'brotherly caveat to the godlye zealous and wyse gentlemen of the parlament house' evidently came from the same pen and belongs to the same circumstances. Pricke searches his heart for the reason why the expectations of the godly have so far been disappointed.

> Then my harte melted with fear and I thought, Oh sinn, sinn, sinn, that thou shouldest soe take from us the favour of God, that in soe fitt a tyme and place, under soe godlye and christian a queen, such godlye zealous and wyse men should have theyre tongs cleve to the roof of theyr mouthes, and be destitute of all power to promote soe worthye, weightye, so nedfull a cause. . . . Consider whether the lettinge passe of this occasion be not in some respect to denye Christe and to be ashamed of him before men.[64]

Here was a prolepsis of the working partnership between Samuel Fairclough and Sir Nathaniel Barnardiston in the early days of the Long Parliament, nearly sixty years later.

In the summer of 1605 there was sickness in Cambridge and fear of the plague. Lewkenor's two sons, both at Emmanuel, were called home to escape the infection and with them came the son of a neighbour. This boy contracted smallpox and Lewkenor and his wife were infected. Lady Susan died on 5 October and Sir Edward on the following day.[65] The double tragedy made a profound impression.

---

[63] No. 37, fols. 68–9.
[64] No. 22, fols. 37–8.
[65] This story can be disentangled from the opening verses of the *Threnodia*, referred to below.

Robert Pricke's funeral sermon, an early example of a still new genre, was preached not long before his own demise and posthumously published by the Suffolk preacher and author Robert Allen.[66] The sermon is notable for its structure deriving from the 'new puritanism' of covenant theology and providing many proofs that both Lewkenor and his wife were 'effectually called'. In addition a copious volume of elegiac verse appeared from the press, a *Threnodia* in Greek, Latin, Hebrew and English, to which many Cambridge luminaries contributed, including the regius professor of Greek and two future and famous bishops, William Bedell and Joseph Hall.[67]

And in the mortuary chapel purposely constructed a truly monstrous tomb was erected: a table with six classical columns in mock porphyry, bearing a canopy with massive armorial achievements. Under the canopy, in life-size effigy, Sir Edward and Lady Susan are found kneeling on cushions in attitudes of strongly-marked devotion, their six surviving children in rows behind them. The heir, Sir Edward the younger, seems to have more than proved his filial piety both by assembling the versifiers of the *Threnodia* and by providing this monument. Aesthetically, there is as much to object to in the one as in the other. Both verge on the grotesque. But the historian cannot pass by with the terse 'not good' of Sir Nikolaus Pevsner.[68] For one thing, the ostentation speaks volumes. At a rough guess the tomb must have cost more than the family home was worth. And the heavy expenditure is a puzzle, for no tomb would be erected for the son, who was said to have deemed the money laid out on funeral expenses 'of all other worst bestowed'.[69] Perhaps this was his rueful conclusion, after his father's obsequies. But what the tomb was meant to say it still says very loudly. Whoever

---

[66] *A verie godlie and learned sermon, treating of mans mortalitie and of the estate both of his bodie and soule after death*, 1608.

[67] *Threnodia in obitum D. Edovardi Lewkenor equitis & D. Susannae coniugis charissimae. Funerall verses upon the death of the right worshipfull Sir Edward Lewkenor knight and Madame Susan his lady. With deaths apologie and a reioynder to the same*, 1606.

[68] *Suffolk*, The Buildings of England, 1961, 168–9.

[69] Oldmayne, Timothy, *Gods rebuke in taking from us . . . Sir Edward Lewkenor knight*, 1619, p. 3. Copies of this sermon are scarce and I am indebted to the Trustees of Dr Williams's Library for my sight of it.

makes his way to Denham will enrich his reading about puritanism by seeing the thing itself, in convincing and concrete representation.

Only twelve years later came the second Lewkenor funeral at Denham. Sir Edward the younger died unseasonably on May Day 1618, in the midst of his year as sheriff, and at the early age of thirty-two. This time there were two orations, the funeral sermon proper preached by Timothy Oldmayne, entitled *God's rebuke in taking from us that worthy and honourable gentleman Sir Edward Lewkenor,* and a sermon volunteered at nearby Cavenham 'upon a lecture day' by Bezaleel Carter, whom Sir Edward had presented to the living.[70] Tragedy continued to stalk the Suffolk Lewkenors. In 1634 the third of the line, aged only twenty-one, succumbed to the same disease which had killed his grandparents. Timothy Oldmayne preached yet another funeral sermon[71] and the widow erected a second prestigious tomb, this one a chaste creation of marble in impeccable taste.[72] In both sermon and monumental inscription much was made of the fact that with this young man's death the race of Lewkenors at Denham was extinguished, although an unmarried sister would continue to live in the village until her death in 1679. The inheritance had by then passed to the Townshends through the marriage of a daughter who was an infant of three months at the time of her father's death. When this daughter herself died as Mary, Lady Townshend, in 1672, she left £100 for the purchase of property, the rent from which was to provide for the apprenticing to useful trades of poor orphans born in Denham.[73] The safe in Denham church contains the crumbling indentures of apprenticeship of children who benefited from this charity in the eighteenth century, and I am told that the fund is still administered to make token contributions to some of the

---

[70] *The wise king and the learned judge: in a sermon out of the 10 verse of the 2 psalme: lamenting the death and proposing the example of Sir Edward Lewkenor, a religious gentleman,* 1618. The biblical reference is to the Geneva version: 'Be wise now therefore ye Kings: be learned ye Judges of the earth'.

[71] *Lifes brevitie and deaths debility. Evidently declared in a sermon preched at the funerall of that hopeful and vertuous yong gentleman Edward Lewkenor esquire, etc. In whose death is ended the name of that renowned family of the Lewkenors in Suffolke,* 1636.

[72] Hervey, 75–6, 243–4.

[73] Ibid., 259–61, 305–6.

young people who go out into the world from Denham. This is the last lingering touch of the charitable puritan piety which was kindled in this village, four hundred years ago.

Finally we turn to the four Lewkenor funeral sermons, not only to satisfy Geoffrey Nuttall's known predilection for this form of literature, but because in themselves they provide a cameo of puritan magistracy in harmonious concert with puritan ministry. In all three generations the preachers discovered a consistent and experienced godliness. Sir Edward and Lady Susan 'accompted all things in the world but drosse' in comparison with Christ. Constant attention was paid to the ministry of the word and devotion was shown to the ministers. Sir Edward the younger was never known to be absent from church when he was at home, morning or evening. He presided over prayers in his family two or three times a day, with reading and a psalm and 'repetition' on the days of exercise, conceiving the prayer himself when no minister was present. His parents 'loved most dearelie the ministerie of the word and ministers thereof . . . with no lesse reverence and tender affection than naturall children doe their naturall parents, of whom they are bred and begotten'. Of the grandson it was noted that in his regard for faithful and diligent ministers he honoured the elder as fathers and the younger as brethren. Sir Edward the younger is said by Bezaleel Carter to have purchased advowsons with which to promote godly ministers. Both Sir Edwards were paragons of philanthropy, which with the younger became an institution. A special building was erected alongside the house (still standing in the nineteenth century) in which the poor were fed daily and 'with more large provision than ordinarie' on three days in the week, and there was an annual distribution of clothing to the destitute of the surrounding villages, as many sets as there were years to the benefactor's life. As for public reputations, Robert Pricke, who had preached on *The doctrine of superioritie,* presented his patron as a model magistrate, with the 'very special grace' of being known to utterly reject all bribes and rewards.

Thus far the sermons contribute to a stereotype, an important part of the integrated ideology of 'the Country', which was set up against not only the corrupt values of 'the

Court' but also in opposition to the mindless vanities of mere rusticity. 'He cannot be a gentleman which loveth not a dogge.'[74] The half-brother of Francis Bacon, the Suffolk gentleman Edward Bacon, was told by an Ipswich preacher: 'Many be the allurements that mighte tie your affection to the glittering delights of this present world: yet have you learned . . . to trample under your feete the vaine glorie thereof and not to spende your witte and your studie and your revenewes upon haukes and dogges and gawdish apparell.'[75] Samuel Ward of Ipswich, or his publisher, made a similar point more economically in an illustrated title page to one of his sermons. A booted and spurred foot, an open Bible and a mailed fist grasping a lance confront a stockinged leg with fashionable shoe, cards, dice and a hand holding an elaborate glass and a smoking pipe of tobacco.[76] Fortunately the characterization of Sir Edward Lewkenor the younger partially escapes the 'pious panegyric'[77] and suggests a more human complexity. There was piety, to be sure, and 'such a piercing insight into points of doctrine'. But we learn that relations with the tenantry were not always harmonious, that he died in debt, and that 'he carried himself like a gentleman in all respects whatsoever, whether you regard his apparell, his attendance, and lastly his pleasure, keeping as he best liked both hawkes and hounds, as well he might'.[78]

We owe to Timothy Oldmayne this fleeting impression of a puritan magistrate whose humanity was generous and approachable, who 'knew right well to put a difference between the use and the abuse'. To Timothy, whose whole existence was involved in the Lewkenors, we allow the final say:

> Foure generations of your honourable *Family* have I seene here upon the *Stage*, successively acting their several *Parts*. . . . But now alas the *Theater* is wholy empted, and all the *Actors* quite gone, the *Stage* hourely expected to be pulled down; and if it

[74] Northbrooke, John, *Spiritus est vicarius Christi in terra*, 1579, fol. 39.
[75] *The lectures of Samuel Bird of Ipswidge upon the 11 chapter of the epistle unto the Hebrewes*, Cambridge 1598, Epistle.
[76] *Woe to drunkards*, 1627 edn.
[77] Stauffer, Donald A., *English Biography Before 1700*, Cambridge Mass. 1930, 71.
[78] Oldmayne, *Gods rebuke*, 11–13, 32–3, 36–7.

stand yet little hope that ever our eyes shall see such *Actors* any more upon it, to play their parts so commendable, as those *Antients* did.[79]

Timothy himself would soon be gone, three or four years before the onset of what used to be called the Puritan Revolution.

---

[79] Oldmayne, *Lifes brevitie and deaths debility*, Sig. A3.

V

Bishops in the Pulpit in the Seventeenth Century: Continuity amid Change

R. BUICK KNOX

AT THE end of the seventeenth century, as at the beginning, England had a monarchy and an established Church. During the century there had been many stark and dramatic events; there had been the Civil War, the execution of Laud, the ascendancy of Cromwell, the execution of Charles I, the restoration of the monarchy and the revolution of 1688. Add to these events the foundation of the Royal Society and the spate of novel opinions set forth in many publications and there is ample evidence of constitutional, ecclesiastical and intellectual change. The century has been called a century of revolution and out of the flux emerged ideas of liberty, legality and constitutionalism which shaped the future outlook of the nation.

Nevertheless, the survival of the monarchy and the episcopate showed that there was a continuity of institutions and beliefs far beyond what is generally acknowledged. The framework and trappings of monarchy proved to be remarkably tough and though it lost much of the prestige of divine right and became accountable to Parliament it offered a stability which proved attractive after the instability of the period of Parliament and of Cromwell and also in spite of the excesses and perils of the reigns of Charles II and James II. The structure of the Church of England proved to be equally resilient and there was a continuity not only in its forms of government and worship but also in the world of thought within which its bishops lived. The correspondence between the teaching of Andrewes at the beginning of the century and that of Tillotson at the end is at least as striking as the difference. In many circles there was a reaction against traditional forms and beliefs but this was not a universal feeling nor indeed was it a majority concern. Nonconformists never became a majority. Most of the landowners and gentry were patriarchal figures upholding their patronage over clergy and people.

The bishops were not isolated figures crying in an inhospitable world of aggressive dissent and incipient democracy. If their sermons were rated by their critics as provocative or laodicean or barren, they were also acceptable to a large constituency and they emerged from a world of thought marked by respect for tradition, morality, authority and learning. During the century the Church of England had three hundred and thirty-four bishops.[1] Sermons by sixty-three of these have been published. Some have left only one, others only a few, and others a profusion. Some are tedious and repetitive, and some won lasting renown either for content or for literary style. In the first rank are the sermons of Andrewes, Hall, Brownrig, Cosin, Sanderson, Taylor, Hacket, Stillingfleet and Tillotson. The reasons for pre-eminence are varied; there is the personal preference of the reader, but there is also the erudition of Taylor, the eloquence of Hacket and the cogency of Stillingfleet. Andrewes has gems which put him in the front rank as a stylist but it must be admitted that his gems are often bedded in arid philological analyses of texts. Substantial evidence of the episcopal outlook is also provided by the collections of sermons by Ussher, Reynolds, Lloyd, Sprat, Burnet, Patrick, Sharp, Kidder, Thomas Tenison and Williams of Chichester. Even when a bishop's remains only provide one sermon, as is the case with Matthew Wren, that sermon usually fits comfortably into the general episcopal outlook.[2]

Bishops were men of ability. All the sixty-three whose sermons survive were university graduates and the dominance of Oxford and Cambridge was well-nigh complete; thirty had taken their first degree at Cambridge, twenty-six at Oxford,

[1] The Church of England included the Church of Ireland and 143 of the 344 bishops were in Ireland.
[2] A list of the sixty-three is given at the end of the essay.

five at Trinity College, Dublin, and two at Aberdeen. Thirty-nine had been Fellows of Colleges, twenty-four at Cambridge and fifteen at Oxford. Twenty-three had been heads of Colleges, nine in Cambridge, thirteen at Oxford, and one, Wilkins, in both Oxford and Cambridge. Many of them found their way to preferment through chaplaincies to the sovereign or to noblemen or to bishops; forty-four passed this way, nineteen of them as chaplains to the Stuart kings. A cathedral stall was a great and almost indispensable asset in the progress to preferment. Thirty-seven had been deans, four at Westminster, five at Christchurch, Oxford, three at St Paul's, and three at Rochester. Suitable family connections were not a disadvantage. Ussher was the nephew of an archbishop; King of London was the father of King of Chichester; Wilkins's step-daughter became the wife of Tillotson; Dolben married a niece of Sheldon. Nepotism was not a serious problem. Few of the sons of the nobility sought to climb the ecclesiastical ladder. Those who rose to eminence were men of ability often from modest backgrounds who had been spotted and assisted by persons of influence.

These bishops had a formidable intellectual equipment. They were steeped in the Bible and for them the unquestioned canon was that prescribed in Article VI. Quotations from the Apocrypha were rare and were not used as definitive in the establishment of any doctrine. The text of the Bible was accepted as that which God intended it should be[3] and through all its diversity the Bible was certain to 'inform the world of the mind and will of God'.[4] Scores of sermons referred to the Bible as the uncorrupt source of all that was fundamental and necessary to salvation and Tillotson referred to it as 'the great and standing revelation of God to mankind', 'the great instrument of our salvation'.[5] The bishops were well versed in textual studies and knew of the variant readings in different manuscripts; Ussher, for example, was a scholar of international repute in this field.[6] However, such issues were not widely aired in sermons and were indeed regarded as

---

[3] Sanderson, R., *Thirty-five Sermons,* 7th edn., 1681, 157.
[4] Tillotson, J., *Works,* edition of 1743, XI, 4930.
[5] Tillotson, J., *Works,* 5th edn., 1707, 350; Tillotson, ed. 1743, XI, 4899.
[6] Knox, R. B., *James Ussher, Archbishop of Armagh,* Cardiff 1967, ch. VI.

unsettling diversions; Bramhall held that even the worst translations were never far off the mark.[7] In interpreting the Bible the predominant line was 'the literal and immediate intendent',[8] but the christological outlook of the preachers was so strong that they saw the literal meaning as that which pointed to Christ. There were also incursions into the allegorical and typological fields; Andrewes made much of the parallel between Moses climbing Sinai, David climbing Zion, and Jesus climbing Calvary.[9] There was an awareness of the variety of literary styles and of levels of revelation in the Law, the Prophets and the Gospels and there was much reference to divine accommodation to human weakness but Hacket held that all parts of the Bible 'make good music when they are parts of one song'.[10] Williams of Chichester was probably the most sensitive to critical problems when he laid stress upon 'the drift and substance' of Scripture.[11] The rapid acceptance of the new translation of 1611 provided a standard text which soon became not just another translation but the very Bible of England. Andrewes was one of the translators and his full use of the new work was a strong influence in ensuring its acceptance.

Quotations from the Fathers showed an acquaintance with their writings which went far beyond the bounds of the Catenae and Florilegia then in circulation. Chrysostom was quoted by almost every preacher and he was much admired for his homiletic gifts, moral earnestness and literary facility. Augustine was quoted by fewer preachers but they used him with far greater frequency than any other writer. His doctrinal teaching, his historical sweep and his penetration into human motives and conduct made him a mighty influence. Jerome was the third most frequently quoted Father and his biblical expositions were highly esteemed. A list of other Fathers less frequently cited would be a veritable patristic catalogue. Taylor held that the Fathers were the best commentators on

[7] Bramhall, J., *Works*, 1845, V, 115.

[8] Brownrig, R., *Forty Sermons*, 1661, 29–30; also Cosin, J., *Works*, 1843–55, I, 226; Hacket, J., *A Century of Sermons*, 1675, 287.

[9] Andrewes, L., *Works*, 1841–54, III, 22; also Brownrig, op. cit., 108, 115, and *Twenty-five Sermons*, 1664, 46.

[10] Hacket, 433; also Cosin, I, 213.

[11] Williams, J. (Chichester), *The Boyle Sermons*, 1707, 208–9.

the Scripture and he commended them with the exhortation, 'Let the consent of the Catholic Church be your measure', but he also insisted that even among the Fathers there was no guaranteed unanimity.[12] Likewise Reynolds pointed to their disagreements while he also respected 'the pious and solid expositions of other learned men'.[13]

The classical grounding in the universities naturally provided ample resources for illustrative material and moral maxims. Cicero's teaching and Plutarch's biographical riches were liberally used to enliven many sermons.

The Jewish writer, Maimonides, was often cited, sometimes with respect for Jewish wisdom, but also to provide justification for the hostility to the Jews which was common in many sermons. The Jewish mob had cried, 'His blood be on us and on our children', and the doom of persecution and dispersion had rightly befallen them as a penalty for their crime.[14]

Medieval writers were drawn upon, sometimes with a recognition of their theological skill, but much more often to provide evidence for the development of corruptions within the Church and for the growth of papal encroachments upon the proper autonomy of nations and of national churches. Far more noticeable was the wide acquaintance with the vast output of controversial literature in the wake of the Council of Trent and of the emergence of the Society of Jesus. Bishops believed it to be incumbent upon them to read and refute these writings and throughout the century they were continually involved in controversy with the Church of Rome.

This controversy placed them firmly within the protestant sector of Christendom. The influence of continental reformers was clear in many sermons yet there were remarkably few specific references to their writings. Quotations were often made without acknowledgement and the words and ideas of Calvin can be traced again and again even when he was not named as their source. When he was mentioned it was often with respect for his gifts as an expositor and it was Laud who

[12] Taylor, J., *Works*, ed. R. Heber, 1839, VI, 520; also Knox, op. cit., 116.
[13] Reynolds, E., *Works*, 1826, V, 154-5.
[14] Wilson, T., *Works*, 1847, III, 161.

referred to him as one of the learned,[15] but this did not pre-
clude acid comments upon the form of church government
which he had set up in Geneva and which was so much
admired by nonconformists in England. The bishops emphasized the distinctive form and tradition of the Church of
England and the paucity of their specific references to the
reformers was due to the desire to obviate any suggestion that
the Church of England was an appendage of a continental
movement.

As the century progressed there was a sharp decline in the
dependence upon past authorities. This was not due to lack of
knowledge; on occasions demanding a defence of the Church
of England preachers such as Tillotson could still deploy all
the resources of the patristic and classical armoury. The
decline was due to a growing reliance upon the cogency and
progression of argument. Tillotson was at his best when he
moved with clear logical steps to present theological and
moral issues and he was less at home when he fell back upon
massive citations of Scripture to make his case. The dependence upon persuasive argument rather than upon weighty
authority did not mark a change of belief but was an attempt
to sustain the same belief by a shift of method.

With such a background of personal, academic and social
interests it is not surprising that the bishops had a common
outlook on the great doctrinal themes of God and the world,
man and salvation, faith and conduct. This outlook persisted
throughout the century and was the framework within which
the bishops sought to assimilate the harvest of their studies
and of their contact with the current winds of intellectual
change.

The bishops constantly affirmed that there was no reasonable ground for doubting the existence of God which was
clearly demonstrated in the aspirations of the human mind and
in the works of creation. Brownrig declared that the history
of all races gave evidence of belief in the existence of a deity.[16]
There was a natural fear in the presence of life's mysteries and
Tillotson, following Calvin, denied that it was the mysteries

---

[15] Laud, W., *Works*, 1847–60, I, 28, 49.
[16] Brownrig, *Twenty-five Sermons*, 58.

which drove people to devise the idea of God; the fear arose
from the presence of God in his creation.[17] Taylor posed the
rhetorical question, 'Can anything in this world be more
foolish than to think that all this rare fabric of heaven and
earth can come by chance when all the skill of art is not able
to make an oyster?'[18] Tillotson drew an analogy from the
marvels of the Henry VII chapel at Westminster; just as the
chapel could not be accounted for as a chance coagulation of
'stone, mortar, timber, iron, lead and glass' so no more could
the universe have come into existence by chance.[19] A similar
confidence spanned the century from Andrewes to Sharp; the
study of history and philosophy fortified belief in the existence
of a deity; truth from whatever source had a self-authenticating
power and there was a consistency within all realms of knowledge, and nowhere more than in the universal witness to the
existence of God.[20] Moreover, God intervened in human
affairs and the increasing awareness of 'secondary causes and
subordinate means' did not lead to any suggestion that God
had bowed out of the world and left it to grind upon its way
by the mechanical sequence of cause and effect.[21] Hall reflected
upon the calamities of famine and disease and he said that
while they could be attributed to a devilish soil, a lukewarm
summer or a blistering autumn he saw a more sombre cause
in 'a displeased God' and 'the inevitable certainties of God's
vengeance'; 'we are like those who think the puppets acting
upon the ledge move alone and fail to see the hand behind the
curtain'.[22] Sancroft, preaching in 1666 after the ravages of the
Great Plague, regarded the pestilences as 'products of God's
righteousness upon our unrighteousness' and unless the
lesson was learned they would return 'whetted with keener
edge and point'.[23] Patrick likewise regarded diseases and wars
as having a place in the 'vast abyss' of God's purposes.[24]

[17] Tillotson, ed. 1707, 16–19.
[18] Taylor, V., 298–9.
[19] Tillotson, ed. 1707, 15, and ed. 1743, VIII, 3413.
[20] Andrewes, I., 245; Sharp, J., *The Theological Works*, 1829, IV, 248–50.
[21] Sanderson, *Twenty-one Sermons*, 1681, 24.
[22] Hall, J., *Works*, 1863, V, 523–5.
[23] Sancroft, W., *A Sermon on October 10, 1666, before the King at the Solemn Fast appointed for the late fire in London*, 1694, 80, 111.
[24] Patrick, S., *Works*, 1858, IX, 148–9.

Bramhall made a similar point when he said that the web of cause and effect in the realm of animal and human fecundity resulted in the 'overrank field of this world' and God had to intervene to 'sweep away whole multitudes by war or famine or pestilence'.[25] Prideaux held that just as the Bible recorded many instances of God's direct intervention so 'all the world is a map of instances of this kind'.[26] Burnet set forth a singularly clear outline of the closely-knit fabric of the world where things acted and reacted according to their own natures but God's power, though unseen, was 'the spring of the whole machine'; nevertheless, God had not limited himself to such regularities but he raised or depressed the sequence as he saw fit; Cyrus, Alexander the Great, Caesar Augustus, Constantine and William of Orange were raised 'by a special providence' and the period of the Reformation was a time when events moved with 'extraordinary heat and giddiness'. All things were not bound to 'go on in a chain'.[27] Kidder also dilated upon the way in which animate and inanimate objects moved by the laws of their own nature but he also pointed to the direct divine intervention in the deliverance of Joseph, Mordecai and Moses and in the use made of the horns at Jericho, of the sling of David, and of the poor Galilean disciples and the helpless babe of Bethlehem.[28] Some sermons also contained cautions against excessive eagerness to discern signs of special divine intervention. Laud held that 'God doth often take unto himself second means and uses them in time to watch over the opportunity which he himself gives'.[29] Moore said that since God himself had established the course of nature he did not avert it for every petty cause and Wilkins spoke of the extent to which an observer's prejudices could shape his reading of the 'perplexed labyrinth' of this world.[30]

Nevertheless, strong as was the evidence for the existence

[25] Bramhall, V, 128.

[26] Prideaux, J., *Higgaion and Selah: For the Discovery of the Powder Plot*, 1636, 5–6.

[27] Burnet, G., *A Sermon preached before the King and Queen at Whitehall on the 19th day of October, 1690*, 1690, 7–10, and *A Sermon preached before the Queen at Whitehall on 29 May 1694 being the anniversary of King Charles II, his Birth and Restoration*, 1694, 7–8.

[28] Kidder, R., *Twelve Sermons preached upon several occasions*, 1697, 35–44, 51.

[29] Laud, I, 114.

[30] Moore, J., *Sermons on several subjects*, 1715, 140; Wilkins, J., *Sermons preached upon several occasions*, 1682, 184–6, 192.

of God, it was not sufficient to satisfy the need of people for assurance and hope or 'to satisfy and compose their doubtful and distracted minds'.[31] People, for all their innate gifts and their creation in the divine image, had incurred the curse laid upon Adam and Eve and so a race intended to be as gods had became as beasts. Hacket put the matter crudely when he said that people left to themselves were 'noisome ulcerous swine wallowing in the mire',[32] but Bramhall, though more refined, was none the less blunt in stating that the human race was infected with 'an hereditary contagion, a spiritual leprosy'.[33] The contrast between man's rich possibilities and his actual depravity was a constant theme. Hall was especially eloquent in expounding the contrast. Man had a glory: 'how doth the head of this microcosm resemble the round celestial globe, and the eyes the glittering stars in that firmament?' Animals could 'bleat or bellow or bray or grunt' and they had an 'inferior mongrel kind of ratiocination' as seen in 'the wily tricks of the fox or the witty feats of the monkey' but man had a tongue, 'this little film' which was capable of 'infinite varieties of expression', and he had the great gift of reason. However, while beasts only acted according to their nature, men sank to a bestiality of which beasts were incapable; they indulged in 'prodigies of sodomitical lewdness' and spent their time in 'hollow visits, in idle courtings, in epicurean pamperings, in fantastic dressings, in lawless disports, in deep plots, crafty conveyances and quarrelsome lawsuits'. Such degeneration was not confined to 'bloody Turks, man-eating cannibals, mongrel troglodytes' or 'miserable Indians idolatrously adoring their devilish pagodas' but was common to all mankind. Their eyes were 'a burning glass of concupiscence', their hearts 'a mint of treasons' and their hands 'engines of fraud and violence'; man was a beast, a monster, 'pardon me, a devil'.[34] Yet no preacher taught that the degradation was complete. There remained a sufficient yearning for survival and social order so that, as Brownrig said, there could be a measure of temporal stability and 'this civil honesty hath a more kindly

[31] Williams (Chichester), 155, 165.
[32] Hacket, 804, also 115, 346, 571.
[33] Bramhall, V, 148.
[34] Hall, V, 342, 454, 457, 461-2.

change into piety and sanctity than unnatural debauchery'.[35] Yet even this love of justice and the forms of piety could be guises assumed by infidelity and be as hard to uncover as 'some Jesuit in a popish dame's chamber'.[36] Sanderson lamented the way in which natural endowments were 'wrapped up in common pollutions'[37] and Cosin saw 'the poor snuff of light' almost extinguished; those who had walked 'no further for their sanctuary than Aristotle's gallery' could not grasp the deep things of God.[38] Taylor listed seventeen categories of falseness of heart and concluded that 'the heart of man hath not strength enough to think one good thought of itself'.[39]

Tillotson had no place for a doctrine of original sin and he avoided any emphasis upon an evil inheritance transmitted from Adam. The moral responsibility of each person was central to his teaching; 'sin is a voluntary evil which men wilfully bring upon themselves; no man is wicked or vicious but by his own choice'.[40] However, people did choose to do evil and Tillotson's picture of the human situation was also gloomy; there was 'a great degeneracy and corruption of human nature' brought about by 'wilfully contracted vicious habits'.[41] Conscience was laid to rest and 'grew brawny and seared as it were with a hot iron'.[42] He said in 1691 that there was 'almost an universal corruption' of the mind of man which was a miracle of God's contrivance.[43] Burnet was also perplexed by the enigma of man who was 'a little lower than the angels, a very little higher than the beasts'.[44] This perplexity was shared by Duppa and Kidder and by Stillingfleet who spoke of 'the antecedent inclination in human nature to the practice of evil'.[45]

[35] Brownrig, *Forty Sermons*, 330.
[36] Hall, V, 164.
[37] Sanderson, *Thirty-five Sermons*, 269.
[38] Cosin, I, 309.
[39] Taylor, V, 498.
[40] Tillotson, ed. 1707, 143.
[41] Ibid., 332–3, also ed. 1743, VII, 1858.
[42] Ibid., ed. 1707, 342–3.
[43] Ibid., 462, and ed. 1743, XI, 5101, and VIII, 3418.
[44] Burnet, *A Sermon preached at the funeral of the Honourable Robert Boyle at St Martin in the Fields, January 7, 1691–2*, 1692, 7.
[45] Stillingfleet, E., *Works*, 1710, I, 220.

People deserved punishment but punishments did not seem to be imposed equitably. Many preachers were troubled by the seeming division between God's justice and the inequalities of life. Few could be as confident as Sharp that on balance godliness paid dividends in prosperity and reputation and that 'honest and upright men for the most part in most public calamities fare well, at least much better than those that are not so'.[46] Bramhall held 'there is a great mist in the ways of God'; there was something monstrous in the thought of blessings upon the unrighteous and if righteous people were not rewarded there would be none to be generous to the poor.[47] Williams of York held it to be 'a cloister conceit' to think that only the poor and needy should be the objects of God's concern. Yet there were the sufferings of individuals, the trial of godly nations and of 'our distressed brethren of the Reformed Churches'.[48] Many bishops wrestled with these problems and there were several arguments commonly used throughout the century.

First, unless God took away human freedom and instituted a system of automatic rewards and punishments hardships were inevitable. Our life, said Bramhall, was such that there could be no certainty that 'this valley of tears could be transformed into a paradise of perpetual bliss'.[49] Brownrig held that while there were 'petty sessions' in this world whereby much judgement was effected it was only at the 'Grand Assize' that all would be clear.[50]

Second, if rewards were given precisely according to merit then people would seek to do good not for the sake of the good but of the profits.[51]

Third, abundance tended to nourish effeminacy and sloth and to miss the 'pearls of patience' to be found in the 'dunghill of sorrow and misery'.[52] Taylor said that a prosperous

---

[46] Sharp, I, 145.

[47] Bramhall, V, 131; also Kidder, 201.

[48] Williams, J. (York), *Perseverantia Sanctorum: A Sermon . . . before the Lords of the Parliament . . . upon Ash Wednesday, the 18th day of February, 1628,* 1628, 15–16, 21.

[49] Bramhall, V, 129; also Hacket, 118; Patrick, VII, 513 and IX, 50.

[50] Brownrig, *Forty Sermons,* 189.

[51] Hacket, 275; Kidder, 86.

[52] Hacket, 535.

iniquity was a hardening for ruin and reprobation.[53] Reynolds found some compensation for inequalities in 'inward and spiritual joy'.[54]

Fourth, hardships on earth could be a preparation for 'the amplitude of our patrimony hereafter'. Nations, according to Tillotson, had no immortality and therefore had to rise and fall in time, and in time the verdict on them was passed; individuals had a redress hereafter.[55]

Fifth, limitations of knowledge prevented exact calculation of consequences and therefore even the best intentions could have quite unintended consequences. As Sanderson put it, a smith while shoeing a horse could prick the hoof and make the horse restless and thus endanger its rider in battle which could then be lost with danger to the kingdom and dire results for other nations as well.[56]

Sixth, the inequalities might not be so great as they seemed; some of the seemingly righteous might be guilty of some secret sin which was receiving its due punishment. 'We are not sure that all are good that seem to be so.'[57]

Seventh, there was the courage displayed by many righteous sufferers and they thus proved the strength of religion.[58]

All these bishops were convinced that within this world with all its enigmas God had made an unique revelation of himself in Jesus Christ. At best all other light was dim whether radiating through other religions or even through the Jewish religion. The eternal Son of God became man in the human life of Jesus Christ. In the words of Cosin, he who was without beginning or ending was born 'in the days'; he who was head of all had to be hidden from Herod, a cruel tyrant.[59] Normally prosaic preachers such as Ussher became lyrical when speaking of Jesus. Hall was moved to even higher than his usual flights of oratory; God had 'put on him the rags of our humanity':

[53] Taylor, V, 590.
[54] Reynolds, III, 177; also Kidder, 86.
[55] Tillotson, ed. 1707, 44, and ed. 1743, VIII, 3481; Kidder, 86; Wilkins, *A Sermon before the King upon 19 March, 1670-1,* 1671, 20-25.
[56] Sanderson, *Twenty-one Sermons,* 308; Bramhall, V, 128-9.
[57] Kidder, 130.
[58] Reynolds, III, 177.
[59] Cosin, I, 11-12.

It is no news for God to be great and glorious, but for the eternal
and everliving God to be abased unto death, to the death of the
Cross, is that which could not but amaze the angels and confound
devils.[60]

Brownrig said the impact of Jesus was overwhelming; Paul
was enraptured; Peter was in a trance; John lay as dead; 'all
human understandings tremble'; Jesus was no stray sheep but
the holy Lamb of God.[61] Tillotson said that the method of
incarnation was not a method which men would naturally
have devised as worthy of God but in the event the example
of Christ, his miracles, his fulfilled predictions about the fall
of Jerusalem and his power for good in shaping the manners
of men were ample justification for the way God had chosen
to act.[62] Lloyd said that the miracles which 'exceed the power of
nature so far as any man is able to judge of it' were a sufficient
attestation of the mission of Jesus to the world.[63]

All the bishops stated that the purpose of the coming of
Christ had been to reconcile men to God but there were also
traces in many sermons of the doctrine that God was reconciled to men. In the early part of the century many sermons
referred to the turning away of the wrath of God by the work
of Christ. 'God is angry with us,' said Ussher, 'and it is no
small satisfaction that can appease God's wrath,' but in Christ
it had been done; he 'pacifieth the wrath of his Father'.[64]
Prideaux attributed part of the agony in the garden to 'the
displeasure of his heavenly Father'.[65] Hall put the point
succinctly: 'An infinite justice is offended; an infinite justice
hath satisfied; an infinite mercy hath applied it'.[66] Brownrig
often stressed the need for satisfaction and said that by
Christ's 'precious death and bloodshed God's wrath was
appeased and satisfied'.[67] Cosin, Hacket, Sanderson, Sprat and

---

[60] Hall, V, 382, also 322.
[61] Brownrig, *Twenty-five Sermons*, 12, 26.
[62] Tillotson, ed. 1743, VII, 1989, 2070.
[63] Lloyd, W., *A Sermon preached before the King at Whitehall on December 1, 1667*, 1668, 11.
[64] Ussher, J., *The Whole Works*, ed. C. R. Elrington, 1847, XIII, 7, 130, 143.
[65] Prideaux, J., *The Draught of the Brooke: A sermon at the Court*, Oxford, 1636, 8–10.
[66] Hall, V, 221.
[67] Brownrig, *Forty Sermons*, 247.

Taylor all echoed the theme of 'the load of infinite anger borne by Christ'.[68] Reynolds spoke much of the love of God but he also spoke of the need to satisfy 'the offended wrath of God'; since Christ's death 'God is placable, sin pardonable, the soul curable'.[69]

The appeasement of an angry deity was an idea which aroused not a little uneasiness in the mind of several of the bishops. Williams of Chichester said it was more fitting to 'a sanguinary sort of demons' than to God the Father. Yet he felt that the idea was deeply embedded in the Old Testament and therefore had its origin in the mind of God; God ordained the system of sacrifices. Jewish sacrificial practices were not the transmuting or adapting of the common practices of primitive people but were a specific ordinance whereby God upheld his holiness. Even a civil ruler could not afford to remit the penalties incurred by a penitent criminal.[70] Tillotson was much more ready to take the view that the idea of appeasement was a divine accommodation to ideas which had their roots in the Jewish and heathen practices of 'substituting one living creature to suffer and die instead of another'. Tillotson did not believe that such practices in fact achieved their aim but they had become the common belief of mankind and they had some foundation in the fact that human beings were 'vile and detestable creatures' and fit objects of divine wrath. Moreover, in getting his message over to mankind God could not ignore common patterns of thought; if the patterns had been different God could simply have offered forgiveness and eternal life to all upon repentance for past sins and upon evidence of a sincere endeavour after obedience in the future, but things being as they were and people being conditioned by ideas of sacrifice and the belief that 'God would not be appeased nor should sin be pardoned without suffering' a simple declaration of forgiveness would be 'encouragement to sin'. Thus, Christ's work could properly be called satisfaction and Tillotson continued to speak of his 'plenary satisfaction', but to the end his reservations came to the surface and he felt

[68] Cosin, I, 281; Hacket, 3, and 530; Sanderson, *Twenty-one Sermons,* 103–4; Sprat, T., *Sermons preached on several Occasions,* 1710, 331, 337–42, 345.
[69] Reynolds, V, 311.
[70] Williams (Chichester), 171, 183, 199–200.

that the imagery of satisfaction went 'almost further than goodness and justice will well admit'.[71] Stillingfleet emphasized again and again the reconciliation of man to God but he never repudiated the idea of God being reconciled to man;[72] he put into the mouth of Jesus the cry, 'Will no other sacrifice appease thine anger but that of Thy Son's blood?' and he also said that 'God was willing to be reconciled'.[73]

Christ having accomplished his mission to the world, there remained the task of moving people to respond to that achievement. Tillotson preferred 'the gentle and peaceable methods of reason and persuasion'[74] but others stressed the need of 'corrosive denunciations' and threats of 'thunderbolts for sinners'.[75] There was also a prevalent thought in the sermons that such was the hardness of sinners only direct divine election could prove effective. The preachers had many reservations and restrictions upon the doctrine of election and they were concerned to preserve human responsibility and divine justice. So Andrewes said, 'God hardened to man's heart but his that first hardeneth his own heart'.[76] Yet there were harsh assertions of God's arbitrary election; none were harsher than Ussher who, echoing Calvin, said that if God chose to elect some to glory and to leave those whom he did not elect to the just reward of damnation there was no ground for complaint. However, even Ussher could not avoid a paradoxical assertion that each individual garden was entrusted to its occupant and it was folly to neglect God's mercy; 'no man can be saved against his will'.[77] Reynolds also stressed God's 'discriminating grace' whereby he had mercy on whom he would and yet he also said that if any were damned it would be due to their rejection of the open invitation.[78]

Tillotson rejected 'as utterly inconsistent with the least measure and degree of goodness' the doctrine of an irresistible

---

[71] Tillotson, ed. 1707, 551, 560–2, 565, and ed. 1743, VIII, 3450, 3455.
[72] Stillingfleet, I, 434, 465, 501, 592.
[73] Ibid, I, 478, 593; see also 85, 496.
[74] Tillotson, ed. 1707, 204.
[75] Hall, V, 573–4, 576; Brownrig, *Forty Sermons,* 216, 514; Hacket, 652, 726; Taylor, V, 596–7.
[76] Andrewes, IV, 447.
[77] Ussher, XIII, 168, also 7; Knox, op. cit., 18ff.
[78] Reynolds, IV, 395; V, 253.

grace which would compel the elect; each person had to decide to respond to the invitation.[79] He managed to keep the language of election by saying that each person by his own choice predestined his own destiny.[80] Nevertheless, Tillotson was so aware of the enfeebled condition of the human will that he admitted it required the stimulation of the Holy Spirit and it was 'no wrong to any man to be made good and happy against his will'.[81] Sharp rejected any doctrine which implied that God decreed any 'from eternity to hell-fire without respect to their evil actions or wicked lives'; 'God never passed any such sentence upon any of his creatures'. There was in all 'a capacity of being saved' but Sharp took the gloomiest view of how people would exercise that capacity; the Scriptures, he held, did not hold out hope for more than one in a million; Christians were still but one quarter of mankind and the greatest part of these were attached to the errors of the Church of Rome but Sharp was confident that in the Church of England there was assurance of salvation 'whatever becomes of those that are without'.[82]

There was unanimity among these preachers that all who claimed to be Christians had to prove themselves by living in obedience to the will of God and by following Christ; 'The Pilot hath swam before thee and thou must also keep stroke to follow'.[83] Outward conduct could be a mask for selfish aims but God was not deceived. Judgements of probability and charity had to be made in assessing the motives of others. Sanderson held that there had to be a cheerful hope that good outward actions were the evidence of inward grace. From a social point of view there was something to be said for fitting outward behaviour even when it was a veneer covering unworthy motives; it was a 'Pelagian conceit' to imagine that such conduct was a prelude to genuine conversion or that it could merit any of 'the unproportionate heavenly rewards' but at least it was preferable to outward 'licentious practices'.[84]

---

[79] Tillotson, ed. 1743, VIII, 3562.
[80] Tillotson, ed. 1707, 118; also Stillingfleet, I, 346.
[81] Tillotson, ed. 1743, VI, 1750; also VI, 1772, 1765; VII, 2091.
[82] Sharp, II, 264–6, 278.
[83] Prideaux, *The Draught of the Brooke*, 8–10.
[84] Sanderson, *Thirty-five Sermons*, 141, 282.

There was also agreement that good works were never of such a perfection as to merit favour in the sight of God. At best such works were an inadequate but necessary effect of 'that grace which brings glory'.[85] Reynolds drew from Augustine, 'the incomparable champion of the grace of God', the maxim that 'our goodness is not the motive of God's love, but his love is the fountain of our goodness'.[86] Even in sermons urging the necessity of good works there were warnings against thinking that such works could gain merit; such an idea was the vain hope of 'the miserable worldling'.[87] Tillotson often spoke of a merciful God who accepted such obedience as people were capable of performing but he set alongside this teaching severe strictures on 'the insolent doctrine of the merit of good works' and said that Christianity was not a moral code but 'a vital principle inwardly to change and transform us'.[88] Taylor in some of his writings did lean to the view that the sinner as much as his sin was distasteful to God and would remain so until he had amended his life but in the sermons there was stress upon the inward motive, the secret thought and the unmerited grace of God. He was much concerned with growth in grace after the initial break with a past sinful life and he saw the arenas of growth as the family, the world of affairs and the nation.[89] He became one of the leading casuists among the preachers.

Taylor was in tune with much medieval thought when he saw the married state as a product of the 'superfoetation of the evil accidents of the world' and as a preventive of fornication and also as a state likely to be filled with much disillusion when people found the valleys of imagined matrimonial refreshment to be vales of sorrow where they were bound by the 'cords of a man's or a woman's peevishness'. Yet, having come to terms with marriage as a necessity he can then say that it is 'the mother of the world and preserves kingdoms and

[85] Hall, V, 144; see Sprat, 289, 294, and also *A Sermon preached before the King and Queen at Whitehall on Good Friday, April 6, 1694,* 1694, 4.

[86] Reynolds, III, 313.

[87] Grove, R., *Profitable Charity: A Sermon before the Rt. Hon. Sir Thomas Lane, Lord Mayor of London, on Easter Monday, 1695,* 1695, 11.

[88] Tillotson, ed. 1707, 85, and ed. 1743, XI, 4717.

[89] Taylor, V, 5–6.

fills cities and churches and heaven itself'.[90] Cosin also said that marriage made possible the replenishing of the earth with godly inhabitants and the augmenting of heaven with glorious saints.[91] Sanderson urged husbands to treat their wives with loving condescension and Taylor counselled wives to be content to shine only by their husbands' light and to avoid 'a studious gallantry' or 'indecent gaieties'.[92] Hall professed a detestation of 'the garish popinjays' who under 'a cloke of modesty hide nothing but pride and fiendishness'.[93] Burnet patronizingly pitied women who had not 'so strong reasonings' as men and were burdened by the death of children.[94]

Parents had a duty to their children. Families with ancestry and inheritance had special opportunities and Sanderson lamented that some parents 'set by the most untoward and misshapen chip of the whole block to make timber for the pulpit'. Those from families of lower standing had to be content with a 'tolerable mediocrity' and society depended upon the readiness of some to 'drudge in the baser and meaner offices'.[95] Tillotson held that 'the gross and shameful neglect' of the upbringing of children was 'one of the great and crying sins of this age and nation' and paved the way for an obstinate growth of lazy habits and a lack of proper respect 'in the presence of their betters'. Children were 'narrow-brimmed vessels' only capable of gradual growth and therefore punishment had to be adjusted to the nature and quality of the fault and a curriculum devised suitable to each 'particular temper and disposition'.[96]

Almsgiving was a constant theme. Andrewes maintained that during the reign of Elizabeth benefactions to schools, colleges and almshouses had been greater than in any other Christian country or in any previous forty years 'during all the time of popery', and he correctly observed that this had, alas, been accompanied by a falling away in generosity to 'the poor

[90] Ibid, V, 254–8.
[91] Cosin, I, 56.
[92] Sanderson, *Twenty-five Sermons*, 30–35; Taylor, V, 264–5, 272, 276–7.
[93] Hall, V, 101, 131–2, 296.
[94] Burnet, *A Sermon at the funeral of the Rt. Hon. Anne, Lady Dowager Brook, the 19th day of February, 1690–1, 1691*, 14–16, 25.
[95] Sanderson, *Thirty-five Sermons*, 205, 213.
[96] Tillotson, ed. 1707, 606, 613, 621, 624, 635–6.

Church and her patrimony'.[97] Patrick, Sharp and Tenison all preached on the growth of London's charities and hospitals.[98] Stillingfleet said that charitable gifts in the sixty years after the accession of Elizabeth had been twice what was given in twice that number of years before the Reformation.[99] Hacket and Sanderson taught that God had made many poor for 'the good use of our riches'; the contrast between surfeited rich and famished poor was a rebuke to the loss of pity for men and reverence for God.[100] Nevertheless, there was no justification for indiscriminate charity which only encouraged idlers who, in the words of Sanderson, were 'the very scabs and filth and vermin of the commonwealth'.[101] Lloyd said that for such 'the vinegar of justice was a bettei restorative than the oil of mercy'. Mistaken charity could be 'the plummet of perdition' but rightly and generously given it could be a sure sign of grace.[102] Riches could be a sign of God's blessing and a fitting resource for those who were fit for them. In many sermons there were sharp attacks upon those who misused their riches by living in 'luxury and intemperance and all manner of excess' and 'bathing in a sea of sensual satieties'. Tillotson rebuked those who wasted 'whole mornings between the comb and the glass and the afternoons at plays and whole nights in gaming or in riot and lewdness and intemperance'.[103]

Some preachers had a concern for all mankind. Sanderson thundered against slavery and the sale of people 'stamped with the image of God, endowed with a reasonable soul, made capable of grace and glory', but he was premature in exonerating 'our Christian religion and pious governors' from countenancing such a traffic which he regarded as the preserve of Turks and pagans.[104] Tillotson was at his most spacious in

<hr />

[97] Andrewes, V, 37, 42.
[98] Patrick, VIII, 513; Sharp, I, 108–110; Tenison, T., *A Sermon concerning Discretion in giving Alms, preached at St Sepulchre's Church in London, April 6, 1681*, 1681, 24–25.
[99] Stillingfleet, I, preface to Sermon XIX, also 316.
[100] Hacket, 9, 857–8, 864, 916; Sanderson, *Twenty-one Sermons*, 256.
[101] Sanderson, *Thirty-five Sermons*, 197; Sharp, I, 110; Patrick, VII, 424.
[102] Lloyd, *The Mammon of Unrighteousness: . . . A Sermon preached in the Cathedral Church of Worcester on Sunday the 19th of August, 1688*, 1688, 10, 21–22; also Wilkins, 474.
[103] Tillotson, ed. 1743, VI, 1638–9; also Ken, T., *Prose Works*, 1838, Sermon II, 162–3; Hall, V, 180, 154; Brownrig, *Forty Sermons*, 454; Croft, H., *A Sermon preached before the King at Whitehall, 12 April, 1674*, 1676, 15–17.
[104] Sanderson, *Twenty-one Sermons*, 95–6.

his appreciation of the virtues to be found in all mankind; in spite of 'the greatest provocations which were committed by men against God' there were lurking virtues in all people and 'an obstinate goodness is apt to conquer even the worst of men'.[105] Sprat gave glowing expression to the ideal of universal accord:

> No difference of outward condition, no calamity, no misery, can make any man not to be equal to me, or to deserve my neglect; no distance of place, no strangeness of country, no contrariety of temper or interest can make any man a stranger to me or deserve my indifference; no ill-will, no ill speech, no ill deed of another against me can make any man an enemy to me or to deserve my hatred.[106]

Thus, on personal morality and on social duty the bishops saw issues with broad unanimity and they prescribed duties with sharp clarity. Yet, they also saw that changing circumstances could alter the form of obligation. Taylor and Sanderson wrestled with many casuistic problems. Sanderson held it to be a duty for a clergyman in England to wear fitting apparel but if he were travelling in Turkey and found himself in danger it could be right for him to disguise himself with 'a green suit, a cap and feather and a long lock on one side, or to work in some mechanic or manual trade'.[107] Or, in some circumstances, it could be justifiable to conduct a service without the use of instrumental music or even to preach without a surplice, but there was no such necessity in England. The laws in church and state emanated from those who were entitled to enact them and the duty of obedience was clear. Each in his own station had obligations to subordinates and also to superiors both spiritual and temporal. Further, when the state no longer attempted to enforce conformity and granted a degree of toleration to nonconformists, the bishops reluctantly had to come to terms with a situation wherein they would have to depend upon persuasion but even then they still held conformity to be the way of wisdom and

---

[105] Tillotson, ed. 1707, 391.
[106] Sprat, 100–101.
[107] Sanderson, *Twenty-one Sermons,* 162; see also 168–70.

especially for 'grown persons who are of very low and mean capacity of understanding'.[108]

Many bishops were influenced by the fresh movements in the worlds of thought and discovery and some of them were influential in so important a pioneering body as the Royal Society, yet to read their sermons is to be taken into a remarkably homogeneous world of belief and precept within which they sought to assimilate the harvest of their studies and researches. The currents which would threaten the foundations of that world were only felt in their full force in the following centuries.[109]

BISHOPS IN THE PULPIT

A list of the sixty-three bishops, in order of consecration, whose sermons are the basis of this essay.

Abbreviations: C–Cambridge: O–Oxford: F–Fellow: M–Master: Ch–Chaplain: D–Dean.

Lancelot Andrewes CFMChD – 1605 – Chichester, Ely, Winchester

William Barlow CFChD – 1605 – Rochester, Lincoln

George Abbot OFMChD – 1609 – Coventry and Lichfield, London, Canterbury

John Buckeridge OFMCh – 1611 – Rochester, Ely

John King OMChD – 1611 – London

Robert Abbot OFM – 1615 – Salisbury

George Downham CFCh – 1616 – Derry

Arthur Lake OFMD – 1616 – Bath and Wells

Thomas Morton OFChD – 1616 – Chester, Coventry and Lichfield, Durham

Martin Fotherby CFChD – 1618 – Salisbury

James Ussher, Trinity College, Dublin – 1621 – Meath, Armagh

William Laud OFMChD – 1621 – St Davids, Bath and Wells, London, Canterbury

John Williams CFChD – 1622 – Lincoln, York

Joseph Hall CFChD – 1627 – Exeter, Norwich

---

[108] Tillotson, ed. 1743, IV, 868–70.
[109] Bennett, G. V., *The Tory Crisis in Church and State, 1688–1730*, Oxford 1975, 309.

Matthew Wren CFMChD – 1634 – Hereford, Norwich, Ely
John Bramhall CCh – 1634 – Derry, Armagh
Roger Manwaring OChD – 1635 – St Davids
Henry Leslie, Aberdeen University, ChD – 1635 – Down and
  Connor, Meath
Brian Duppa OFMChD – 1638 – Chichester, Salisbury,
  Winchester
John Prideaux OFMCh – 1641 – Worcester
Ralph Brownrig CFMCh – 1642 – Exeter
Henry King OChD – 1642 – Chichester
Henry Jones, Trinity College, Dublin – 1645 – Clogher,
  Meath
John Gauden CCh – 1660 – Exeter, Worcester
John Cosin CFMChD – 1660 – Durham
Gilbert Sheldon OFMCh – 1660 – London, Canterbury
Robert Sanderson OCh – 1660 – Lincoln
George Morley OMD – 1660 – Worcester, Winchester
Jeremy Taylor CFCh – 1660 – Down and Connor, Dromore
Benjamin Laney CFMChD – 1660 – Peterborough, Lincoln,
  Ely
John Hacket CF – 1661 – Coventry and Lichfield
Edward Reynolds OFMChD – 1661 – Norwich
Herbert Croft OChD – 1662 – Hereford
Seth Ward CF – 1662 – Salisbury
Robert Mossom CD – 1666 – Derry
John Dolben OD – 1666 – Rochester, York
Anthony Sparrow CFM – 1667 – Exeter, Norwich
John Wilkins OM (in O&C) – 1668 – Chester
Peter Gunning CFM – 1669 – Chichester, Ely
John Pearson CFM – 1673 – Chester
John Vesey, Trinity College, Dublin, D – 1673 – Limerick,
  Tuam
John Fell OFMChD – 1676 – Oxford
Thomas Lamplugh OFD – 1676 – Exeter, York
William Sancroft CFMChD – 1677 – Canterbury
Edward Wetenhall C – 1678 – Cork and Ross, Kilmore and
  Ardagh
William Lloyd OFChD—1680—St Asaph, Coventry and
  Lichfield, Worcester.

Richard Tenison, Trinity College, Dublin, ChD – 1682 –
Killala, Clogher, Meath
Francis Turner OMChD – 1683 – Rochester, Ely
Thomas Sprat OFD – 1684 – Rochester
Thomas Ken OFCh – 1684 – Bath and Wells
Gilbert Burnet, Aberdeen University – 1689 – Salisbury
Edward Stillingfleet CFD – 1689 – Worcester
Simon Patrick CD – 1689 – Chichester, Ely
Nicholas Stratford OFChD – 1689 – Chester
John Tillotson CFChD – 1691 – Canterbury
John Sharp CChD – 1691 – York
Edward Fowler O&C – 1691 – Gloucester
John Moore CFCh – 1691 – Norwich, Ely
Richard Kidder CFChD – 1691 – Bath and Wells
Robert Grove CFCh – 1691 – Chichester
Thomas Tenison CFCh – 1692 – Lincoln, Canterbury
John Williams OCh – 1696 – Chichester
Thomas Wilson, Trinity College, Dublin, Ch – 1698 – Sodor
and Man

VI

A Devotion of Rapture in English Puritanism

GORDON RUPP

ONE fine day, somebody will write about the relation between spirituality and geography. There seem to be places in the world with an affinity for contemplative men, like the deserts of Libya or Goreme, or that north-eastern corner of Scotland which in the seventeenth century produced Samuel Rutherford, Henry Scougal, Patrick Forbes, the Chevalier Ramsay and the Garden brothers.[1] Such a place is that part of Thuringian Saxony where among the 'grey sisters' of Helfta, there was a remarkable flowering of devotion and holiness. The Gertrudes and the Mechtilds owed something both to the Benedictine and the Cistercian tradition, but they also developed what Pere Doyère has called 'the style of Helfta' – a devotion centred on the love of God, and the sacred humanity of Christ, anticipating by many centuries later devotion to the Sacred Heart.

Only half a mile from Helfta is the little town of Eisleben, where, two centuries later, Martin Luther was born, and where he died. Of this district he too was a 'Landeskind' and the Count of Mansfeld was the one to whom Luther, like the nuns of Helfta, owed civil obedience.

Gerard Manley Hopkins dismissed the coincidence roughly enough:

> Gertrude, lily, and Luther were two of a town
> Christ's lily and beast of the waste wood. . . .

---

[1] Henderson, G. D., *The Burning Bush*, 1957; chs 6–8 in *Mystics of the North East*, 1934.

In regard to Luther, as with the fate of his beloved Henry Purcell, Hopkins' 'thinking with the Church' was well behind Vatican II. It is ironical, because 'The Wreck of the Deutschland' is the finest exposition in non-theological English of what Luther meant by the 'Righteousness of God'. A modern Catholic, Josef Lortz, is nearer the truth:

> Luther possessed a mighty power of prayer . . . he never had to jump over any ditch before beginning to speak with God . . . there is a robust solidarity about Luther's prayer . . . he interpreted many things in the Bible in a quite inadmissably private way, but he did not play at Christianity.[2]

Though Luther came to denounce the monastic life, and indeed the life of contemplation, he remained a man of prayer.[3] And for him, as for the ladies of Helfta, the Psalms were the heart of his devotion. Curiously like Gertrude of Helfta,[4] he was wont to meditate on the meaning of his Baptism, and on the faith of the Church as it is expressed in the Te Deum.

Moreover, Luther's devotion to the humanity of Christ is an important part of this theology.[5] In his sermons, especially those on the Fourth Gospel this is evident, for it is important to remember that the Reformation was a Johannine as well as a Pauline renaissance, and Luther was very much a John man. For Luther, as for the other Reformers, the preaching of the Word implies on the part of the congregation devout meditation: on the part of the preacher, too, meditation on the sacred text. But Luther's continuities with medieval religion did not end there. The label 'Theology of the Cross' has been aptly applied to Luther's theology and to stresses within it which endured throughout his life and which appear indeed in his very last sermon.[6]

---

[2] Lortz, J., *The Reformation in Germany*, E.T. 1968, Vol. 1, 434.

[3] On Luther's prayers, see Wertelius, G., *Oratio Continua*, Lund 1970; Schmidt, K. D., *Luther lehrt beten*, Gesammelte Aufsätze 1967; *Luther's Devotional Writings* (Works, American ed.), Vols. 42, 43.

[4] Gertrude d'Helfta, *Oevres Spirituelles*, 2v; P. Doyère (ed.), *Sources Chrétiennes*, Paris 1967–8; Leclercq, *History of Christian Spirituality*, Vol. 2, E.T. 1968, chs 5, 6.

[5] Lienhard, M., *Luther, Témoin de Jésus Christ*, Paris 1973.

[6] Von Loewenich, W., *Luther's Theology of the Cross* E.T. Philadelphia 1976; E. G. Rupp, 'Luthers 95 Theses and the "Theology of the Cross" ' in *Luther for an Ecumenical age* (ed. Meyer) 1967, 67ff.

We know that Luther's teacher and patron John Staupitz turned his attention to the 'Wounds of Jesus' as the place where we see the mind of God towards us. The first publication of Luther was an edition of the little German treatise – perhaps written in Frankfurt by one of the Teutonic knights – which has become known as the *Theologia Germanica*. Among his earliest books was a copy of the sermons of John Tauler, the Dominican of Strasbourg whose addresses to devout women reflect an earlier German mystical tradition. The thought of the essence of sin as egocentricity, the need for the Christian to be crucified with Christ, for the extermination of the Old Adam that the new man in Christ may be born, and the belief that the Christian is called to share the fellowship of Christ's sufferings, all these were in that older German tradition, and what Luther owed to them became explicit in his brilliant Heidelberg Theses of 1518 and underlay, to a surprising extent, his more famous 95 Theses against indulgences. But the 'Theology of the Cross' was not only to be found in books. The Churches of Germany – like that of St George in Eisenach which Luther attended as a boy, or the Sebaldus Kirche in Nuremberg – had poignant effigies of the Cross which seemed almost to exaggerate physical suffering, while the altar pieces of Luther's friend, Lukas Cranach the Older, make so much of the 'blood of Jesus' as to anticipate the 'blood and wounds' theology of eighteenth-century Pietism.

But Luther's is not the only link with Thuringian mysticism. Thomas Müntzer, the famous radical figure of the Peasants' War, was born in Thuringia and this locality was his stamping ground. He began as chaplain and confessor in two nunneries and a fragment of an early sermon is in praise of the Virgin Mary and draws heavily on St Bernard. He is said to have carried round with him a great double volume. In one half were Tauler's sermons, and if Tauler influenced the young Luther he dominated for a time Müntzer whose theology is saturated in Tauler, not least in the theme of the regeneration of the Christian through the Work and Will of God, who ploughs up the ground of the human heart, and who through the experience of suffering and the good fight against temptation, destroys the weeds of creaturely desire, and implants the good seed of Christ.

Müntzer's other half volume was edited by the French biblical humanist, Le Fèvre of Etaples, *The Lives of Three Spiritual Men and Three Spiritual Women* (1513). In this exotic and indeed explosive volume it is the three women who have most interest. St Hildegarde of Bingen, one of the great women of history, is represented by her vision of the Two Ways-'Scivias'. St Elizabeth of Schönau is a lesser mortal, but one whose imaginative vision of the story of St Bridget helped to make it a medieval favourite. These two women represent Rhineland mysticism. But the third is one of the Thuringian ladies – Mechtild of Hackeborn, and her treatise 'Of Special Grace'.

It is true that this is but one strand of Müntzer's thought, and the Christocentric core of his devotion is not apparent in his few writings. He was a man of original and complex mind: debtor to Scripture and the Fathers, to Plato, as also to medieval apocalyptic via the Spiritual Franciscans and the Hussites. When in 1525, his Thuringian peasants burst into the convent at Helfta and looted and destroyed the books and manuscripts, we may hope that Müntzer left those sombre proceedings to his more militant comrade Thomas Pfeiffer.

There is nothing to link Helfta and Eisleben with the English Reformation. We are concerned in this essay rather with affinity than with pedigree. But it is true that the first English Protestant Reformers inherit, like their German comrades, the late medieval 'Theology of the Cross'. William Tyndale owed much to Luther and supremely the doctrines of justification, the dialectic of Law and Gospel, the themes of Christian liberty and Christian vocation. Like Luther he becomes most eloquent when he writes about Christ and about forgiveness.

The Communion services of 1549 and 1552 with their emphasis on the sufficiency and once for all-ness of Christ's sacrifice on the Cross have been seen by some, including Gregory Dix, as a reflection of medieval western piety. The sermons of the Edwardian preachers, especially Bradford and Knox, stress repentance and are often in a minor key. But the heirs of this theology of the Cross are not only those who belong to what became the Puritan tradition. Lancelot Andrewes, John Donne, George Herbert are as concerned with Christ and with His passion. Both wings of English Protestantism represent the sixteenth-century crisis of Augustinianism.

As the rules of a sonnet make possible its spontaneity, and as the devotion of the ladies of Helfta is to be explained against a strict discipline, liturgical and ascetic, so the Puritan devotion of the heart was imbedded in an often complex rationalism, and is to be set against an austere pattern of religious life, in community, in family worship, in Bible study and in concern for conscience, as well as in adherence to the sacramental ordinances, and the observance of the Sabbath. The English Puritans, like the ladies of Helfta, set a great store by the Psalms.

In the last thirty years attention has centred on first one and then another aspect of Puritanism, on logic and theology, on ecclesiastical polity, on casuistry, on developing notions of freedom and toleration which presaged the future, and mil-lenarian ideas which seem to peg down prophecy, together with the sociological context and the implications, conscious and unconscious, of their beliefs, for the development of political ideas and of science. Too little attention has been paid to their spirituality, to what they have to say of Christian experience, of their devotion to Christ, and about the joy of the Christian religion. But the evidence is abundant, at almost every level of religious and theological writing. It is time to look at Puritanism from the other side of the (Christopher) Hill.

What we have called a devotion of rapture[7] is to be found not in the cloister but in crowded congregations in the Inns of Court, and in the Universities, and even before the House of Commons. Not that these things were confined to the academic and upper classes. We must never forget those old ladies whom John Bunyan overheard in Bedford, sitting on

[7] See Wakefield, G. S., *Puritan Devotion*, London 1957, ch. 7; Bouyer, L., 'Orthodox Spirituality and Protestant and Anglican Spirituality' in *History of Christian Spirituality*, Vol. 3, E.T. 1969, Pt. 2, ch. 2.

their doorsteps in the sun, and discussing Christian doctrines with precise and scientific accuracy – the kind of lay articulateness which occurred in Byzantium in the fifth century, in Scotland in the nineteenth but not often elsewhere and nowadays nowhere at all.

It was a devotion of the heart, of Christian experience. It is at the points of forgiveness and the assurance of faith that the experience of conversion becomes eloquent. Many of the leading Puritans came to religion reluctantly, out of the worldliness of the permissive society of Elizabethan England.

> As once at a crash Paul
> Or as Austin, a lingering-out sweet skill.

We hear of forty Cambridge divines converted through the influence of Laurence Chaderton, the first master of Emmanuel College, whose long life – 1536–1640 – spans the whole English Reformation. At a time when dons were advising their bright students to turn to medicine rather than theology, amid a hubbub of possible repression, it was significant when a John Preston or Samuel Ward turned back to divinity.

Robert Bolton (1572–1681) is typical of the massive learning of Puritan biblical humanism, only untypical in that he came from Oxford. Throughout his edifying discourses there runs a formidable critical apparatus of Biblical, patristic and scholastic learning; at the fundament are the sacred languages, the first hand study of the Bible in its original tongues, a massive Puritan tradition joining Chaderton, Preston, Bedell, Clark, with Meade, Worthington and John Milton. He read contemporary Protestant theology, Beza rather than Calvin, Chemnitz rather than Luther, and of course Bellarmine and the divines of Trent. Even more notable is his patristic learning, Augustine of course, but also Bernard and Chrysostom and Cyprian.

In a slightly over-stated argument Louis Martz has suggested that behind Puritan patterns of contemplation there are precise medieval Catholic models, and he instances Joseph Hall and Richard Baxter.[8] That there was blood transfusion between the

---

[8] Martz, Louis L., *The Poetry of Meditation*, 1954.

two traditions is not to be denied. But thirty years before Baxter's *Everlasting Rest* Bolton, resting on his reading of the Fathers, had given similar advice:

> Feed, enlarge, improve . . . to the uttermost, with meditation, prayer and practice, so shalt thou preserve thine heart in a soft, holy comfortable temper which is singular happiness . . . what Christian heart can endure to discontinue its sweet and humble intercourse with God for one day? Let thy broken heart therefore everyday, besides solemn and ordinary ejaculations be sure . . . to bathe itself deliciously in the blissful depths of God's boundless mercies in Christ, that he be kept spiritually merry, thankful and in heart to all holy duties. To kiss sweetly the glorified body of our crucified lord with the lips of infinitely dearest and inexpressible affectionate love: though the distance be great, yet the hand of faith will bring them easily together.[9]

In another treatise he turns to the theme of eternal life, the New Jerusalem, the beatific vision,

> that heart ravishing contemplation, the very life of everlasting life, and the soul of heavenly joys and bliss: to be admitted to the face of God, by beatifical vision and fruition of the most glorious and blessed Trinity, by immediate communion and so consequently of those torrents of pleasure and fulness of joy flowing thence. The other innumerable inestimable joys of heaven are I deny not transcendant and ravishing, but they are all but accessories of this principle, drops of this ocean, glimpses to this sun.[10]

John Preston is sometimes thought of as a political Puritan and his cloak and dagger activities on the Continent and his involvement in the Duke of Buckingham's ploys attest his activities as a diplomat, which led to his being offered the post of Lord Keeper of the Great Seal. All this activity among University doings in the corridors of power led to his cozening old Chaderton out of the Mastership of Emmanuel. As in the case of his more right-wing contemporary Joseph Hall, his devotional utterances are the more startling against this more secular background, and though in both cases the idea that

[9] *Directions for a Comfortable Walk with God*, 1636, 93.
[10] *Of the Four Last Things*, 163, 5 113.

this is a kind of evangelical cant springs to mind, the idea is to be resisted.

> The bowels of compassion in Christ melt over a straying sinner and he is ready to receive them . . . we that are the ministers of Christ are bound to press it on you . . . invite you to a banquet . . in a banquet there is a concourse of all spiritual things – such things are in Christ: there is a concourse of spiritual joy and comfort: of all the precious things you can find. And if you will come and take it, you shall have his jewels, all his graces to adorn you. Let this persuade you to come.[11]

Richard Sibbes (1577–1635) was Master of St Catherine's College, Cambridge, and preached some of his most powerful sermons to the lawyers of the Inns of Court in London.

> But what (some say) must nothing be preached but Christ? I answer, nothing but Christ or that which tends to Christ. If we preach threatenings it is to cast men down that we may raise them up . . . all make way for Christ . . . whatever we preach it may be reduced to Christ, that men may walk worthy of Christ.[12]

Nor did Sibbes neglect the doctrine of the Incarnation, for he has a powerful oration on 'The Nativity of Christ celebrated by Angels'. Perhaps the most remarkable of all his sermons are those on the fifth and sixth chapters of the Song of Songs, 'A Discovery of the Union and Communion betwixt Christ and the Church, and consequently between Him and every believing soul'.

> Let us then often warm our hearts with the consideration hereof, because all our love is from this love of his. Oh! the wonderful love of God, that both such transcendent majesty and such infinite love should dwell together . . . in the heart of one Christ . . . the consideration of these things is wondrously effectual as to strengthen faith, so to kindle love.[13]

[11] Preston, J., 'The Breastplate of faith and love', in Wesley, J., *Christian Library*, 1819, 5, 361.
[12] Sibbes, R., 'The Fountain open'd or the Mystery of Godliness', in Wesley, J., op. cit., 1820, 6, 84.
[13] Ibid., 176.

The most excellent thing we can think of, is the expression of the heart of God in Christ and of Christ's love to us. 'He is altogether lovely' – lovely to God, to us, to the soul: lovely to him that can best judge of loveliness: God cannot but love his own image.[14]

Whatsoever hath the stamp of Christ upon it, let us love it: we cannot bestow our hearts better. To lose ourselves in the love of Christ, and to forget ourselves . . . is the only way to find ourselves. . . . Therefore let us labour to kindle in our hearts an affection towards Christ, all that we can considering that he is thus lovely.[15]

Francis Rouse (1579–1669) was a Cornish layman, among other things a notable Provost of Eton and Speaker of the House of Commons. He wrote a treatise on 'Mysticall Marriage' turning also to the Song of Songs and a variety of images derived from St Bernard. His rather odd treatise on 'The Heavenly University' returns to the same themes:

There is a marriage between Christ and his Church: the church in this marriage is one spirit with him, as in natural marriages, two are one flesh. And if there is such a marriage, there is also a marriage love between them . . . will not this husband who is light itself, and love itself teach his own spouse by this most perfect light and from this most perfect love? Yea, certainly he will not only tell her the words of his counsel, but by a sacred unction (being one spirit with her), he will make her to see the counsels of his words: he will give her an inward and spiritual eye, to see the inward riches and realities of his counsels.[16]

The treatise ends with 'Aspirations of a student in the Celestial University', a series of prayers which include the following:

Welcome, thou Christ, Son of the Living God, the end of my desire and my love. Welcome, blessed Jesus! Behold, while my mind breatheth and panteth after thee, while my soul, sweetly resting in the secret closet of thy mysteries, contemplateth thy admirable presence . . . the insurrection and tumult of thoughts

[14] Ibid., 211.
[15] Ibid., 213.
[16] Ibid., 9, 344–5.

ceaseth . . . all things are silent: the heart is on fire: the spirit
rejoiceth: the understanding shineth: the whole affection, inflamed
by the desire of thee, sees itself ravished into the love of the
things which are not seen.[17]

More significant, perhaps is the treatise of 'Mysticall Marriage'.
E. I. Watkin has pointed out the similarity, even down to
technical terms, between Rouse and the writings of St John
of the Cross, not least in his distinction between the actual
presence of Christ and a mere feeling of his presence:

> He and his love are better than the seeing and feeling of him and
> his love . . . better for thee that they are thine than that they appear
> to be thine. . . .

Fr Bouyer comments, 'It would be hard to find a more complete expression of the most traditional Christian mysticism
and impossible to show better how this mysticism, far from
being in opposition to the true notion of salvation by faith
alone in the sole grace of Christ, is no more than its fulfilment
in the faithful soul'.[18]

Thomas Goodwin (1600–79) after a distinguished beginning
in Cambridge, when he held the important lectureship at Holy
Trinity, went into exile and became pastor at Arnhem in
Holland, returning under Cromwell to be President of
Magdalen College, Oxford. His sermons abound in passages
of Christocentric devotion, but his tract 'The Heart of Christ
in heaven towards sinners on Earth' (1651) so remarkably
anticipates the devotion to the Sacred Heart at Paray le
Monial that Fr Bouyer cannot escape a wild surmise that here
may not be affinity, but pedigree. For Goodwin's reiterated
theme is the constancy of Christ, the fact that at God's right
hand He is still the friend of sinners:

> All our sermons and your prayers are evidences to you, that
> Christ's heart is still the same towards sinners that ever it was, for
> the Spirit that assists in all these, comes in his name, and works all
> by commission from him . . . the Spirit prays in you, because

[17] Ibid., 365–6.
[18] Bouyer, L., op. cit., 137.

Christ prays for you; he is an intercessor on earth because Christ is an intercessor in heaven. . . . He also follows us to the sacrament, and in that Glass shows us Christ's face smiling on us, and through his face, his heart, and thus helping us to a sight of him, we go away rejoicing that we saw our Saviour that day.[19]

His taking our nature not only adds to our faith, but some way or other, even to his being merciful . . . the greatest of that mercy that was in God, that contributes the stock and treasury of those mercies to be bestowed on us: and unto the greatness of these mercies nothing is, or could be added by the human nature assumed: but rather Christ's manhood had all the largeness of mercy from the Deity: so that had he not had all the mercies of God to enlarge his heart towards us he could never have held out to have for ever been merciful to us. But then, this human nature assumed, that adds a new way of being merciful: it assimilates all these mercies and makes them the mercies of a Man: it makes them human mercies, and so gives a naturalness and kindness unto them to our capacities. So that God doth now in as kindly and as natural a way pity us who are flesh of his flesh and bone of his bone, as a man pities a man: thereby to encourage us to come to him and to be familiar with God, and treat with him for grace and mercy as a man would do with a man: as knowing that in that man Christ Jesus (whom we believe upon) God dwells and his mercies work in and through his heart in an human way.[20]

Some of those we have quoted were Independent divines, but there is no doubt of the sturdy Presbyterianism of the Scot, Samuel Rutherford (1600–61). Fr Bouyer dismisses him, quite wrongly, as a trivial sentimentalist, and perhaps he does not understand the Celtic temperament which accounts for the pre-echoes of J. M. Barrie, of *Beside the Bonnie Briar Bush*, or of Thrums and Tannochbrae. Sentimentalism does indeed lie perilously close to all affective religion, but in Rutherford's case we need to remember that he was a bonnie fighter, and a vitriolic polemic divine, and that his devotional utterances are not to be found in sermons so much as in letters of spiritual counsel to godly women. What he says about devotion

[19] *Christian Library*, 6, 157.
[20] Ibid., 203.

to Christ is set against a background of persecution and physical suffering:

> I urge upon you, Madam, a nearer communion to Christ, and a growing communion. There are curtains to be drawn aside in Christ that we never saw, and new foldings of his love in him . . . I know not what to do with Christ: his love surroundeth and surchargeth me: I am burdened with it, but O how sweet and lovely is that burden. I cannot keep it within me. I am so in love with his love that if his love were not in heaven, I would be unwilling to go there.[21]

A good deal has been written of late of the origins of Puritan scholasticism, which is not to be isolated from the growth of Protestant scholasticism, Calvinist and Lutheran, on the Continent. But no explanations of it will do, unless the revival of medieval currents of inward religion are also accounted for. And when we come to the end of the Puritan period, amid the violence of Civil War and the aftermath, we seem indeed to see the wholeness of faith dissolve into the three strands of rationalism, moralism and mysticism. In the notable generation clash in Cambridge which worked out in three generations – between tutors and undergraduates in one decade, between younger fellows in the next, and between Heads of Houses in the third – Emmanuel college was of central importance. The climax, in the public controversy between Andrew Tuckney and Benjamin Whichcote shows us the abandonment of Puritan rationalism for the new rationalism of the Cambridge Platonists. But it is easy to forget how much they all had in common, not only massive Biblical learning but also a devotion to Christ, of which the Cambridge Platonist return to the thought of the imitation of Christ and the divine life in the soul is no innovation.

Among the finest utterances of these learned men is the noble oration of Ralph Cudworth before the House of Commons in 1647. Central to it, is the thought of the love of God.

[21] Ibid., 16, 155.

He loveth everything that is lovely, beginning at God, and descending down to all his creatures, according to the several degrees of perfection in them. He enjoys a boundless liberty and a boundless sweetness according to his boundless love. He enclaspeth the whole world within his outstretched arms, his soul is as wide as the whole universe, as big as yesterday, today and for ever.

The discourse abounds in epigram:

Grace is holiness militant . . . glory is nothing else but holiness triumphant . . . holiness with a palm of victory in her hand, a crown upon her head.[22]

Two of the greatest of these men are on the margin of the company, Peter Sterry and Nathaniel Culverwell. Peter Sterry, whom F. D. Maurice and T. S. Eliot both singled out for nobility of spirit and majesty of English, reflects a new eirenical temper; he pleads for an end of polemic and for a Christian toleration grounded in the love of God.

If thou hadst any taste or glimpse of the glory of God in thy soul, thou wouldst feel a sweet peace within Thee, with thy God, with thyself, and with all things. . . . The soul that swells in this love thinks no evil of God, of itself, of anything, but is at peace with all, hath sweet thoughts of all. For God is its eye by which it sees and its heart by which it thinks. . . . Abide in the Father's love by spiritual joy. Joy is love flaming. One saith, that laughter is the dance of the spirits, their freest motion in harmony, and that the light of the heavens is the laughter of angels. Spiritual joy is the laughter of divine love, of the Eternal Spirit which is in our spirits.[23]

It will already have been noted in how many of these passages the note of joy recurs, and how removed is this world of thought from the received notion of Puritan piety as sombre, sad and altogether in the minor key. There is perhaps nothing to surpass a passage in one of Nathaniel Culverwell's superb sermons.

[22] Cudworth, R., in Patrides, C. A. (ed.), *The Cambridge Platonists*, 90ff.
[23] Sterry, P., *Discourse of the Freedom of the Will*, 1675.

Men look upon religion as a rigid and austere thing that comes to rob them of their joy, they must never have a smile more, they must never have a summer day after it, but thou canst tell them of the sweetness and deliciousness that is in the ways of grace, thou canst assure them that all the ways of wisdom are pleasantness: thou canst assure them that grace does not mean to take away their joy, but only to refine it, that it does not mean to put out the light, but only to snuff it, that it may burn brighter and clearer ... spiritual joy, t'is the most clarified joy, aye, and t'is solid and massy joy, beaten joy like beaten gold.[24]

He has another fine sermon on 'The Child's return' with the text 'My son, give me thine heart' (Proverbs 23:26):

Give it Him that He may make it happy, that He may fill it with His love, that He may satisfy it with Himself, that He may seal it with His spirit ... go then to the fountain to the ocean, and there fill thyself. Dost thou think thou canst suck any sweetness from the breast of a creature? No but go to the fulness of a Deity, and then stretch thy desires to the uttermost: widen thy heart as much as thou canst, yet there will be enough to make thee run over with happiness.[25]

Devotion to Christ: a religion of the heart: happy delight in God. Let it not be thought that those we have cited are rare and isolated passages. In these authors there are scores of such pages, and the number of preachers could be doubled and trebled.

I do not think this can be called a baroque piety though one must make allowance for the prose of that age, which at its best is a kind of literary counterpart of the music of Henry Purcell, or the carving of Grinling Gibbons.

But this is not something confined to eminent preachers still less to University men. That prince of mechanic preachers, John Bunyan, in his 'Jerusalem sinner saved' and in his 'Heavenly Footman' knows well how to rhapsodize about the divine mercy. In a little cemetery in the town of Hitchin lies the grave of Agnes Beaumont. In 1674 she got a lift to church, riding pillion behind John Bunyan:

[24] Culverwell, N., *The White Stone*, 1654, 133.
[25] 'The Child's return' (*Christian Library*, 10, 17).

... and so we came to Gamlingay, and after a while the meeting began and made it a blessed meeting to my soul indeed. Oh, it was a feast of fat things to me. My soul was filled with consolation and I sat under His shadow with great delight and His fruit was pleasant to my taste when I was at the Lord's table . . . I found such a return of prayer I was scarce able to bear up under it. . . . Oh I had such a sight of Jesus Christ that brake my heart to pieces . . . a sense of my sins and of His dying love made me love him and long to be with him: and truly it was infinite condescension in Him and I have often thought of His gracious goodness to me that Jesus Christ should so graciously visit my poor soul that day.[26]

Agnes needed ghostly comfort, for when she got home she found her father had locked her out, and the result was an angry confrontation in which her father fell dead with a seizure. A suitor, jealous of her friendship with Bunyan, accused her of poisoning her father and there was a coroner's inquest, and a jury; the story reads comically today but no doubt was tragic enough then. For Agnes soon had the court on her side, and the coroner, like the Judge in another 'Trial by Jury', could not be too kind and encouraging. She herself became a notable preacher and her memoirs which have survived are a minor classic of Puritan literature.

The appeal to violence, the Civil War and its aftermath, the events of 1660–2, have provided a distorting mirror to all of us who have come after, Anglicans and Free Churchmen. There was no doubt too, a changing mood and temper of the age which was reflected in new kinds of Christian preaching. Certainly this religion of the heart seems to have disappeared, like an underground stream to emerge in the Evangelical Revival. Perhaps it never wholly returned, and there are colours missing from the wide spectrum of English religion.

This is not to under-estimate the lyric qualities of the Evangelical Revival. Most of the quotations we have given are to be found in that library of Christian classics which Wesley edited for his preachers but which were perhaps only appreciated by a few, most of them devout and godly ladies.

[26] Harrison, G. B. (ed.), *The Narrative of the persecution of Agnes Beaumont in 1674*, 1929.

Wesley's *Christian Library* consisted of fifty-two volumes of what that age called 'Practical Divinity', works which build up the soul and have as their background the Church as an edified and edifying community. The hymns of Doddridge and Watts, of the brothers Wesley, of John Newton and William Cowper have real continuity with this devotion of rapture:

> O happy Day that fixed my choice
> On Thee my Saviour and my God,
> Well may this glowing heart rejoice
> And tell its raptures all abroad.
> (Doddridge)

> The opening heavens around me shine
> With beams of sacred bliss,
> If Jesus shows His mercy mine
> And whispers I am His.
> (I. Watts)

> Ah! show me that happiest place,
> The place of Thy people's abode,
> Where saints in an ecstasy gaze,
> And hang on a crucified God.
> (C. Wesley)

> In the heavenly Lamb
> Thrice happy I am,
> And my heart it doth dance
> at the sound of His name.
> (C. Wesley)

And so we come full circle from St Bernard to John Newton:

> How sweet the Name of Jesus sounds
> In a believer's ear. . . .

The failure of much contemporary religion to meet not only the intellectual but also the emotional needs of men may have deep roots: a mere charismatic movement, loosely theologically orientated would seem to have less prospect of meeting such needs than a christocentric piety within a properly Trinitarian theology.

When John Henry Newman reacted so sharply against the fervour of Frederick Faber and Wilfred Ward and stood a little aloof from their Italianate devotions, did this not represent something very Oxford and very English which had come to look upon rapturous devotion with suspicion?

In the crypt of St Paul's cathedral at Christmas, may be seen three figures of the Wise Men, carved by one of the Wantage sisters. The first stands with head bowed as one facing a great light, in awe. The second kneels with outstretched arms, in wonder. But the third, the African, lies on the ground his arms outstretched in commitment and rapture. It is this third dimension which the sisters of Helfta and the Puritans of Oxford and Cambridge knew very well.

Peter Sterry was no poet, but among his papers there is a haunting little verse:

> I sing thy praise, my Jesus, all along.
> Thou art my glorious subject, my sweet song.
> Thus let me pass into those joys on high
> In the soft bosom wrapt of this sweet harmony.

Not perhaps so very far from St Gertrude of Helfta.

> *Eia nunc, o amor, rex meus et deus meus*
> *Nunc o Jesu mi, chare meus, in*
> *benignissimam curam tui divini cordis*
> *suscipe me. Ibi, ibi, ut tota vivam tibi,*
> *amore tuo conglutina me. Eia nunc in*
> *agnmum mare abyssalis misericordiae tuae*
> *dimitte me.*[27]

[27] *Oevres Spirituelles*, 1, Les Exercices, Paris 1967, 152.

VII

Henry Jessey in the Great Rebellion

B. R. WHITE

H ENRY JESSEY (1601–63) has hitherto existed only in the margins of the ecclesiastical history of the period of the Great Rebellion. Historians have been content to label him, rather inadequately, a Baptist and, usually without further exploration, have noted his links with some of the Fifth Monarchists. This essay attempts to explore his relationships and the part he played among the sectaries of the time.

The outline of Jessey's early life is quite well known and can be easily summarized. He was born 3 September 1601 at West Rounton in Yorkshire where his father, David Jessey, had been rector since 1574 and was to remain until his death in 1623. David Jessey was probably Welsh since he had entered Brasenose College, Oxford, from Laugharne in Carmarthenshire. Nevertheless, in the summer of 1618, Henry went up to Cambridge as a pensioner at St John's College. It appears that he was always a diligent student but that it was not until September 1622 that he was converted to a Puritan position. Shortly after his graduation the following summer his father died, yet, although this left Henry very short of money, he did not leave Cambridge to become chaplain to Brampton Gurdon at Assington, Suffolk, until November 1624.[1]

He was ordained priest by the bishop of Llandaff in June 1626, was licensed to preach by the bishop of Norwich in January 1627 and was recorded as curate of Assington that

---

[1] The major source for Jessey is Anon., *The life and death of Mr Henry Jessey*, 1671, cited here as *Life*. Details of David Jessey's career are derived from records at the Borthwick Institute of Historical Research, University of York, kindly communicated by Mrs N. K. M. Gurney.

same year. During his time with Brampton Gurdon, Henry Jessey came to know the Winthrop family and was to keep up an occasional correspondence with them even after their settlement in New England. Gradually he seems to have become uneasy about holding a public appointment in the Church of England so he began to work informally with 'the most tender Christians and suffering ministers' in the district round about. Nevertheless in 1633 he was invited back to Yorkshire, perhaps to act as curate to William Alder who, as vicar of Aughton, was himself in trouble with the church authorities. Jessey's own conscience proved, however, even less flexible than Alder's and he was, in 1634, 'also removed from that place for not using the ceremonies then imposed as well as for the removing of a crucifix there'. Fortunately he was again able to find employment in the household of a substantial country gentleman, Sir Matthew Boynton, and he was even able to preach in two parish churches which came within the latter's sphere of influence.[2]

Soon, however, Sir Matthew was himself thinking of emigrating and, in 1635, he took Jessey and the rest of his family down to London and, the following year, moved to Uxbridge, Middlesex. The move to the capital proved momentous for Henry Jessey since it brought him into touch with the illegal congregation founded there by Henry Jacob in 1616 which had been without a pastor since the departure of John Lathrop for New England in 1634. On 18 August 1637 Jessey wrote to tell John Winthrop junior that the Lord had convinced him of 'the necessity and beauty of being under Christ's government' (that is, in a gathered church) and that he had accepted the pressing invitation of the underground congregation to join them while not immediately accepting any office among them 'though now urged to it'. His reason, he explained, was because he was awaiting advice 'from some in New England'.[3]

[2] Consignation Book 1627 fol. 16, Norwich Diocesan Archives, Norwich Record Office; Life, 4–7; Marchant, R. A., The Puritans and the Church Courts in the diocese of York 1560–1642, 1960, 122f.; Cliffe, J. T., The Yorkshire gentry from the Reformation to the Civil War, 1969, 273.
[3] Life, 7ff.; Winthrop Papers (Massachusetts Historical Soc., Cambridge, Mass., 1929–47), III, 484–8.

Since its foundation the church Jessey had now joined had tried to keep in fellowship with others who sought the further reformation of the Church of England from within. So, unlike the strict Separatists and those who were to follow their example, this group, sometimes known by the names of its three pastors as the Jacob-Lathrop-Jessey congregation, steadily refused to unchurch those who remained within the Anglican establishment. However, partly due to the pressures of persecution and consequent debates over the administration of true Christian baptism, a rigorist party developed in the congregation and at various times in the 1630s more rigorist groups withdrew to form their own congregations while the majority maintained their more tolerant stance.[4]

While a number of attempts have been made to reconstruct the development of these more rigorist daughter congregations of Jessey's church one important question about the interpretation of the fragmentary evidence remaining has often been overlooked. This, since it bears immediately upon Henry Jessey's own relationship to the Calvinistic Baptists in the early 1640s, needs to be examined. The question concerns the nature of the relationships between the various underground churches in the last years before the outbreak of the Civil War including not only those actually referred to in the Jacob-Lathrop-Jessey materials but also the others which developed at that time. From the fragmentary evidence now extant it seems probable that the various groups, often not much larger than small house churches, shared a common looseknit interdependence. It must not be supposed that their

---

[4] The records concerning Jessey's church and its daughter congregations down to 1645 are only available today in the transcript made by Benjamin Stinton (1676–1719) and deposited in the Angus Library, Regent's Park College, Oxford. The MS volume is entitled 'A repository of divers historical matters relating to the English Antipedobaptists . . .' and is dated on the title page, 'Anno 1712'. The three relevant transcripts (nos. 1, 2 and 4 in Stinton's MS) are all said to be from MSS which came to Stinton from Richard Adams, once co-pastor with William Kiffin. T. Crosby, in *History of the English Baptists*, 1738–40, III, 100, explains that after Jessey's death the members of his church who opposed 'mixed communion' were led by Henry Forty but after his removal to Abingdon they joined Kiffin's congregation. It is likely that by this means the records reached Richard Adams (d. 1716). Transcripts 1 and 4 were said by Stinton to be respectively 'Ex MSS of Mr H. Jessey' and 'supposed to be written by Mr Jessey or transcribed from his journal'. The MS will be cited here as 'A Repository'. Transcripts 1 and 2 were published in Burrage, C., *Early English Dissenters*, 1912, II, 292–305. All three were published by W. T. Whitley, TBHS (1908–9), I, 203–45.

relationships were formally structured but it does mean that they co-operated with each other sufficiently to arrange for joint meetings for prayer and it seems that members of the rigorist daughter congregations of Jessey's church still sometimes attended its meetings: the records indicate that there were no high walls of bitterness between them and even the withdrawals are recorded as brotherly.[5]

Hence Samuel Eaton, who had left Lathrop's congregation in 1633, was arrested in January 1638 while worshipping with some of Jessey's people; Richard Blunt, who had also withdrawn in 1633, discussed the question of immersionist baptism with them in 1640, and William Kiffin, who may actually never have been a member with Jessey's church, seems also to have taken part in the arguments within Jessey's congregation about believer's baptism in 1644–5. In May 1638 it seems that Walter Cradock was caught worshipping with Jessey's friends but the very next year Jessey, Cradock and William Wroth shared in the foundation of the Independent congregation at Llanvaches, Monmouthshire, which became known as the mother-church of the Independents in Wales.[6]

While the early years of Jessey's leadership were times of persecution the church seems to have continued to grow so that, even after further withdrawals over the issue of believer's baptism, it became too large to continue to meet in one place. In consequence, after May 1640, one half was led by Praisegod Barbone while Jessey himself continued as pastor of the other. About the same time Richard Blunt raised the issue of the correct mode of baptism. This soon led to two consequences: first, some of those from the underground congregations who had already been baptized by sprinkling as believers were baptized by immersion in January 1642 and, secondly, Henry Jessey continued to baptize babies but by immersion.[7]

This compromise failed to settle the matter for long and

---

[5] 'A Repository', 8, entry for 21 April 1640, where there is no suggestion that this was other than a meeting of Jessey's church, but cf. *Life*, 10 where it is shown to have been inter-congregational.

[6] 'A Repository', 7, 10, 25–8; White, B. R., 'How did William Kiffin join the Baptists?' BQ (1969–70), 201–7; *Life*, 9f.

[7] 'A Repository', 10; *Life*, 10f.; Crosby, op. cit., I, 310f.

such books as John Spilbury's *A treatise concerning the lawfull subiect of baptisme* (1643) helped to keep the question before the attention of the London sectaries. However, it was apparently Hanserd Knollys, freshly home from New England and for a while in membership with Jessey's church, who opened up the matter again. Unconvinced by Jessey's arguments for baptizing his child, Knollys sought, and obtained, agreement that some informal meetings should be held at which the whole question could be thrashed out. By 17 March 1644 a number in the congregation were ready to repudiate infant baptism although Jessey himself remained convinced that it was right. Since some of those who repudiated infant baptism were withdrawing from the meetings of the church on the grounds that it, being not rightly baptized, was no true church some of the rest of the congregation wanted to censure them. It was, however, decided, as in the case of the division of the congregation into two four years earlier, to seek the advice of 'the elders and brethren of other churches'. Among those from whom therefore counsel was sought was Praisegod Barbone and such outstanding leaders among the growing number of Independents as Thomas Goodwin, Philip Nye, Sydrach Simpson and Jeremiah Burroughes. The counsel given was to be fairly characteristic of the not intolerant attitude of many Independents during coming years to those in their congregations who nevertheless held to believer's baptism. They judged that the position taken was held not out of 'obstinacy but tender conscience and holiness' so that the people concerned should be treated as church members in good standing until either they returned or grew 'giddy and scandalous'. The recognition that some at least might fall into such a condition may reflect their knowledge of the unstable state of sectarian opinion in the capital at the time rather than the traditional fear of anabaptism.[8]

---

[8] 'A Repository', 25–8. About June 1645 a group of English Independents including Thomas Goodwin, John Owen, and Philip Nye wrote asking the Massachusetts General Court not to penalize Baptists for their dissent and in March 1648 Jessey wrote to the Governor pleading for 'tenderness' to them (*Winthrop Papers*, V. 23f., 204f.). He also pleaded for mixed communion between Independents and Baptists in a letter dated 22 June 1645 (a week before his baptism by Knollys). McLoughlin, W. G., *New England Dissent, 1630–1833*, 1971, 54, note 9.

Meanwhile some of those who accepted believer's baptism remained uncertain whether a properly authorized administrator of the ordnance could be found. Of this group of twenty-six, nine (including apparently Mrs Hanserd Knollys) eventually concluded that 'such disciples as are gifted to teach and evangelize may also baptize'. Although this coincided with the teaching of the Particular Baptist *Confession* first published that year it sidestepped a major aspect of the question which would continue to concern a number of the sectaries of the time, namely, where authority must be sought for the restoration of true baptism in an apostate church.[9]

During this time Henry Jessey was himself becoming uneasy about infant baptism, but before he came to a clear decision in the matter a number of those who had come to accept believer's baptism left him to join groups led by Hanserd Knollys and William Kiffin. Meanwhile, characteristically, Jessey continued to consult with other Independents such as Burroughes, Cradock, Goodwin, Nye and William Greenhill. Finally, however, he decided and Hanserd Knollys baptized him on 29 June 1645. One consequence was the return of seven members who had previously withdrawn, but some continued in membership and held to infant baptism down to the time of Jessey's death. While Jessey maintained this 'mixed' or 'open' communion position Knollys and Kiffin were to be leaders among the rigorist Calvinistic Baptist movement who insisted on acceptance of their 'closed' communion position in which every member had to be baptized as a believer, hence Jessey always remained outside the mainstream of the Calvinistic Baptists.[10]

In consequence it is hardly surprising that, while Jessey maintained a number of individual links across the years with the Calvinistic Baptists, he did not apparently share in their national programme of outreach and organization during the years 1644–60. The individual relationships, as will later be seen, sometimes led to Jessey's being associated with them in political matters, but neither he nor his church co-operated in

[9] 'A Repository', 27.
[10] Ibid., 28. See my 'The organisation of the Particular Baptists 1644–1660', in JEH, 1966, XVII, 209–26, and also *Association Records of the Particular Baptists . . . to 1660*, pts. 1–3, 1971–4.

the evangelistic programme of the men who published the successive editions of the London *Confession* and stood behind the strict policy first clearly enunciated in Benjamin Cox's publication *An appendix to a Confession of Faith* (1646). On the other hand Thomas Edwards reported that Jessey (presumably some time in the first half of 1646) had been present at a healing meeting at Aldgate, London, conducted by Hanserd Knollys, and it is known that he sought to rent a room for some joint purpose with William Kiffin and others at a date after the organization of the Presbyterians in London in June 1646. Later, almost incidental, contacts with Calvinistic Baptist leaders included support for his calendar reformation schemes from John Pendarves, information upon matters of missionary interest from Edward Cresset, signatures to two joint Baptist/Independent documents with Kiffin and Knollys, signatures to radical political/Fifth Monarchist documents with such as Edward Harrison, William Allen and John Vernon and a signature (with John Tombes who also stood for 'mixed' communion) to a defensive statement in 1659 with a number of Calvinistic Baptists in London.[11]

Henry Jessey believed and published his views that believer's baptism was the baptism the Bible taught but there is no doubt that he was interested in keeping close links with the Independents while seeking to draw together, in particular, the 'mixed' communion churches. In October 1653, Thomas Tillam, who had founded the church at Hexham, Northumberland, after being sent out by Hanserd Knolly's church as an evangelist in 1651, received a letter from a group of churches mostly in the south-west midlands in an area where the influence of John Tombes was very strong. With it came a covering letter from Jessey's church and among the congregations who had signed it was Abergavenny whose temporary erring from the paths marked

[11] Edwards, T., *Gangraena*, 1646, III, 19; *Reasons humbly offered in justification* lacks a title page and name of author with whatever followed p. 8. It is undated but the Bodleian catalogue suggests 1642. Internal evidence points to a time after Jessey had adopted believer's baptism and after the Presbyterian classical system had been set up in London during June 1646; White, B. R., 'John Pendarves, the Calvinistic Baptists and the Fifth Monarchy', BQ, 1973–4, 257, where it is suggested that Pendarves borrowed a piece written against the Quakers by Jessey and himself to include in his *Arrowes against Babylon*, 1656.

down for them by John Miles has been noted elsewhere. Tillam had apparently abandoned the closed-membership stance of his home church in London so Jessey and his friends were able to seek 'a holy union and correspondence' with Hexham. The October letter had been preceded by another seeking 'nearer communion' and a more personal letter from Tillam to Tombes at the end of July. The covering letter from Jessey's congregation, apparently a near neighbour of Hanserd Knollys in Swan Alley, Coleman Street, London, speaks of links with churches 'sound in the faith and holy in life' though differing among themselves over, among other matters, 'the subject and manner of the ordinance of baptism'. The response from Hexham, held up until April 1654 because of a crisis within that congregation, mentioned that the Calvinistic Baptists of Newcastle had disowned Hexham 'because we can own unbaptized churches and ministers for churches of Christ and ministers of Christ; though we also judge in those churches and ministers something as to order wanting'. What came of these moves towards a closer union between the churches practising 'mixed' communion is unknown, but it is perhaps important to note that 1653 was the year of the foundation of Baxter's Worcestershire Association, of a new initiative to closer links among the closed membership Calvinistic Baptists and also of the summoning of the Parliament of the Saints.[12]

The links between Henry Jessey, his church and other, often non-Baptist, congregations and leaders can be documented from various sources. It may well have been his links with Llanvaches church, which had joined the Broadmead people for a time during the Civil War, which introduced him to the Broadmead congregation. In 1653 they sent one of their members for believer's baptism at Jessey's hands (presumably because the Bristol Calvinistic Baptist church at the Pithay would not baptize for a congregation practising 'mixed'

---

[12] Jessey, H., *A Storehouse of provision,* 1650, 60, 74f.; White, B. R., 'John Miles and the structure of the Calvinistic Baptist Mission to South Wales, 1649–1660', in *Welsh Baptist Studies,* 1974, ed. Mansel John; Underhill, E. B., *Records of the Churches of Christ gathered at Fenstanton Warboys and Hexham* 1854, 341–51. Nuttall, G. F., 'The Worcestershire Association: its membership', in JEH, i, 1950, 197–206. *Association Records* op. cit., 111–18.

communion). The following year, in all probability, the pastor Thomas Ewins and their ruling elder, Robert Purnell, also came to Henry Jessey for baptism. By 1655 Broadmead was seriously divided over the teaching of the Quakers and, as Thomas Ewins later wrote, Jessey came to Bristol 'to endeavour the settling and establishing the minds of the people of this city against the pernicious doctrine of the Quakers and I believe his endeavours were not successless in this thing'.[13]

In the same year and perhaps at the same time Jessey visited a succession of other churches in the south and west of the country – at Wells, Cirencester, Somerton, Chard, Taunton, Honiton, Exeter, Dartmouth, Plymouth, Lyme, Weymouth, Dorchester, Southampton and Chichester. It has normally been assumed that these were Calvinistic Baptist churches since there is clear evidence of the existence of such congregations in or near almost all the places named. Yet their churches in this area were led by Thomas Collier who was committed to the rigorist, 'closed-membership' position. Furthermore, the Pithay church which was presumably not prepared to baptize people for Broadmead was linked with Collier's association. It hardly seems likely that they would have welcomed a preaching tour by Henry Jessey. While the silence of the Western Association records concerning Jessey is hardly conclusive proof that he did not visit their churches there is the likelihood, according to *Calamy Revised*, that there were Independent churches to welcome him in or near most if not all these places.[14]

Henry Jessey's personal relationships and desires for cooperation across as wide a spectrum of theological conviction as possible led him to be 'a main promoter of and helper in a meeting of some eminent persons of the parochial and congregational way who in 1651 assembled frequently, sometimes at his own lodgings . . . for the furtherance of peace and communion among brethren that differed not fundamentally'. The preaching tour which Jessey, accompanied by John Simpson

[13] Hayden, R. (ed.), *The Records of a Church of Christ in Bristol* (Bristol Record Soc. Vol. XXVII), 1974, 97f., 105, 111; Purnell, R. (et al.), *The Church of Christ in Bristol recovering her Vail*, 1657, 58.
[14] *Life*, 84.

from the All Hallows congregation, made during the summer of 1653 was also quite obviously intended to link together like-minded congregations in Essex, Suffolk and Norfolk. Apparently they succeeded in visiting some thirty churches 'to understand their way and order, and to further love amongst all that love the Lord Jesus in sincerity, and communion with them'.[15]

One other area of co-operative work in which Jessey was engaged throughout the 1650s was that of producing a new translation of the Bible with a committee including, among others, John Owen and John Row, professor of Hebrew at the University of Aberdeen. The *Life* clearly implies that the whole project was initiated and given most of its momentum by Jessey. First, he apparently produced a paper arguing the need for a new translation, then he urged the appointment by 'public authority' of a committee to carry through the work composed of 'learned persons sound in the fundamentals of religion' so that it would not represent the idiosyncrasies of any one man. On 11 January 1653 the House of Commons set up a committee to make recommendations for the new version of the Bible and on 4 March they were agreed. According to the author of the *Life* the scheme was virtually complete by the end of the Protectorate 'and stayed for nothing but the appointment of commissioners to examine it and warrant its publication'. He gave very considerable attention to this project (nearly a fifth of the *Life* was taken up with details about it) because, the author asserted, Jessey had made the project of a new translation 'the master study of his life'.[16]

Henry Jessey's own pastoral and preaching programme was divided between his own congregation and more general work. He spent Sunday afternoons teaching his church and answering their questions and had a weekly meeting with the brethren of the church for business and discipline. His visitation was systematic and was based on a fourfold division of the city. He normally lectured at St George's, Southwark, on Sunday mornings, at Ely House to the crippled soldiers and at the

---

[15] Ibid., 86; *Records of the Churches*, op. cit., 346f.
[16] *Life*, 46f.; CJ, 1651–9, 245, 264; CSPD, 1652–3, 73f.

Savoy during the week. His most successful publication was an account of the case of a young woman delivered from the depths of spiritual despair who herself became something of a sensation in London sectarian circles. Most of the book is concerned with interviews between the woman, Sarah Wight, and those who came to her for counsel. It appears he was a considerable success with children and certainly his *Catechisme for babes or little ones* (1652), an expanded version of an original he had prepared twelve years earlier, with some questions and answers in smaller print that the youngest children could at first omit, showed a refreshing sense of the limitations of the very young. He even collected, in the manner of the time, some improving anecdotes concerning the godly (and, it seems, inevitably sickly) young.[17]

Perhaps the most enlightening of Jessey's books, because it clearly reflects the ecclesiological issues with which he was most concerned, is *A storehouse of provision* (1650). Like his other writings it is comparatively brief but is overwhelmingly concerned with questions of churchmanship: about the continuing value and significance of the ordinances, especially of baptism and the Lord's Supper, about church discipline, about right relationships between those with opposing views about baptism. The *Storehouse* suggests that in 1650 he was feeling increasing pressure from and exerting a widening influence upon those who, on the one side, devalued the ordinances and would even omit them altogether and those who, on the other side, emphasized that the practice of the baptism of believers only was a fundamental condition for church communion. On the latter issue he reprinted two letters he had written, one in 1647 and one in January 1650, urging that believers differing about baptism might join in church fellowship none the less. The question of the ordinances continued to be discussed in the circle of Jessey's friends and it is hardly surprising that correspondence with Morgan Lloyd in 1656 touched both on

[17] *Life,* 40ff.; Jessey, H., *The exceeding riches of grace advanced . . . in . . . Sarah Wight,* 1647. Here, note first the list of those who visited Sarah Wight in the postscript to the Christian Reader and pages 8–9; cf. Nuttall, G. F., *James Nayler: a fresh approach* 1954, 9–15, which helps to provide a context. Secondly, John Saltmarsh (d. December 1647) provided a commendatory letter addressed to 'my dear and honoured friend and cousin, H. Jessey'.

that issue and the other absorbing question of the Second Coming. While Lloyd casually asked Jessey to remind John Goodwin, the Arminian Independent vicar of St Stephen's, Coleman Street, that he owed him a letter and asked for an introduction to Samuel Hartlib, the letter from Jessey's church (on which their pastor scribbled a personal note) dealt with largely theological matters. They stressed their concern not to idolize God's ordinances 'as too many do' (with a side glance at the rigorist Calvinistic Baptists) but also not to go to the other extreme like 'the Ranters and people called Quakers'. Evidently Jessey's people at this time, perhaps under their pastor's influence, were not sure that the Return of Christ was immediately imminent, for they mentioned that the vials of *Revelation* 16 would not be poured out until the two witnesses of *Revelation* 11 had completed their ministry, had been slain and raised to life, 'near the time of the end'. This apparent sense that the end was not yet – in December 1656 – may have strengthened Jessey's position as a moderate Fifth Monarchist.[18]

His missionary enthusiasm was also encouraged by his eager anticipation of the Second Advent, for before that event both the fulness of the Gentiles had to be gathered in and God's ancient people, Israel, must be saved. In 1650 Henry Jessey published a pamphlet reporting numerous conversions among the people of Formosa by means of a Dutch preacher and among the North American Indians by John Eliot of the Society for the Propagation of the Gospel in New England. Jessey's first introduction to the Dutch work had been through Edward Cresset, later to be a leading Calvinistic Baptist in London, who had apparently heard of events in Formosa while on business in the Netherlands in 1646. The pamphlet, after reporting that by 1649 there were already four Dutch ministers in Formosa and that it was now proposed to send three more, ended with detailed news of John Eliot's work. Jessey continued to take a practical interest in this enterprise for, in the files of the New England Company, there is a letter from Eliot to the treasurer thanking him for £11 worth of goods which had come through the good offices of Henry

18 National Library of Wales MSS 11438, 11439.

Jessey and 'a small packet of books from Mr Jessey which I distributed . . . according to Mr Jessey's appointment'.[19]

Superficially, Henry Jessey's earliest publication, an almanac which came out every year from 1645 onwards and settled down to the name *The Scripture Calendar* from 1649, appears unlikely to provide much of great interest but, in fact, it offers some very significant hints concerning his thinking. Primarily, it bore testimony, from the beginning, to his great reverence for the Bible. In the 1645 edition the climactic date in England's history was given as that of the summoning of the Long Parliament because it committed itself to 'a reformation according to the Word of God'. Just how far that reformation should go Jessey showed by his consistent advocacy of the replacement of the common heathen names for the days of the week and the months of the year by the biblical names. Two things that did not change across the years were Jessey's belief that the Long Parliament was an instrument of God's purposes for England and his anticipation of the Fifth Monarchy – Christ's millennial reign upon earth. Each year he included the image of the man made of four metals created on the basis of Daniel 2. Those four kingdoms had come to pass and many sectarians waited, breathless, for the Second Advent. In the *Scripture Calendar* for 1655 the list of changes in recent British history was greatly enlarged. Among the more notable additions was the note 'Normans began October 14 1066, ended in Charles beheaded 30 January 1649'. This suggests that Jessey accepted the theory of the Norman yoke: the view of English history which saw the alien monarchy founded in the blood of the battle of Hastings purged in the blood of the executed Charles I. Like many others, and not only those in the gathered churches, Henry Jessey believed that with the execution of the king a long sad chapter of England's history was ended and a new day was dawning. In the 1660 edition, put to the printers presumably months before the shape of a Stuart restoration became clear or was even seriously feared, Jessey noted that there had been fourteen changes of the supreme power in England in twenty years. In

[19] Jessey, H., *Of the conversion of five thousand and nine hundred East-Indians*, 1650; Guildhall Lib. MS 7936 fol. 2.

the 1661 edition he listed twenty-five changes of political direction in the previous seven years and, while he made no other explicit political comment, his Scripture citation at the end might rightly be considered thoroughly subversive by the new government of Charles II. It was Ezekiel 21:26, 27 'Take off the crown . . . I will overturn, overturn, overturn it . . . until he come whose right it is and I will give it to him'. So the *Scripture Calendar* underlined the instability of the times and warned that the restoration itself was but one more step in the outworking of the divine will.[20]

The setting then, for Jessey's political commitment was his sense that history was moving to its last crisis and the visible reign of Christ upon earth: all other rulers were at best caretakers, at worst usurpers, of the crown rights of the Redeemer. Since the days when he had first opposed his conscience to the policy of those who administered the English Church and the period which followed as he led the illegal, hunted, congregation bequeathed him by John Lathrop, Henry Jessey had always known that obedience to his understanding of the will of God could certainly bring him into conflict with the powers that temporarily be.

In late November 1647 an unsigned pamphlet entitled *A declaration by congregational societies in and about the city of London as well of those commonly called Anabaptists as others* was published. As a later edition was to indicate, its signatories included, among others, William Greenhill, John Simpson, Christopher Feake, Hanserd Knollys and Jessey himself. Simpson must probably be considered Jessey's closest friend and colleague among the London ministers during the period 1647–61 although there may have been a measure of disagreement between them during 1654–5 when Simpson on the Fifth Monarchy issue was for a while closely identified with the extremely belligerent position of Christopher Feake. It was to be Henry Jessey who was one of those leaders who supported Simpson's congregation at Allhallows in the negotiations over the withdrawal from it of the hard-line Fifth Monarchists during the early summer of 1656 and thereafter.[21]

[20] Hill, C., *Puritanism and Revolution*, 1958, 67–71.
[21] Jessey and Simpson were linked together in pastoral care for Sarah Wight in 1647.

However, the aim of the 1647 pamphlet was to stress the general soundness of the sectarian congregations both in faith and morals in the face of the attacks which had followed the publication of *Gangraena* the previous year. Characteristically they insisted that in spiritual matters the censures of the churches alone should be used to correct the erring and that it would be wrong for the state 'to exercise a coercive and worldly power therein'. At the same time they recognized the need of society to be protected from the wickedness of men and were quite prepared to acknowledge 'a kingly government, bounded by just and wholesome laws' to be allowed by God and to be useful for men and that 'the ranging of men into several and subordinate ranks and degrees is a thing necessary for the common good'. They also affirmed that it was right that there should be private property and they repudiated polygamy. These two matters were probably raised in the public mind by the ghost of Munster.[22]

It was a cautious, conservative document, published at a time when hardly anyone had thought of ending the monarchy, much less of executing the king. The re-issue and expansion of the document came about in very different circumstances. During the autumn after the battle of Worcester both Cromwell and many officers of the Army were, with other radical elements, looking for the dissolution of the Rump Parliament and the election of a new one. It was in this situation that two pamphlets came out arguing that any new parliament should be chosen from and elected by the members of the gathered churches. The London leaders who had produced the 1651 *Declaration* may possibly have known no more of the origin of the two tracts than can the modern reader: one may have been serious, the other seems to have been, at least in part, an attempt to ridicule John Goodwin and his church. At all events the leaders hastened to reject the idea out of hand apparently fearing that, whether or not the two writers were enemies trying to make the gathered churches

---

(*Exceeding Riches*, 3rd ed., 1648, 29, 34), and in visiting the child, Mary Warren, 8 November 1661 (Jessey, H. and Cheare, Abraham, *A looking-glass for children*, 2nd ed., 1673, 12); *The old leaven purged out*, 1658, 22, 49.

[22] *A declaration of the congregationall societies*, 1647, was reprinted in E. B. Underhill (ed.), *Confessions of faith and other public documents*, 1854, 273–87.

seem hungry for political power, this would certainly be their effect. They quickly, therefore, denied they held that both the electorate and the elected should be limited 'to the Gathered-Congregational-Churches' and looked forward to the time when 'all that fear the Lord shall be of one mind and of one heart' and have 'such external visible union and communion that shall convince the world . . . as our Lord Jesus prayed'. The pamphlet was dated 10 November 1651.[23] It should be noted that when the Barebones Parliament was summoned less than two years later the members were in part nominated by the gathered churches! It is certainly possible that the meeting Cromwell had with Owen, Nye, Stephen Marshall, Jessey and Thomas Harrison in the late autumn of 1653 while Barebones Parliament was sitting was less to exhort them to unity among themselves, as Dr Tai Liu apparently believed, than to enlist their efforts as responsible and reasonable leaders to unite the various parties among the gathered churches.[24]

Earlier, on 19 June 1653, Jessey's friend, the Independent minister Nathaniel Robinson, wrote from Southampton seeking information about two Jews who had apparently approached him for financial aid. While Robinson asserted that he would rejoice to be used in any way towards the conversion of the Jews he yet needed to know something of their *bona fides*. He did not, he said, want to find himself supporting a Jesuit instead of a Jew for something like that had actually happened to Thomas Tillam, Jessey's correspondent in Hexham a few months earlier. At all events Jessey passed Robinson's query to another friend in London, John More, whose church had actually been joined by one of the two men in question.[25]

It seems likely that Henry Jessey wrote *A narrative of the late proceeds at Whitehall* (1656), a very sympathetic treatment of the application of the Jews to return to trade in England and of the London debates about the proposal during

[23] *A declaration of divers elders and brethren of congregational societies*, 1651, 3, 7, 8.
[24] Tai Liu, *Discord in Zion*, 1973, 133.
[25] Bodley, Rawlinson MS D. 828 fols. 7, 8. Cf. Burrage, C., 'A true and short declaration', TBHS II (1910–11), 129–60, for a partial transcript of the records of the church to which More belonged; Howell, R., *Newcastle-upon-Tyne and the Puritan Revolution*, 1967, 250f.; *Records of the Churches*, op. cit., 343.

December 1655. Although no clear decision was reached, the preachers being divided and the merchants uneasy, Jessey had apparently suggested a compromise, namely that they should be allowed to trade only in certain specified decayed ports and pay double customs, but this also had been unacceptable. His concern for the conversion of the Jews was strong and he argued that if they were allowed entry this might well follow since there were more praying for their conversion in England than anywhere else and there were more able to win them over by Scripture proofs and holy living in England than in any other country. In 1651 Jessey had committed himself to the view that the conversion of the Jews might take place before 1658 and in a writing of 1654 he clearly expected they would shortly be freed from captivity to the Fourth (Roman) Monarchy by Christ who would then set up the Fifth Monarchy.[26]

Even after the comparative failure of his attempts to secure permission for the Jews to re-enter England Jessey's concern for them continued to be shown in the relief funds he raised for the needy Jews of Jerusalem with the support of the ministers of many London congregations and the active help of John Dury between 1656 and April 1659 when he apparently sent a lengthy covering letter with one of the gifts.[27]

By February 1654 Jessey was fairly closely involved with the Fifth Monarchy movement and, especially, the meetings held at Allhallows. The evidence seems clear that throughout the period of the Protectorate Henry Jessey, like John Pendarves who died in 1656, was identified with the moderate, non-violent wing of the party. Jessey, Samuel Highland and John Spencer were speaking at the meeting in February 1654 soon after Christopher Feake and John Simpson had been imprisoned. None of the trio speaking on this occasion carried the weight or stirred the enthusiasm of the other two, and Jessey proved virtually inaudible, so Marchamont Needham, who was reporting it to the Protector, departed. Nevertheless,

[26] Jessey, H., *A narrative of the late proceeds at Whitehall*, 1656, 4, 9f., where Jessey and Cresset and Kiffin were listed among those who shared the debates; *Life*, 67; Cary, Mary, *The little horns doom and downfall*,1651, Preface by Jessey; Jessey, H., *A description and explanation of 268 places in Jerusalem*, 1654, 3.
[27] *Life*, 69–77.

Needham strongly advised the Protector to prohibit further meetings which were, he claimed, very bad for the government's image abroad. It was certainly odd that, a month later, it could be announced that Jessey had accepted appointment to serve as one of the Triers responsible for checking the qualifications of those ministers who were to receive state appointments and state pay. One possible explanation, made in an earlier article on Jessey, is that he had agreed to serve after Cromwell had, as he understood, promised to bring tithes to an end by September 1654.[28]

On 2 September 1654 Thomason added to his collection a Fifth Monarchy manifesto entitled *A declaration of several of the churches of Christ*. It was signed by representatives of a number of radical congregations including several of Jessey's people. In this document the writers complained that the Army had gone back on its own principles and, among other things, had tolerated the setting up of the court of Triers 'of like make with the bishops' high commission court'. This attack was hardly fair but it is hard to see how, in such circumstances, Jessey could have continued as a member.[29]

Whether it was due to disappointment over tithes or not, by October 1655 Henry Jessey was certainly in opposition for it was then that Jerome Sankey wrote to tell Henry Cromwell that Simpson, Jessey and some others of the same outlook had been given a meeting with the Protector in order to discuss various matters over which they were dissatisfied. A week later Sankey wrote to report that the meeting had borne no other fruit than an arrangement to meet again. Nevertheless, as was noted earlier, Jessey was involved in official discussions that December at Whitehall about whether Jews should be allowed to re-enter the country.[30]

Only one other political action by Jessey is known between the Whitehall debates of December 1655 and the letter he signed with other London ministers addressed to the Protector on 3 April 1657. This was a speech at a meeting held in Allhallows on 5 January 1657 and it appears to mark a

[28] Public Record Office SP/18/66/20; cf. White, B.R., 'Henry Jessey: a pastor in politics', BQ. (1973–4), XXV, 104–6.
[29] Reprinted in TBHS. (1912–13), 129–153.
[30] BM, Lansdowne MSS 823 fol. 120, 821 fol. 24.

public breach between Feake and the hard-line Fifth Monarchists on one side and Jessey and Simpson on the other. Nevertheless it must be recognized this does not mean that Jessey had abandoned his fundamental republicanism. Hence his appearance that April as a signatory to the letter urging Cromwell not to allow himself to be made king. In it the authors urged Cromwell to refuse the crown and the monarchical form of government which had previously been repudiated as 'unnecessary, burdensome and destructive to the safety and liberty of the people'. Cromwell did refuse but was to die on 3 September 1658. Within a few months his son Richard had been deprived of power by the Army and the remnant of the members of the Long Parliament were recalled to take over the government. Jessey joined the aged John Canne and the Calvinistic Baptist Edward Harrison to summon the saints to a grand act of rejoicing over God's 'late most glorious and never to be forgotten shaking and over-turning providence', but time was running out for the republicans also.[31]

A Fifth Monarchy petition presented to Parliament on 17 September and apparently published as a broadsheet virtually simultaneously was signed by Jessey and a number of com-mitted radicals. It spoke, as a document endorsed by Jessey and his circle might be expected to speak, with some hostility of the Protectorate. Then its signatories repudiated in turn government by a single person and any unrepentant politician or by military or naval servants of the Protectorate and demanded government by the godly party, laws intelligible to all and in line with the Bible, and churches without state supported clergy or compulsion of conscience over matters of worship. This *Essay toward settlement upon a sure foundation,* while it did provoke critical replies and some support, was quite ineffectual in changing the course of events. An attempt to turn the London militia against George Monck failed and some of the Baptist leaders in the capital appear to have panicked.[32]

[31] Underhill, E. B., op. cit., 335–8; Thurloe, J., *State Papers,* 1742, V. 755–9; *The Publick Intelligencer,* 9–16 May 1659.

[32] Brown, L. F., *The political activities of Baptists and Fifth Monarchy men in England during the interregnum,* 1912, 192f.

The consequence was a *Declaration* put out by twenty-four Baptist leaders in London including such men as Kiffin, Knollys and Spilsbury and also Henry Jessey and John Tombes. It seems to have been printed and reprinted in December 1659 and the British Library copy has no signatures – the names are derived from a Quaker criticism of it by Richard Hubberthorne entitled *An answer to a declaration put forth by the general consent of the people called Anabaptists* (1659). In their *Declaration* the various Calvinistic Baptist leaders proclaimed their obedience to the state, their hostility to the Quakers, their tolerance of episcopacy, presbyterianism and infant baptism, their intolerance of Roman Catholicism, idolatry, and blasphemy and, finally, their desire 'that every man may be preserved in his own just rights' (including the Quakers 'while they live morally honest and peaceable in the nation'). Their haste to issue the document was because they sensed a campaign of vilification against them and they feared that this might be effective 'to incense the rude multitude against us, purposely to provoke them (if possible) to destroy us'.[33]

Jessey's interest in the prophetic writings and his general Biblical studies continued to shape his mind throughout the 1650s although it is not quite clear at what point he adopted the belief that the Seventh-day Sabbath was still obligatory for Christians. More dangerously his habit of collecting what he believed to be acts of divine justice and mercy in everyday life was to lead him to publish *The Lord's loud call to England* (1660). This summons to national repentance supported by accounts of the persecution of gathered saints and the judgements which overtook their persecutors could easily be looked upon as subversive by a government still unsure of the security of its own position. He would probably have survived this unscathed (as he did a rather half-hearted attempt to assert that he and William Kiffin were involved in plotting a

---

[33] Hubberthorne attacked the *Declaration* as a sell-out to right wing ecclesiastical policies; Henry Adis, leader of a group of General Baptists, in *A declaration of a small society of baptised believers*, 1659, insisted upon their policy of total dissociation from political commitments of any kind; John Griffiths, with other General Baptist leaders, criticized the Calvinists' *Declaration* in *A declaration of some of those people*, 1660, for limiting toleration too narrowly.

rising against the king) had he not contributed material for the publication of *Annus Mirabilis* (1661) the following summer. This laid great stress upon the portents which were understood to imply divine displeasure with the restored monarchy. In August 1661 Jessey was regularly preaching at Great Allhallows with Hanserd Knollys and John Simpson. When, in December 1661, he was examined for complicity in the production of *Annus Mirabilis* he admitted an interest in the type of events there recorded and to knowing Henry Danvers (an incorrigible plotter) and Francis Smith the General Baptist bookseller. It appears that Jessey had been arrested the previous August as actively opposed to the government although he was, so his own petition claimed, 'known to be of peaceable principles, practices and expressions'. At all events he did not secure his release until the early spring of 1663. He died 4 September 1663 (John Simpson had died the previous year) with Hanserd Knollys standing by, as a hostile witness noted 'to take his dying words'. It was claimed that 'he said the Lord would destroy the power that now is in being and did much encourage all the people to put their helping hand to that great work', but this was denied by his friends and seems unlikely in the light of his consistent reputation for moderation over the years.[34]

It seems from all this that Henry Jessey's place in the ecclesiastical history of the period of the Great Rebellion needs location and relocation as his career advances. It is clear that throughout his sectarian career he moved easily and co-operatively among the gathered churches and their leaders, especially the Independents. For, although he became a Baptist in a formal sense and published his Baptist opinions, neither he nor his church was actively involved with the nationwide programme and organization of the closed-membership Calvinistic Baptists. Rather were they close to those who held Fifth Monarchy opinions during the 1650s, whether moderate or violent, both Baptists and Independents: there are signs also that they sought to build a pattern of formal co-operation in 1653 with other churches which practised 'mixed' communion. Then, although Jessey was

[34] *Life*, 87f.; Public Record Office SP 29/41/39; 29/45/28; 29/65/85; 29/80/101.

close to John Simpson, it does not seem that he ever shared Simpson's more extreme Fifth Monarchy views, rather did he draw Simpson back from these to his own consistently moderate position.

Jessey appears throughout his life to have kept in personal touch with old friends like William Kiffin and Hanserd Knollys even though he disagreed with elements in their policy.

However, he was certainly prepared to work within the political framework provided by the Protectorate – hence his continued reliance upon public authority for his Bible translation project and the question of the re-entry of the Jews. On the other hand he expected neither the Protectorate nor the restored Monarchy to last and he believed steadfastly in the coming of King Jesus.

VIII

The Healing Herb and the Rose of Love:
The Piety of Two Welsh Puritans

R. TUDUR JONES

DR GEOFFREY NUTTALL'S admirers hardly need to be reminded of the sensitive and sympathetic pen-portraits of Vavasor Powell and Morgan Llwyd in his book *The Welsh Saints 1640–1660*. As he has shown, Vavasor Powell (1617–70) deserves better of historians than to be dismissed as a millenarian enthusiast. In many ways, Powell was the most striking personality amongst the Welsh Puritans. But he was also a man of deep spirituality and that aspect of his character has hitherto been little studied, partly perhaps because it follows a well-recognized pattern amongst Puritans. Morgan Llwyd 'o Wynedd' (1619–59) is greatly revered amongst all lovers of Welsh as one of the greatest prose writers in the nation's literature. And that has made him inaccessible to those who are ignorant of the language. But apart from his literary distinction, he is also a fascinating guide into the mysteries of the spiritual life. Powell and Llwyd were close colleagues in the tempestuous years of the Civil Wars and the Protectorate. Despite the estrangement that clouded their friendship for a short period in the later sixteen-fifties, Powell magnanimously wrote an apologetic letter to heal the breach. But Llwyd had died while the letter was on its way. He was only forty years of age. Powell survived him for eleven years and, apart from a couple of short breaks, those years were spent in prison. Despite their close association their respective patterns of piety differed in a striking way. A study of them will throw light on the men themselves and reveal the characteristics of two different Puritan paths towards communion with God.

I

In his book *Christ and Moses Excellency, or Sion and Sinai's Glory* (1650), Vavasor Powell discourses upon the two covenants, of the Law and of Grace, and then proceeds to inform his readers how to understand and apply those Scripture promises that are appended to both covenants. The book, therefore, reveals Powell's theological position as being that of the Federal Theology, a form of Calvinism that became immensely influential in Wales (as in other countries) and continued in vogue down to the Victorian Age. But the book also reveals the presuppositions of Powell's piety. He becomes ecstatic as he apostrophizes the wonder of divine grace:

> Oh soule, consider how the God of grace owned thee, how the Lord of grace bought thee, how the Word of grace called thee, how the Herbe of grace healed thee, and how the Spirit of grace wrought in thee, and sealed thee. . . .[1]

Although man is justified by grace alone and thereby brought into the Covenant of Grace, he is still bound to discharge duties. But he performs these duties to God and his neighbour not in order that he may be justified, but 'to express our love to Christ'.[2] And it is in this context that Powell sees the duties that have to do with the promotion of piety.

The Life and Death of Mr. Vavasor Powell (1671) provides us with a full and vivid portrayal of the spiritual discipline which sustained the faith of this vigorous Welsh Puritan. We catch glimpses of it as practised at his home at Ceri in the beautiful and placid Montgomeryshire countryside, as well as in the stinking prisons in which he spent so many years. He was profoundly concerned about the condition of the human heart.

---

[1] Powell, Vavasor, *Christ and Moses Excellency*, 1650, 155.
[2] Ibid., 169.

As he says in a recommendation he wrote to *Spiritual Experiences of Sundry Beleevers* (1655), 'herein you may see not only your owne hearts, but many hearts, and heart-knowledge is both necessary and precious to sincere soules'. And this promise is echoed in the 'Preface' (possibly by Edward Bagshaw) to his own *Life*, for it tells the reader that in the selections of Powell's Diary printed in the book 'You have some discovery of his heart-walk'. For the Puritan the seat of real religious experience was the heart, and 'experimental knowledge' (as they called it) of God's dealings with man was to be had by studying the heart. Sharing 'heart-knowledge' was consequently a recognized means of helping others to walk with God. In the *Life* also, so the Preface tells us, the reader will find

> his vigilant, vigorous, and steady watch, not only to improve the motions of the Spirit, but to withstand the motions of sin and Satan: his close and hard persuit after God, by all ways and means to keep the heart clean, and the life holy, to keep up grace in the act, & godliness in the power thereof, observing daily his spiritual experiences both in his gettings & losings.

And the promise is well kept. The individual believer's exertions were part of the momentous war that was being waged between God and Satan on the wider stage of the world. Powell was noted in his day for his untiring vigour in his public life. He was not less vigorous in his private spiritual discipline. As he put it,

> As a Watch must be dayly wound up by him that carries it: So the Soul must be wound up by Christ, else it will be unuseful and unserviceable.[3]

The struggle, however, is not inspired by any suspicion that man's ultimate fate may be in doubt. Powell's Confession of Faith makes that quite clear.[4] Those who truly believe are in the New Covenant and 'cannot absolutely fall and utterly perish'. They are 'in Christ and God the Father's' hand and they have the Spirit 'abiding in them unto eternal life'.[5] The

[3] *Life*, 51.
[4] Ibid., 20–45.
[5] Ibid., 32.

spiritual struggle is a confirming of this condition. To have grace is to be eager 'to add one Grace to another, going from strength to strength'.

In order to assess his growth in grace, the believer needs to know what a true Christian is. This motive explains the appendix which follows Powell's Confession of Faith in which he lists thirty-nine 'Signs of a True Believer'. The true believer is characterized by 'affection to Christ', hatred of his own sin, the eagerness to cultivate holiness, humility, self-denial, love for the saints and zeal for God's glory. The moral element is embedded in the personal relationships of the Covenant, personal love towards God in Christ and one's fellow-men. But sin is more than moral failure. It is a breach of these personal relationships and is due to the incursion of alien evil powers into man's life. It is precisely this conviction that sin is powerful that animates Powell's fear of it. 'Learn to know sin, to disallow of it, dispise it, overcome it inwardly, and to put it from thee, to fear its return. . . .'[6]

Powell found several forms of discipline useful in the spiritual warfare. In common with many other Puritans, he found the diary a valuable means of reviewing daily his spiritual condition, of recalling God's dealings with him and of registering the lessons he had learnt during the day. Puritan diaries are often disappointing to the twentieth-century reader because they concentrate so consistently on spiritual matters to the exclusion of those disclosures of facts and motive which fascinate the people of our own day. But the Puritan diary is personal but not necessarily private in the way that Pepys' diary for example was a private document with its secrets hidden behind a shorthand. The individual believer's spiritual struggles were recorded for the edification of other believers. Although the battle was a private one, the war was everybody's business. The experience of the Christian heart was a testimony to divine grace and consequently to be shared in the communion of the saints in order that personal experience of God's reality and love could strengthen others. Powell believed that 'amongst the various wayes of Gods teaching Experience is one of the chiefest'. And he goes on to make the

[6] Ibid., 34.

striking statement (in his recommendatory preface to *Spiritual Experiences*) '*Experience* is a copy written by the Spirit of God upon the hearts of beleevers'. So, in a very real sense, the Puritan did not glory in a private life, carefully screened from public view. What the Spirit of God had written on his heart was for the public benefit of the whole Christian community. In the eighteenth century this use of private experience for public edification found a new and influential setting in the Experience Meetings (the Welsh 'seiat') of the Methodists.

Another element which Powell, in common with his generation, found of great spiritual assistance was the telling phrase or the memorable saying. This found its greatest master, it must be admitted, in Morgan Llwyd who had a positive and sophisticated doctrine about the role of words and language in the spiritual life. But collections of sayings and last words were immensely popular in the Puritan period. The distillation of wisdom and experience in epigram and adage has been pitifully despised in our present culture, except as a means of amusement. But the Puritans shared the partiality of their age for the well-turned phrase and scintillating metaphysical wit. Not that Powell was adept at this sort of thing, but his friends when compiling his *Life* obviously treasured his sayings and printed a selection of them under the title, 'Some gratious Experimental and very choyce Sayings, and Sentences . . .'. And 'experimental' here means that they bore the marks of experienced reality. Such were, to quote a few of them,

> Bad times well improved, are far better than good times, not redeemed, or mispent.
> I never trusted Christ but I found him faithful, nor my own Heart but I found it false.
> The Devil is like the Turkycock (or Crocodile), if you turn upon him he will fly from you, but if you fly from him, he will pursue you.
> He that will not take an Example shall make an Example.
> A Christians Soul should be like the Dial going according to the Sun, or following Christ.
> Careless learning makes carnal Hearts, and carnal Hearts makes cursed lives.

Powell put great store by 'sanctifying thoughts'. The twentieth-century idea that no great harm comes from entertaining evil or corrupt thoughts was quite foreign to Puritan conceptions. Morgan Llwyd put the Puritan view succinctly when he wrote, 'One vain thought outweighs the whole world, because the earth is temporal, but thought is eternal'.[7] For Llwyd man's inner life is of eternal significance precisely because 'the Lord's temple is man's pure mind' and to defile that is corruption indeed. And Powell would have agreed warmly with his friend. To occupy the mind, in case of temptation, with 'sanctifying thoughts' was to guard oneself against corruption. And so Powell lists his favourite sanctifying thoughts, such as 'The thoughts of God's free and constant love to me' and 'The thoughts of what Christ hath done for me'. Obviously, the Bible itself was the most lucrative source of sanctifying thoughts. Its words were an unfailing help in the battle against temptation. An entry from his diary will illustrate this use of the Bible,

> This day in the morning my Heart was very free to pray for my Persecutors, and Enemies as freely as *I* was to seek and receive pardon for my own sins. I had power also to apply those words to my self, Psal. 62. 2. *He is onely my Rock, and my Salvation, he is my defence I shall not greatly be moved* and in verse 6, *I shall not be moved*. God did bring this Scripture as an Antidote for that Evening, there came several persons one after another, to tell me that I and several others were to be tryed at the Sessions, and I observed that my Heart was very little moved thereat, but could willingly refer myself to the Lord, and be quiet in, and contented with his will, though never so contrary to my own carnal and natural will.[8]

And that excerpt also contains an excellent example of his 'heart-walk' in distressing circumstances and one can appreciate how that little piece of 'heart-knowledge' would strengthen others who might be under strain when threatened with persecution in the courts.

In one of his sayings, Powell mentions four aids to piety,

[7] *Gweithiau Morgan Llwyd*, 2 v., 1899 and 1908, I, 225.
[8] *Life*, 60.

'By Prayer God doth converse with me, by Meditation he doth fill me, by singing Hymnes he doth ravish me, by his Supper he doth feed me'.[9] It is worth noting, in order to capture the flavour of his devotional discipline, that he writes of these in terms of God's action upon him rather than in terms of fulfilling duties towards God. Prayer and meditation he found absolutely necessary for his soul's health,

> The more a soul is exercised by spiritual meditation, the less with carnal Temptation.
> The more frequent and powerful in private Prayer, the more free from, and the more potent against Corruptions.[10]

We not only have Powell's own words to help us reconstruct his spiritual exercises but we have also the testimonies of his friends about his devotional habits at home at Ceri. First of all, it is fascinating to discover in Vavasor Powell a form of piety that one would certainly expect to find in nineteenth-century Wales, but which must be quite rare in the Puritan period; that is a passion for hymn-singing. Mention has already been made of Powell's confession that when he sang hymns God 'ravished' him. It adds a vivid touch to this statement to know that his home rang with his hymn-singing:

> He was very heavenly, his Heart so set with diligence and intent-ness upon the things of God, that when he was alone, and none to discourse with, he would many times be singing of Hymns in his house and elsewhere, and often in his Bed as soon as he awaked in the morning, being excellent at extempory Hymns, which have been to the refreching of many, who have declared to have injoyed as much of God in joyning with him therein, as in any other ordinance.[11]

So his passion was infectious! Hymnody in both England and Wales was in its infancy at this time and Powell's productions cannot claim any lasting merit, but the practice of extem-porizing hymns was popular in millenarian circles in Powell's

[9] Ibid., 50.
[10] Ibid., 47.
[11] Ibid., 114.

time, although it is possible that he had been inspired by the popularity of extemporary poetical composition as a source of entertainment at social evenings in Wales.

He insisted strictly on the practice of piety at home. He used to tell his servants 'that they should at any time leave work to pray or read' and if he did come upon them at any time 'in the Fields reading or conferring about the things of God, he would bid them go on and continue in it'.[12] He used various means to instil piety in his household. One way was to 'repeat' a sermon and question the servants about its contents. Another way was to ask them about their private Scripture reading. Or again he would read and expound a portion of the Bible and catechize them to ensure that they had understood its meaning. This was no mere formality. A servant's future employment might depend on it. If servants were forgetful or lax in their spiritual discipline Powell would 'threaten to turn them out of his doors, if they did not reform'. Family prayers were held at least twice a day and consisted of Bible reading and prayer. Sometimes he would indulge his enthusiasm for hymn-singing.[13]

His wife Katherine added her own testimony in support of all this:

A man much in prayer, he set aside one part of the day alone, to seek God for *Sion*, not mixing other requests at that time, and constant in Family duty, morning and night at least, and with his Wife he went to Bed (notwithstanding which) immediately before he composed himself to rest, took leave by committing himself again by a few words in Prayer to the Lord, and so in the morning when he awoke renewed Communion afresh with God, sometimes, first by Prayer, then sometimes (when his heart overflowed with spiritual joy) in Songs or Hymns of Praises, and that with a very broken and melting Frame.[14]

Students of the unconscious mind will be interested to hear that he could sometimes be heard praying in his sleep 'and yet know it not when he awaked'. It is perhaps no wonder that

[12] Ibid., 116.
[13] Ibid., 117.
[14] Ibid., 118–19.

he was 'a great observer of dreams' and believed that 'God might speak to himself or others by them'.[15]

To what extent was this piety centred on the promotion of otherworldliness? Powell is best known for his vigorous zeal in 'advancing the Name, Interest, Kingdome, and Sovereignty of Jesus Christ', as his biographers put it. He was one 'of a worthy publick Spirit' who became a well-known political figure during the Fifth Monarchy agitations of 1653 which led to the convening of the Saints' Parliament and subsequently in the millenarian campaign which he organized in Wales against the Protectorate. Was his spirituality a means of escape from the tensions of public and political life? There is certainly a critical attitude towards the 'world' in his devotional writing. The 'world' is a snare and a temptation. As he puts it in one of his aphorisms, 'The world is a great nothing, deluding the bad, disturbing and distracting the good'.[16] Christians should not grasp the 'world' too tightly: 'When God makes the world to hot for his People to hold, they will let it go'.[17] Unfortunately, his biographers have not seen fit to date the selections from his diary. It is obvious from internal evidence that they belong to different periods in his career. Some of the 'experiences' printed in the *Life* are dated 3 May 1658.[18] But otherwise it seems that much of the material comes from the last period of his life which he spent in prison. There is, for example, the touching saying, 'A Prison or persecution is to a Christian as some scaring thing, that one sees in the Night at a distance, but when he comes near it, and to know it, he is not at all afraid of it'.[19] Confinement in prison cuts people off from public activity, however much their interest might be in the progress of events, and it would have been interesting to be able to compare Powell's devotional life when he was immersed in public and political activity with his spirituality during the long years of imprisonment. In any case, the idea that political life or 'secular' activity was outside the responsibility of Christians would have been unacceptable

[15] Ibid., 114.
[16] Ibid., 36.
[17] Ibid., 46.
[18] Ibid., 92-5.
[19] Ibid., 41-2.

to Calvinistic Puritans. And even more so to Powell who, as a Fifth Monarchist, saw the political realm as a very significant field of Christian activity. When Powell writes disparagingly of the 'world' he is not advocating a quietistic and pietistic attitude towards society and politics. He is thinking rather of the realm of human life – and of material things – as a possible rival to God in the affections of Christians.

There is clear evidence that Powell had a deep interest in suffering. This is revealed not only by his book *The Sufferers-Catechism* of 1664 but by references in his diary and sayings, as for example, when he says, 'As the Martyr professed he had rather be a Martyr than a Monarch, so should every Christian. It is a special favour, and great promotion to suffer.' The suffering he was most especially concerned with was the suffering which the saints endured under persecution. And this goes to show that his piety was by no means a retreat from anxiety into otherworldliness. Rather was the devotional life understood as a necessary means to strengthen the Christian for his warfare in the world. Powell certainly mellowed during the years of imprisonment. The significance of toleration became clearer to him as the years passed by and the ferocity which sometimes marked his attitudes to his opponents in the days of the Puritan ascendancy gave way to a deep concern for love and reconciliation. One of his manuscript notebooks preserves a beautiful meditation he wrote in Welsh on Love:

> The God of Heaven, grant us those graces that will carry us above the world, especially that grace of Love which makes all the Lord's ways gentle and easy. Unless we receive that true grace of love towards the Lord and his ways, a godly Christian life will be but a load and a burden. But where that Grace of Love has been received, the ways of the Lord are lovely, easy and light. It was Love that made the Church say of Christ that her Beloved is fair. Oh God of Heaven help us to contemplate the free gracious Love of the Lord towards us, who so loved the world that he gave his only begotten Son to die for sinners. Oh that the Love of Christ would compel us to judge that it is no longer meet for us to live according to the lust of the Flesh, but for Him who lived and died for us.[20]

[20] National Library of Wales, Add. MS. 366 A.

As this meditation puts it, the Christian ideal is to live 'above the world'. Piety can suffer when Christians are tempted to put the world above Christ and so worship the creature rather than the Creator. Another meditation in the same manuscript touches upon the point:

> Oh Holy God, how we consider it a waste to practise piety or to seek to live a holy life! And how sweet it is unto us to practise those things that are but for a moment! The world is such a burden on our heart that we cannot live above the world and creatures because of the love we bear towards them.

And so in this manuscript Powell asserts with vigour the necessity for love to be transformed into toleration in public life. A person may be in error but no one has anything 'to do with him by way of cruelty to guide him out of it'. The duty of citizens is to persuade those who hold unacceptable opinions. 'If you use violence you are undertaking to exceed the commission granted you by God', he tells the magistrate.

It needs hardly to be said that the whole of Powell's devotional life is permeated through and through by the Bible. The *Life* tells us that he was 'mighty in the Scriptures, which was so admirably imprinted in his memory, that he was as a Concordance wherever he came, so that a Scripture could hardly be named to him, but he could tell you the Chapter and Verse'.[21] His unfinished *A New and Useful Concordance to the Holy Bible,* posthumously published in 1671, was more than a handbook for finding texts. It was intended to serve as an aid to private devotion. As the title page informs us, it had, more than any other Concordance, 'Marks to distinguish The Commands Promises and Threatenings' of Scripture. It was several times reprinted and enlarged with the passing years and served to make a contribution to that form of Christian piety which uses the Bible, to the virtual exclusion of other books, as a primer of devotion. It is quite obvious that Powell was a vigorous exerciser of this form of devotional discipline. He found in the Bible an inexhaustible source of instruction, encouragement and delight.

[21] *Life,* 109.

II

In the case of Vavasor Powell, we have abundant materials for describing his devotional life. We can observe his piety directly in his own writings and see it in practice through the eyes of his friends. The case is rather different with Morgan Llwyd. There is no escaping his burning concern for the spiritual life. No Welsh Puritan expressed that concern with greater vigour and brilliance than he did. But in his published writings he is concerned with the conditions that make true piety possible. We have to deduce the characteristics of the resulting piety by reading between the lines. That he was a man of impressive personality is suggested by a vivid snapshot of him preserved by Robert Jones, Rhos-lan, in his book *Drych yr Amseroedd* (1820):

> Morgan Llwyd used to preach at Pwllheli on market days, and his custom was to walk through the market with his hands on his back, holding his Bible in one of them; and the people would retreat before him, as though a chariot were rushing through the streets.

Would that we had many more such descriptions of his public and private life!

The promotion of true piety was the master concern of his life. This can be seen in the opening sentences of his first published work, *Llythur ir Cymru Cariadus* (1653), 'But seek, O Man, to know thyself, and to enter through the strait gate'. He goes on to describe those who pursue vanity and says of them that they 'know not goodness, nor practice piety, nor fly above the sun to Him who inhabiteth eternity'. The concern runs through his published work like a golden thread. In his last book, *Gair o'r Gair: neu Son am Swn* (1656), he described the preconditions of Christian piety,

> Your first task is to become silent, and to silence absolutely every other Sound that is in your heart, and to exclude every mental voice within you, except the Voice of God within you. . . . Therefore seek of God until you receive a quiet heart within. . . .[22]

[22] *Gweithiau Morgan Llwyd*, II, 190-1.

His grand theme throughout is that man must seek God in his own heart. Searching for God in books, or amidst the ideas and arguments of men is burdensome and pointless. It does not bring man face-to-face with God. God confronts man ultimately in the depths of his own being. But it is the tragedy of the Welsh people, as of sinners everywhere, that they have not even embarked on the search for God. They devote themselves to outward things, to the flesh and its lusts, to the material world and its attractions.

> Woe, woe, woe it is that so many of the Welsh people, the wise as well as the foolish amongst them, live in the sieve of vanity, in the spleen of bitterness, lying in the bonds of falsehood on the bed of Babel, grazing in the devil's meadow to feed the flesh, without knowing the God who made them.[23]

This quotation introduces us to one of the key symbols in Llwyd's thought. 'Flesh' is a comprehensive term for those things which obscure man's vision of God.

> The flesh is everything under the sun that is outside the inner man. Whatever is transient and not eternal – that is flesh. Man's senses are flesh, as well as the pleasures of the world. Playfulness in old and young is flesh. . . . Time and all that is limited by it is flesh. Flesh is the will and mystery of man. Prayers and innumerable sermons are flesh. The honour of great men and the snobbishness of small men are flesh. Flesh is all that the natural man can see, and hear, and get, and absorb.[24]

So the word has an extremely comprehensive denotation. The reader naturally asks why the word should be understood in this way. Llwyd's answer is that it is because 'it surrounds man like a garment. It is loved by him, it is near him, is part of him, and grows in him and rots about him.' Perhaps it can be better understood as existence seen from the standpoint of sinful man. And so it has a portentous theological significance, for flesh is 'God's enemy, man's poison, the livery of

[23] Ibid., I, 116.
[24] Ibid., I, 219-20.

hell, the image of the beast, the darling of the sinner' and many other terrible things besides.

To escape this thraldom man must penetrate through the flesh to God, through the transient to the eternal. And this is a journey inwards. Flesh encircles the heart, the existential centre of man's being, and man must penetrate through the flesh to it. So 'mask' (*mwgwd*) becomes an appropriate metaphor for the flesh: 'Lucifer keeps the mask of the flesh over the eyes of man's mind.'[25] The mask has to be torn away so that man can confront God in his heart. This process of penetration inwards is described in a crucial passage in *Llythur ir Cymru Cariadus*:

> You must understand that the whole universe that you see is like the bark of a tree, or the crust of a loaf, or a bone amongst dogs. And there is a spirit or humour in creation that conforms with your nature and makes you covetous. Then next within the natural life, is your spirit walking and running without ceasing amongst angels. Next within that is the infinite, blessed Trinity, the Father, the Word and the Spirit (that is, the will, the joy and the power, and these three are one). And this is as far as the mind of man can see in the spirit. But at the farthest and deepest point is the root and the ground in the eternal, immeasurable, still unity that eye cannot gaze upon nor anyone's mind grasp but He himself.[26]

Students of Jacob Böhme will immediately recognize the echo of that teacher's doctrine in this passage. But as Mr Hugh Bowen has so rightly emphasized in his brilliant study, *Morgan Llwyd y Llenor* (1954), Llwyd, despite his intense interest in Böhme, dispensed with the German mystic's obscurer metaphysical speculations. All the same, Llwyd in the above passage makes room for the inscrutability of God as expressed in Isaiah 45:15, 'Thou art a God that hidest thyself'. No human mind can comprehend God entirely, because our knowledge of God is limited to what He has chosen to reveal of Himself. But the spiritual pilgrimage inwards does take

---

[25] Ibid., I, 234.
[26] Ibid., I, 119.

man to the fringes of the ultimate mystery precisely because it brings man into confrontation with the true God.

Llwyd is fascinated by the mystery of God's reality and the wonder of human communion with Him. And this mystery and wonder cannot be expressed in human words in a direct way. To use modern jargon, the existential moment can only be pointed to; it cannot be expressed. Even the most sublime talk about that moment is not to be confused with the moment itself. Otherwise words become 'flesh'; they hide the reality instead of pointing towards it; they become a 'mask' concealing what is always beyond them. On no account – and this point is sometimes forgotten by commentators on Llwyd – on no account must the Creator and the creature be confused (to adopt a technical term from the Chalcedonian Definition!), nor must experience of created things be identified with experience of the Eternal. These insights have a profound reference to Llwyd's conception of his literary task. God cannot be conveyed in a formula. The writer therefore has to hint, to suggest, to point towards God. His message is of necessity an oblique one, always straining to turn the eye from itself to the divine subject. God cannot be encapsulated in human words and sentences otherwise men's attention is directed towards human literature or human speech. If man is to come to faith, he must be directed and persuaded and invited to look away from men and the created world. So Llwyd's literary style is itself governed by principles which stem from his theological convictions and his evangelistic task. Much of his prose is direct admonition to the reader. It is the very reverse of cool academic analysis. In Welsh, the second person singular has not disappeared as it has in English. Llwyd's constant use of this verbal form therefore gives his prose an urgency and a directness which is no longer possible in English by the use of the 'thou' and 'thee' forms. So Llwyd's prose comes hot from the heart and is addressed to individual people.

And even more significantly, the Christian author must use symbols to convey his message. Llwyd uses an exceptionally rich variety of metaphors, symbols, 'emblems', comparisons and Biblical references, not in order to describe the eternal realities, but in order to compel his readers to make that momentous journey inwards which is also the great existential decision of faith. To apply the vocabulary of existentialism to Llwyd is by no means inappropriate. Together with his contemporary Blaise Pascal he has a claim to be considered one of the many founders of modern Christian existentialism. Once this is grasped, the syntax, as well as the vocabulary, of his writing can be better appreciated. Since he is confronted with the problem of bringing men face-to-face with the mystery of the loving and saving God, he cannot indulge in straightforward logical discourse in the manner of a theological *summa* or a philosophical treatise. His interest is not in logical precision, nor in academic accuracy, nor yet in intellectual comprehension of God and his love, but in leading men into that confrontation with God which will transform their existence. The literary method that he has adopted to do this subtle work is to combine symbols, allusions, metaphors and comparisons in carefully constructed paragraphs so that within the compass of a few lines the reader glimpses something of God's divinity from several different standpoints. Moreover, such is Llwyd's mastery over language that he can by the felicities of his style create the emotional quality which should characterize the person who has accepted his invitation to look at the reality beyond the words and symbols. This, after all, is the mysterious alchemy which makes great literature. In Llwyd's case (as in the case of a Bunyan or a Milton in English) it is also that which makes great Christian literature. (It is this aspect of Llwyd's work which has been examined in Mr Hugh Bowen's book to which reference has already been made.)

In describing the salvific movement by which man penetrates the mask of the flesh to the heart, one of Llwyd's suggestive images is that of the secret chamber. The Spirit of God takes the believer 'to converse with God in the chamber of the heart'.[27] That is why Llwyd urges men to 'seek God in your heart, because no one sees Him but the one who sees within himself'.[28]

[27] Ibid., I, 232.
[28] Ibid., I, 122.

Again, the symbols of light and darkness play a large role in his thinking, as they have in so much religious thinking throughout the ages. 'Welshman! look for the light of God in your mind.'[29] Again in *Gwaedd Ynghymru,* he says, 'Oh man, God has shown you what is good. He has set a candle within you to light your way'.[30] In a later passage in the same book he links this symbol with his concept of flesh and the candle is transformed into a purifying fire,

> Remember always that God has set a candle within you and that hitherto it has burned but weakly. If the flesh is allowed to oppress it and to extinguish it, it will produce smoke and a nasty smell for ever within you. But if you allow the Holy Spirit to flame up in it, it will burn up all the flesh, and purify the soul for God.[31]

In that way, the soul is illumined by God's bright light. Otherwise, man is enveloped in darkness, like the sleeper in a seventeenth-century four-poster bed:

> Man does not see where he is, any more than a person sleeping in his bed who has the curtains of flesh drawn about him, and all the windows closed. But the time to wake up is near when the flesh is buried or burnt. . . .[32]

Man's heart lies under a pall of darkness and he is 'unable to see how empty, shapeless and chaotic his internal world is'. It is therefore a great consolation to know 'that God commands light to shine out of darkness, and to separate night from day in the individual soul'.[33] By intertwining symbols in this way, Llwyd conveys the essential unity of the process of salvation so that the moral and the intellectual, the will and the mind, are not divorced from each other. But the metaphors of light and darkness emphasize the element of vision, of perceiving more clearly. When he urges man 'to seek God's

29 Ibid., I, 119.
30 Ibid., I, 130.
31 Ibid., I, 140.
32 Ibid., I, 213.
33 Ibid., I, 140.

light in your mind', he adds, 'Ask for the fountain of understanding and drink often of it'.[34] There is no question in
Llwyd of embracing the obscurantist position which would
deny the place of intellectual apprehension in salvation. And
yet the Scriptural overtones of the symbol 'fountain' reminds
us that the 'fountain of understanding' is more than that – it
is the fountain of eternal life welling up in the heart.

The symbols connected with reading belong here. Puritans
generally were fascinated by the evangelistic possibilities of
the printing press. Welsh Puritans like Stephen Hughes,
William Jones, Richard Jones and Charles Edwards, assisted
by patrons like Thomas Gouge, worked hard to publish 'good
books'. And Llwyd shared their enthusiasm. But still books
vary in value and even the 'good books' could become an
end in themselves and hinder true spiritual penetration to God.
For Llwyd, the best book of all lies in the heart. And so he
pleads, 'Read the book which is within you'.[35] For him it was
regrettable that people should waste their time 'reading
obscene dirty books and poisoning the pure root' within
them. But it is by reading the book in the heart that men can
grasp spiritual reality. Even the Bible itself can become one
of the veils of flesh unless men follow this advice as they read
it. 'Books and letters are but straw. Life lies in the spirit not
in the letter.'[36] Llwyd does not wish to disparage the letter,
but to emphasize that it is not rightly understood except by
the light of the Spirit. Thus, he urges his readers to take his
own books seriously:

> Do not, on your peril, despise what is written here, and do not
> read lightly and throw it into a corner to rust as a testimony
> against you, without understanding it down to the fundamentals.
> Because here and there the deep things of God appear. . . .

The 'book of the heart' does not displace other books. Thus,
it is clear from his attitude to the Bible that it is not replaced
by the knowledge which comes from confrontation with God
in the heart. He writes in *Gair o'r Gair*:

[34] Ibid., I, 119
[35] Ibid., I, 193–4.
[36] Ibid., I, 251.

You are familiar with Scripture, its chapters are at your finger-tips. But have you ever heard the Mystery of the Thunder-clap and the Heavenly Song together within yourself? . . . If you have read the letter, have you understood the Spirit in it after all your reading?[37]

There seems to be a two-way traffic here. One reads the Bible 'in the Spirit' and is led thereby to the 'book of the heart'. And reading the 'book of the heart' leads back to a new appreciation of the significance of Scripture.

Scripture immediately raises the question of the Word of God. In dealing with this topic Llwyd introduces a posy of symbols that have to do with 'Word', 'Sound', 'Voice', 'Hearing' and 'Understanding'. Again the symbols illustrate the theme of the journey inward. Here 'flesh' or 'veils' or 'masks' upon the existential truth are to be understood in terms of sinful man's ceaseless and pointless chatter. Chatter leads men astray. Even the chatterers themselves are duped by their own verbosity. 'He who talks much amongst men can hear little of the voice of God and Paradise.' 'Paradise', again, is a symbol he sometimes uses, and he says that 'Paradise is not far from you but is everywhere where the love of God appears'.[38] God makes Himself known in his Word:

> Therefore, oh immortal mind of man, choose to listen to God's Word and you shall live. Oh Man-King, live for ever! And before you know anything, enter into yourself to know yourself more and more, to perceive how the Word of God is in you, and how God is in the Word, that is, Christ in you, and God in Christ, and you in Christ in God, if you are in the Spirit of Christ. . . .[39]

The title 'Man-King' (Dyn-frenin) in this quotation has led some commentators to speak of Llwyd's humanism. But care must be taken not to confuse Llwyd's teaching with the secular form of humanism that was already gathering strength in his time. A Scripture reference in the margin, relevant to this word, directs the reader to 'Esay. 55. 2'. It is not quite clear why this verse in Isaiah should cast light on the title,

[37] Ibid., II, 168.
[38] Ibid., I, 213.
[39] Ibid., II, 196.

but the third verse, 'Incline your ear, and come unto me: hear, and your soul shall live', connects the paragraph as a whole with one of the best known passages in the Bible dealing with the significance of listening to the Word of God. Only so will man be received into 'the sure mercies' of King David. The theme of man's dominion over nature is prominent in the Creation narrative and is taken up again in Psalm 8. But this kingly dominion of man in Llwyd's thought is offered anew to fallen man as a consequence of obedience to God's Word. And this is the theme of the book from which the quotation comes. *Gair o'r Gair* is an extended meditation on the significance of the Word as reality and symbol. God's voice permeates creation. To hear God's Word, man must not rest with merely formal knowledge of the Bible or of Christ. 'The danger of the soul is that it knows Christ, and self, and his brother, and his duty, and Scripture, and the Churches, and the world and everything else by the light of the flesh . . .'. But, 'If knowledge of God's Word is merely carnal, it must be left behind'.[40] Which is to say that in that case it is not God's Word. Or, more accurately, the sinner is hearing a word that is not God's and confusing the two. Only when the heart is engaged – when there is total attention by man to the very roots of his being – is it possible to hear God's Word. Once that condition supervenes, the light of revelation illuminates man's thoughts and the Bible is recognized for what it is. 'The Word within and the Scriptures without harmonise and agree and testify in unison. The former is written with an external pen in the holy Bible, the latter in the other Bible, namely the Book of Conscience.'[41] And so Llwyd is able to intertwine several of the symbols that have already been mentioned in a beautiful paragraph:

We have the true preacher standing in the pulpit of our hearts, and a book within us that will be serviceable if we follow it, and if we attend upon it as a Word or candle burning in a dark place. And we shall follow and obey the Voice and Light within rather than every external voice.[42]

[40] Ibid., II, 197.
[41] Ibid., II, 183.
[42] Ibid., II, 174–5.

So he begs his readers to bring their minds to meditate and their hearts to believe. This is also a plea to cultivate an inner quietness. Believing, for Llwyd, is receptive attention to what God says. 'Your first task is to be quiet and to silence absolutely every other noise in your heart . . . and think of nothing but God.' Man should seek of God 'the silent heart within . . . to sink down into thyself and so out of thy self into God thy root'.[43] It is useless to emulate those people who 'gaze upon God from afar, and who call for him from outside, without realising that a fountain and a root within them is seeking to spring up and grow . . .'.[44] One must walk through the inner door which is in his own heart. That is the way to enter 'the glorious eternal palace'.[45] And there, all that is necessary for eternal felicity is to be had, 'There is within the godly the Morning Star and the Sun, a fountain and eternal life, as John says. Make the most of the treasure that is in your own field.'[46]

At this point it is necessary to warn against possible misunderstanding of Llwyd's position. His interest in Böhme and the debt he owes him are both obvious. But Llwyd was a critical admirer of Böhme and only adopted what he needed for his own purposes from his system. And Böhme is the link which explains some coincidences between Llwyd's ideas and those of later thinkers of the Idealistic School and of Paul Tillich. He was in sympathy with the ideas of contemporaries like John Saltmarsh, William Dell, Samuel Hartlib, George Fox, and his own teacher William Erbery. And there was a strong bond of friendship between him and Peter Sterry. However, his voracious appetite for ideas, new and old, did not deprive him of his critical faculty and he moulded his borrowings into an impressive theological pattern which still allowed him to accommodate insights from the millenarianism of Vavasor Powell and the genial Calvinism of Walter Cradock.

Llwyd was not a pantheist. Nor was he a Gnostic. He was

[43] Ibid., II, 189–92.
[44] Ibid., I, 227.
[45] Ibid., I, 243.
[46] Ibid., II, 196.

not engaged in a ruthless subjectivization of Christian faith in the manner of Schleiermacher and the nineteenth-century Romantics. Nor did he embark upon a humanistic programme which was tantamount to divinizing man. Even Professor W. J. Gruffydd's attempt in his *Llen Cymru* to make a mystic – in the classical sense of the term – of Llwyd fails to carry conviction in the light of subsequent scholarly work on Llwyd. Dr E. Lewis Evans, apart from providing us in a masterly way with the materials for tracing the various influences on Llwyd's thinking, has also concluded that 'Wales has not produced a more original teacher and interpreter than Morgan Llwyd'.[47] And Dr Evans's conclusion is a warning not to jump to hasty conclusions in assessing Llwyd's thought.

In his published books, Llwyd's overriding concern is the evangelization of Wales. He wishes to bring his people to a saving knowledge of God. This is because God is a loving God who desires to bring his erring children into communion with Himself. In an age when interest in religious matters was universal and when theological debate was part and parcel of everyday life, formal profession of faith paid large dividends, but at the cost of undermining the spiritual power of Christianity. Llwyd wished above all to guide his readers into a real and vital knowledge of God. This is why his mind grappled with the question of the epistemology of faith. How precisely do we come to a real, sincere, saving knowledge of God? His answer was that God in his love meets man in the depths of his own personality.

Two things comfort many. But the third is the foundation of all. The first is that Christ, the Son of God, died for us, and paid all our debt to God. But to talk of that is nothing, unless the second follows, and that is that Christ lives in us, and rules over us and through us, as light, and comfort and power in the bosom of the soul.

But this is not sufficient either, this is not the root of the matter, but the union between the Father and the soul, in the Spirit of the

[47] Evans, E. L., 'Cyfundrefn Feddyliol Morgan Llwyd' in *Efrydiau Athronyddol,* 1942, 31.

Son, in the infinite love. That is, the same union that exists between God and his own Son. . . .[48]

It will be observed that Llwyd is not recommending a flight from history. Indeed, even the casual reader of his work will sense his keen sensitivity to the spiritual urgency that follows the passing of time. Time is running out for the sinner and he must make his peace with God before death catches up with him. Nor does he despise God's work in the history of Wales and the world. The historical work of Christ and his atoning death are of supreme importance to him. But a merely historical faith is of no avail. The true import of Christ's sacrificial death is only realized when its benefits are appropriated in the inward man. 'It is your corruptible flesh that Christ put to death on the Cross: and it is righteousness before God to crucify you on the Cross within, to save your spirit from death and bitterness.'[49] It is clear that it is not Llwyd's intention so to internalize Christ's death and resurrection as to deprive them of their objective historical validity. But to be saving events in the life of a citizen of Wrexham in 1653, these events on the stage of history many centuries previously have to be paralleled by a spiritual appropriation in which the believer becomes involved directly in them.

Similarly with the externals of religion. Llwyd does not wish to dispense with Bible, sacraments, churches and public worship. If they are conceived of as the ultimate substance of Christianity, then they are of no avail. Without union with God, apart from the existential cleaving to the Eternal, they become a snare. As he puts it in a moving autobiographical passage, in *Llyfr y Tri Aderyn* (1653):

> Once upon a time I heard sermons, but I was not listening. I said prayers but I was not praying. I sang Psalms, but my heart was dumb. I took communion but saw not the Body of the Lord. I conversed and said many things, but not sincerely from my heart, until the rose sprang up in me. . . .[50]

[48] *Gweithiau Morgan Llwyd*, I, 143.
[49] Ibid., I, 144–5.
[50] Ibid., I, 258.

The queen of flowers, the rose, is the traditional symbol for the *unio mystica*. But with the flowering of 'the rose' in man the ordinances of Christianity take on a new and profound significance.

Again, Llwyd carefully maintains the distinction between God and man. Despite his insistence that God ultimately confronts man in the heart, he does not wish to imply that there is in man, by nature, an aspect of his personality which is a divine emanation. The light in the heart is not a human light but God's light. There is throughout a firm insistence on the objectivity of God even though that objectivity is only fully revealed in man's internal life. There is no confusing of the divine and human nature in Llwyd's doctrine of man.

It is true that Llwyd's main interest is in bringing people to repentance rather than in describing the piety that would flourish after conversion. But at one point in *Llyfr y Tri Aderyn* he does address himself to the question what a Christian should do when he falls away from 'his first love'. He answers:

> Oh, take heed lest your candle go out on the earth, so that there be no light in you to show you your destiny when you die. Be courageous. Increase in knowledge and humility and boldness with God. Hold on to the goodness you have received. Let the mustard seed grow within you and thrive within you. Exclude evil and shout for help and the Saviour will draw near.[51]

The style is highly allusive but the thrust of the advice is that in the case of backsliding man must make the effort to retrace his steps along the path that leads him through the door in the heart to Paradise. Piety in this context becomes a spiritual recapitulation. This means effort, perhaps struggle. But Llwyd is careful to set the elements of gift and effort alongside each other. The human initiative and the divine initiative go together in his thinking. 'The man who does what he can through God, will receive power from Almighty God to do everything that is good.'[52]

[51] Ibid., I, 245.
[52] Ibid., I, 142.

But if anyone wishes to know what he thought piety was, his answer is simple and straightforward, 'the sum of piety is, Love God with all your heart, and your neighbour as your-self.'[53]

III

When Powell's conception of piety is put alongside that of his friend Llwyd, it can be seen that they represent two different emphases in Christian spirituality. The Puritan move-ment was able to embrace both because there is a considerable overlap between them. To talk of Llwyd abandoning Calvinism entirely is as misleading as to assert that Powell rejected the indwelling of Christ in the believer's heart. Both men revered the Bible, both were passionately committed to the propagation of the Gospel in Wales, both exalted the historical saving work of Jesus Christ, both were excited by the likelihood of Christ's imminent Second Coming, both taught the basic importance of the love of God. But they parted company because Llwyd's understanding of the way in which salvation is appropriated differed from that of Powell, and his teaching involved a rejection of the Calvinistic teach-ing of his day about Election and Limited Atonement. Their respective understanding of the nature of piety consequently possessed a distinctly different flavour. Despite his interest in the need for righteousness in public life, Llwyd tended to promote a quietist piety which moved people away from involvement in public controversy. Powell, despite his pro-found commitment to deepening the spiritual life, promoted a piety that was productive of vigorous activism.

In the main, it was Powell's type of piety that carried the day in Wales. It would, however, be a mistake to assert with Professor W. J. Gruffydd that Llwyd was entirely forgotten. Not only were his books frequently republished and used by the discerning as devotional handbooks of great value, but his concern about the reality of the sinner's confrontation with God in the depths of his own personality was an emphasis

[53] Ibid., I, 254.

that received its due in the Evangelical Revival of the eighteenth century. William Williams, Pantycelyn, and Howel Harris were indebted to both Powell and Llwyd. And so, therefore, are the Welsh Christians of today.

IX

Quaker and Chiliast: the 'contrary thoughts' of William Ames and Petrus Serrarius[1]

J. VAN DEN BERG

IN THE year 1662 there appeared in the Netherlands a little book, written in the Dutch language, which on its title-page mentioned the name of one of the leaders of the early Quaker movement, William Ames; an English edition, also bearing the name of Ames, appeared in the course of the following year under the title *The Light upon the Candlestick*.[2] Already William Sewel, who possessed so much first-hand information on what had happened in the early period of Quaker history, found reason to deny the authorship of Ames, who however, according to Sewel, had approved of the contents of the work; and indeed, while the style and the method of reasoning are different from those of Ames, the spirit of the work is in full conformity with the central emphasis of his authentic publications.[3] It is the message of the Light, 'the inward ear, by which alone, and by no other, the voice of God, that is the Truth, can be heard',[4] which is the main theme of the work.

On the first page the author, dealing indirectly with the religious controversies of his times, remarks 'that two men, speaking or writing the same words, may nevertheless have

---

[1] I thank Dr Norma E. Emerton for her correction of the English text, and my assistant, Miss Ernestine G. E. van der Wall, for her help in the preparation of this study, in particular with regard to the problems around the biography of Serrarius.

[2] I quote from the English edition: Ames, W., *The Light upon the Candlestick*. Serving for observation of the principal things in the Book called The Mysteries of the Kingdom of God, etc., London 1663.

[3] See for the question of the authorship: Hull, W. I., *The Rise of Quakerism in Amsterdam 1655–1665*, Swarthmore 1938, 214f.

[4] Op. cit., 9.

different, yea sometimes contrary thoughts'. This sentence sums up quite well what happened in the Netherlands, when English Quakers first came into contact with Dutch 'Collegiants'; we receive the impression that in the initial stage the two groups felt attracted to each other because they seemed to speak the same language; soon, however, it became clear that on many points their ideas diverged rather widely. Yet, at the end we may wonder whether under the surface there was not still present a common spirituality, rooted in what R. M. Jones, speaking of 'mystical religion', calls 'a direct and intimate consciousness of the Divine Presence'.[5] We shall meet with all the tensions, but perhaps also with something of the underlying affinity, in the discussions which took place in the years around 1660 between William Ames and the Dutch Collegiant and Chiliast Petrus Serrarius.

William Ames set foot on Dutch soil for the first time in the spring of 1656, driven by an indomitable urge to spread the message of the Light also in the Low Countries, where only six years later, at the end of 1662, he was to find his grave.[6] It seems that he already possessed some knowledge of the Dutch language, with which he came to be well acquainted within a short time. We do not know the date of his birth, but probably on his arrival in Holland he was middle-aged; he had served in the army of the King, with the navy and in the Parliamentary army, and after that he had worked as a Baptist minister in Ireland. From Sewel's work as well as from his own writings we get the impression that he was an intelligent, courageous and energetic man, eager to convert others to the doctrine which had 'pierced through' him, when 'one who was sent by the Lord . . . declared that that which convinced man of Sin, was the Light of Christ'.[7]

Ames was not the first English Quaker who worked in the Netherlands, but soon he became the recognized leader of the

[5] Jones, R. M., *Studies in Mystical Religion*, London 1909, XV.

[6] See for the following passage: Hull, op. cit., and Kannegieter, J. Z., *Geschiedenis van de vroegere Quakergemeenschap te Amsterdam*, Amsterdam and Haarlem 1971. Hull often refers to the classic works of G. Croese, *Historia Quakeriana*, Amsteodami 1695, and of W. Sewel, *Histori van de opkomste, aanwas en voortgang der . . . Quakers*, Amsterdam 1717; Kannegieter gives additional information of the grounds of his researches in the Amsterdam archives.

[7] Ames, *A Declaration of the Witness of God, manifested in the Inward Parts*, 1681[2], 12.

Dutch Quaker community. His task was not an easy one. There were difficulties within the Quaker community, caused by unbalanced people: W. C. Braithwaite remarks, that the soil in Holland was not stony as it had been in Ireland and Scotland, but shallow, bringing forth rank and short-lived growths.[8] And the magistrates, though in general rather tolerant, could be hostile towards strangers who seemed to upset the stabilized order in church and society. More than once Ames was led before the magistrates and even imprisoned, but he bore his adversities with that mixture of quiet patience and almost defiant boldness, which is one of the secrets of the early Quaker movement. To those, and particularly to the Amsterdam magistrates, who in 1657 wronged him, and in him the Light, he announced the judgement of the Lord in words which have an apocalyptic ring:

> Cry and complain about the misery which shall come over you, for the Lord is coming with a retaliation, vengeance and heat, to avenge the innocents' blood, and he wants to root out totally the evil-doers and the hypocrites from the earth, and the beast and the false Prophet will perish together, who have arranged themselves against the light. . . .[9]

But there were also softer tones:

> . . . and we do not wish evil to those who have wronged us, but we rather wish that the Lord may open their eyes, and that they may follow the light in their consciences, which will show them the evil they have brought about, and their injustice. . . .[10]

In view of all the troubles they met, it is amazing to see with how many people and groups Ames and his friends came into contact. Only in passing do we mention Ames's visit to 'a Jew at Amsterdam that by the Jews is cast out',[11] no doubt

---

[8] Braithwaite, W. C., *The Beginnings of Quakerism*, London 1970, reprint of 2nd ed., 408.

[9] *Een verklaringe van den onrechtvaerdighen handel van de Magistraten van Amsterdam, tegens Willem Ames, ende Humble Thatcher, voorghevallen in den jare 1657*, 7.

[10] Op. cit., 1.

[11] Ames in a letter to Margaret Fell, 17 April (O.S.) 1657, found and printed by Hull, op. cit., 205.

Spinoza,[12] to whom Ames may have been introduced by one or more of Spinoza's friends in the circle of the Amsterdam Collegiants, perhaps by Serrarius, who only a few years later acted as an intermediary between Spinoza and the secretary of the Royal Society at London, Henry Oldenburg.[13] With the dominant Reformed Church, relations were strained to the utmost. The ministers looked with deep disapproval upon people who not only bitterly attacked the existing churches, but who even 'disturbed' the church services by interrupting the preacher; it was the Amsterdam consistory which in 1657 directed the attention of the magistrates to the actions of the Quakers.[14] In their turn, the Quakers were shocked by what they considered the persecuting spirit in the 'official' church. Ames wrote to Jacobus Koelman, one of the protagonists of the 'Second Reformation', who had attacked the Quakers:

> I believe that such a pretended congregation which persecutes, banishes, imprisons, strikes, stones, reviles, etc., those of which they must confess that they are of a better conversation than they themselves are . . . are not the congregation of Christ but the synagogue of Satan. Oh, how appears the devouring wolf under the sheep's clothing.[15]

The Remonstrants, too, were severely criticized: over against the Rotterdam minister Albertus Holthenus, who, according to Ames, held the religion of the Remonstrants to be a perfect religion, Ames remarked that 'this people', while singing with David that they were enfeebled and broken-hearted, is 'neither enfeebled nor broken or bowed down, but many of them are adorned with gold, pearls, knots of ribbons and costly apparel, thereby showing that they follow the lust of their eyes and the greatness of life . . .'.[16] Besides, the Remonstrants whom Ames met denied the continuation of

---

[12] Thus, more positive still than Hull, Kannegieter, op. cit., 328f.

[13] See: Meinsma, K. O., *Spinoza en zijn Kring*, 's-Gravenhage 1896, 227, 244f., 251; Hall, A. R., and Hall, M. B. (eds.), *The Correspondence of Henry Oldenburg* II, Amsterdam 1966, 97, 381, 391, 567.

[14] Kannegieter, op. cit., 17; Evenhuis, R. B., *Ook dat was Amsterdam* III, Amsterdam 1971, 331ff.

[15] 'Aen Jacobus Coelman, Prediker, door William Ames', in [William Ames and John Higgins], *De valsche propheten bekent aen haere vrughten*, 1659, 26f.

[16] 'Eenige dwaelingen der Remonstranten . . .', in *De valsche propheten*, op. cit., 17–20.

special revelations and emphasized that in these present times Scripture is the only way and means to come to the knowledge of God and of his will.[17]

Only with the Mennonites were relations somewhat different. Ames chided the Leiden Mennonites because in a dispute they had called in the help of an Arminian – it was like Saul going to the witch of Endor – but he felt obliged to add:

> Now let no one apply this to himself who is not guilty! for I do not accuse all for the faults of some; for I know that there are many amongst you in several places, in whom there is a hunger and thirst after righteousness. . . .[18]

In Amsterdam, Ames had come into contact with Mennonites who were also members of the Collegiants' society. Now the Collegiants – most of whom were at the same time members of a Remonstrant or a Mennonite congregation – had a number of things in common with the Quakers.[19] They came together in meetings for mutual edification and there was full freedom of speech though not for the women; they were critical of the institutional aspects of church life; in particular, some of the early Collegiants believed in the possibility of a direct inspiration by the Holy Spirit, and, while at a later stage most of the Collegiants moved in a more rationalist direction, in the period around 1660 at least a number of Collegiants, such as Adam Boreel, a patrician from Zeeland,[20] and Petrus Serrarius, were of a mystical and chiliastic bent. One of the leading Collegiants was the Amsterdam Mennonite preacher Galenus Abrahamsz, who at first had some sympathy with the Quakers, even so that his opponents (belonging to the more conservative Mennonite group) accused him of having both his feet in the Quakers' barge.[21] But this was not true. Sewel writes in his *History*:

[17] *De valsche propheten,* 19; Ames, *Een ghetuyghenis des Wets van de Geest des Levens in de binnenste deelen* . . ., 1659, 3.
[18] *Een ghetuyghenis des Wets* . . . , 6f.
[19] See for the Collegiants: van Slee, J. C., *De Rijnsburger Collegianten,* Haarlem 1895; for the contacts between Collegiants and Quakers esp. 386–92.
[20] See for him as a representative of the Collegiant movement: Lindeboom, J., *Stiefkinderen van het Christendom,* 's-Gravenhage 1929, 342ff.
[21] Meihuizen, H. W., *Galenus Abrahamsz 1622–1706,* Haarlem 1954, 60.

W. Ames found also some reception among the Baptists there, who at first were pleased with him, but J. Stubs did not use them so well, as Dr. *Galenus Abrahams* once told me, who compared *Ames* to a Musician that play'd a very melodious tune, and Stubs to a Disturber of the harmonious Musick, tho' *Ames* afterwards for his great Zeal, was found Fault with also.[22]

The 'XIX Articles' of 1657, written by Galenus and D. Spruyt, contained an implicit criticism of Quakerism; Ames in his turn attacked Galenus; others also took part in the discussion (on the side of Galenus, among others, Petrus Serrarius); the number of pamphlets and the vehemence of the attacks and counter-attacks make W. I. Hull use the term, 'the war of pamphlets'.[23] According to Sewel, during Ames's lifetime the conflict between him and the Collegiants remained unsolved.

In his Sickness, which was a lingring Disease, he was told, that among the Baptists and Collegians, it was said of him, That he had changed his Judgment, and was grieved for having judged them wrongfully. But to this he said, It was not so, but that he still judged their Way of Worship, especially their Disputations and Will-Worship, to be out of the Way of the Lord. And in this belief he died in peace.[24]

The message of Ames, as we meet it in the pamphlets he wrote, was concentrated upon the one great theme of the Light, which convinces of sin and thus enables man to overcome the world[25] and to enter into the Kingdom of Christ. Was it this central theme of his message, was it something which radiated from his personality, or perhaps a combination of these and other factors, which attracted some of the Collegiants when they came into contact with Ames? No

---

[22] Sewel, W., *The History of the Rise, Increase and Progress of the Christian People called Quakers*, London 1725², 133.

[23] Hull, op. cit., 232ff. The large number of Quaker tracts, published in the Netherlands in this period, corresponds with the peak in the publication of English Quaker tracts in the same years. See Mrs M. J. F. Bitterman, 'The Early Quaker Literature of Defense', *Church History* XLII (1973), esp. 204.

[24] Op. cit., 366.

[25] See for the various aspects of this expression, used by Ames in his *A Declaration of the Witness of God*, op. cit., 15: Nuttall, G. F., 'Overcoming the world: the early Quaker programme' in D. Baker (ed.), *Sanctity and Secularity: The Church and the World*, Oxford 1973, 145–64.

doubt it was in their circle that the first meeting between Ames and Serrarius took place. From a few remarks, made by Serrarius in a pamphlet against Ames, we may conclude that initially not only was he himself impressed by the Quaker message, but also through him others came under Quaker influence: 'a number of plain pious souls, who are deceived and ensnared by these false *Lights* (to which, inadvertently, I may have given some occasion) . . . '.[26] Already the way in which Ames and Serrarius addressed each other in their pamphlets makes it clear that the two men knew each other rather intimately; at any rate we know that the meeting between Collegiants and Quakers, in which Adam Boreel bitterly attacked the Quakers because of the Nayler affair[27] and the young Quaker John Higgins no less vehemently inveighed against Boreel, was held in the house of Serrarius;[28] at this meeting, which took place on 24 August 1660, Ames, too, was present.[29] The clash marked the break between Quakers and Collegiants; 'the war of pamphlets', in which Ames and Serrarius came to take opposite sides, had already begun some years earlier.

Petrus Serrarius or Serarius, whom Ames – in a rather rash judgement – considered the most bitter opponent of the Quakers in the Netherlands,[30] was born in London, where he was baptized as Pierre Serrurier in the French Church of Threadneedle Street on the 11 May 1600.[31] In 1620, he was admitted to the Walloon College at Leiden,[32] where he stayed

[26] Serarius, P., *Van den Waere Wegh tot God, Tot Bewijs Dat niet alle LICHT dat in de Duysternisse schijnt, den Wegh zy tot God. Gestelt Tegens 't Voorgeven van William Ames . . .*, Alckmaer 1661, A12ro. Possibly Serrarius was even the translator of the first Quaker pamphlet which was translated into Dutch, that of William Dewsbury, *The Discovery of Man's Returne to his first Estate* (1654); the Dutch ed. of 1656 was translated by 'P. S.': Cadbury, H. J., 'Joshua Sprigge on the Continent', *JFHS*, XLV (1953), 60–3.

[27] The conduct of James Nayler soon became known in Holland and led to a strong anti-Quaker agitation. See: Hull, op. cit., 237–54.

[28] *Adam Boreel/ontdeckt door sijn Vruchten*, Amsterdam 1662.

[29] Serrarius gives his account of the meeting (with its date) in his: *Van den Wegh tot God*, op. cit., A2ro, vo; Ames in his: *De Misslagen en Valscheden Wederleydt, die gevonden zijn in de Extracten uyt de Schriften van Jacob Adriaensz Waere*, Amsterdam 1661, 12ff.

[30] Ames, *Het waere Licht beschermt, Ende de Onnooselheydt van de Eenvoudige bevrijt van de onwaerheden ende valsche Beschuldigingen/door Petrus Serrarius op haer geleyt . . .*, 1661, A1vo.

[31] Moens, W. J. C., *The Registers of the French Church of Threadneedle Street, London*, Lymington 1896, Pub. Huguenot Society London, IX, 35.

[32] *Livre Synodal* I, La Haye 1897, 285, 287.

till 1623.[33] No doubt, already there he met John Dury, whom some years afterwards he was to succeed as a minister in Cologne and with whom he was to have such friendly contacts at a later stage of their lives.[34] In 1623 Serrarius was accepted as a probationer in the Walloon churches. From 1624 to 1626 we find him in the province of Zeeland working as an assistant in Middelburg, Flushing and Groede.[35] In the spring of 1626, he was inducted as a minister in the Walloon church of 'Du Verger' (secret name for Cologne); the acts of the consistory contain the interesting detail, that he had in his house a number of books, left by Dury.[36] We may just wonder whether perhaps it was the reading of these books which made him leave the ministry of the church at Cologne and ultimately brought him to proclaim himself '*Ministrum Euangelii in Ecclesia universali*'.[37] We know that when he left Cologne in 1628 he was suspected of doctrinal errors,[38] though the nature of these errors does not become quite clear. It is sometimes assumed that he was dismissed in Cologne on account of chiliastic ideas, but we have grounds to suppose that at that time he was not yet a chiliast; it seems, however, that he had come under the influence of mystical tendencies which somehow alienated him from the strict Calvinism of his church.[39] In a work which he wrote shortly before his death, he confessed his sympathy for the great mystics: the author of the *Theologia Germanica*, Tauler, Ruysbroeck, Suso, Thomas à Kempis, John of the Cross and Dionysius the Carthusian;[40]

[33] Posthumus Meyjes, G. H. M., *Geschiedenis van het Waalse College te Leiden 1606–1699*, Leiden 1975, 191.

[34] Turnbull, G. H., *Hartlib, Dury and Comenius*, London 1947, 273, 293, 296f., 382. Dury stayed in the Walloon College till about March 1621: Posthumus Meyjes, loc. cit.

[35] *Livre Synodal* I, 315, 317, 319.

[36] Löhr, R., (Hrsg.), *Protokolle der Wallonischen Gemeinde in Köln von 1600–1776*, Köln 1975, 128f.

[37] Crenius, Th., *Animadversiones Philologicae et Historicae* II, Lugd. Bat. 1696, 47 (quoting Maresius).

[38] *Livres des Actes* 1 (Bibl. Wallone, Amsterdam), 145ro: '*Notre frere Pierre Serrurier venu du Verger pour voir ses parents ayant donné quelque soubcon d'erreur en la doctrine, a esté trouvé bon que l'Eglise d'Amsterdam en prenne exacte cognoissance. . . .*'

[39] W. Rood in his *Comenius and the Low Countries*, Amsterdam 1970, 149, states that he was dismissed as a result of his chiliastic views; D. Nauta, however, quoting Bayle's *Dict. hist. et crit.* III, fol. 325, mentions '*les erreurs fanatiques de Swenckveldius*' as the cause of the conflict: *Samuel Maresius*, Amsterdam 1935, 332 note 199.

[40] *Responsio ad Exercitationem Paradoxam Anonymi cujusdam, Cartesianae Sectae Discipuli*, Amsterodami 1667, 52.

at any rate, this is the line which runs through almost all his works and made him feel sympathetic, though sometimes only for a time, to those who shared his mystical interest. Gottfried Arnold, himself so deeply influenced by the mystical tradition, recognized in Serrarius a kindred spirit: he called him 'an impartial teacher and witness of the truth'.[41]

After some wanderings – in 1629 he wrote a letter to Dury from Groningen[42] – Serrarius settled in Amsterdam, where in 1630 he married Sara Paul van Offenbach.[43] In 1640 the Walloon synod, probably on behalf of or at the instigation of the Middelburg consistory, thought of making use again of the services of Serrarius, but – apparently on the grounds of information obtained from the Walloon consistory at Amsterdam – the Walloon synod, held at Zierikzee, decided not to go further in this matter, but to recommend him to the care and the prudence of the Amsterdam church.[44] Still, from the fact that in 1640 the Walloon brethren in Zeeland initially were inclined to renew the contact with Serrarius, we may gather that at least at that time they did not consider him a real heretic.

The information we possess about his Amsterdam period – he lived there until his death in 1669[45] – is of a very fragmentary character. We receive the impression that he lived in an *otium* of a probably rather comfortable character; the Groningen professor Samuel Maresius, speaking of the chiliastic speculations of Serrarius, ironically remarks: '*qui eo quod abundes otio istis speculationibus libentius indulges*'.[46] He found time to translate from German, English and Latin, to write a number of theological works, to travel frequently in England,[47]

---

[41] Arnold, G., *Fortsetzung und Erläuterung oder Dritter und Vierdter Theil der unparthey-ischen Kirchen- und Ketzer- Historie*, Franckfurt a/Mayn 1729, 1092.

[42] Turnbull, op. cit., p. 127.

[43] *Doop- en Trouwboeken* [hereafter: *D.T.B.*] Frans-Ger. Kerk [Walloon Church], Gemeente Archief [Municipal Archives; hereafter: G.A.] Amsterdam, nr 437, 11.

[44] *Livre Synodal* I, 421, 423. Here I differ from Goeters, who gives the impression that it was Serrarius himself who refused to come to Middelburg; see Goeters, W., *Die Vorbereitung des Pietismus in der reformierten Kirche der Niederlande*, Leipzig 1911, 48.

[45] He was buried on 1 October 1669: *D.T.B.* Frans-Ger. Kerk, G.A. Amsterdam, nr 1130, 295.

[46] Maresius, S., *Chiliasmus Enervatus ad D. P. Serarium*, Groningae 1664, 2vo; see for the controversy between Maresius and Serrarius: Nauta, D., op. cit., esp. 332–5.

[47] Goeters, loc. cit.

and to have personal contacts with a variety of people. An impartial judgement of his character is that of his opponent Maresius: '*Est certe vir ille, bonus, pius ac bene doctus*'.[48] Serrarius moved in the circle of the Amsterdam Collegiants and was a great friend and admirer of Galenus Abrahamsz,[49] though we have no reason to suppose that he joined the Mennonite community. For a time, he was under the spell of the world of ideas of Antoinette Bourignon, from whom at last he was alienated by a deep conflict, in which their common friend Comenius took the side of Antoinette.[50] The friendship with Dury – based on a spiritual affinity, though perhaps they did not agree in all things[51] – lasted till the end. A special mention must be made of his interest in the alchemical activities of Franciscus Mercurius van Helmont,[52] to all intents a mystic, who because of this was even held to be a Quaker in the latter part of his life.[53] Serrarius was also known for his friendly contacts with a number of Amsterdam Jews; we shall return to this in the context of an exposition of his eschatology.

The '*primitiae*' of his studies are the theses on the question whether the church can totally decline, which he defended on the 6 July 1622 in the Walloon College at Leiden; his conclusion is, that in a period of general persecution and apostasy the church can totally lose its external splendour, while yet the internal (and essential) state of the church remains intact.[54] It would be tempting to see at least something of his later ideas on the church prefigured in these theses, and indeed, the anti-triumphalist emphasis returns in more than one of his later publications, but we should not forget that often theses like these were no more than an echo of the teacher's views;

[48] Maresius, op. cit., 6.

[49] Hylkema, C. B., *Reformateurs* I–II, Haarlem 1900, 1902, *sparsim*; Meihuizen, op. cit., 63.

[50] Marthe van der Does, *Antoinette Bourignon, Sa vie (1616–80), son oeuvre*, Groningen 1974, 109, 120, 134.

[51] See Dury's reaction to the criticism of the Amsterdam minister John Rulice with regard to his contacts with Serrarius and his circle: Turnbull, op. cit., 296.

[52] Crossley, J. (ed.), *The Diary and Correspondence of Dr John Worthington* . . . III, Part I (Chetham Society), 1855, 105ff.

[53] Op. cit., 100.

[54] *Explicatio Quaestionis an Ecclesia possit deficere* . . . quam favente Deo Opt. Max. praeside . . . D. Danielo Colonio . . . tueri annitat in collegio Petrus Serrarius Londino-Anglus . . . Lugd. Bat. 1622, *passim*.

and no doubt what Serrarius defended was quite in accordance with orthodox doctrine and theology (cf. art. XXVII of the *Confessio Belgica*). In 1647 there appeared a new Dutch translation of Tauler's works from the German 'to the service of the general impartial Christendom', partly or even wholly made by Serrarius.[55] In 1654, Serrarius wrote a foreword to a translation of seventeen sermons of Joshua Sprigge on the future glory of the church.[56] Now Sprigge's eschatology had a mystical character; he emphasized the fact that the second coming of Christ is a spiritual matter, a coming of Christ in the heart of man; in this, as we shall see, his views resemble those of the Quakers. It is exactly this element by which Serrarius was deeply moved: he thoroughly sympathized with Sprigge's view that the 'future glory' does not refer to the external form of the church, but to the internal work of God in the conscience of man. 'There are some to whom Christ has already come and who are day by day enjoying him, while others look forward in painful suspense, calculating the times and the years of his coming according to the Scriptures, without knowing it is so close at hand.'[57]

Here, like Sprigge, Serrarius speaks more the language of a mystic than that of a millenarian. But only a few years later we find him defending, though not without hesitation, the chiliast position over against Moyse Amyraut, who in 1654 had attacked chiliasm in his *Du Regne de Mille Ans*; according to Wallmann (who, with Goeters, is inclined to seek the source of Serrarius' chiliasm in England), his work against Amyraut is the best introduction in the chiliastic world of thought of those times.[58] It is not easy to combine the more

[55] *Johannis Tauleri Opera . . .*, Hoorn 1647.

[56] See for Sprigge: *DNB* LIII, 426f.; Braithwaite, op. cit., 264, 566f.; Th. Sippell, 'The Testimony of Joshua Sprigge', *J.F.H.S.* XXXVIII (1946), 24, 28; and the article by H. J. Cadbury, mentioned in note 26.

[57] Sprigge, J., *De Getuygenisse Eener Aenstaende Heerlijkheyt . . .* in 't Nederlands getrouwelijk overgezet door P.S., Amsterdam 1716², 4vo.

[58] Wallmann, J., *Philipp Jakob Spener und die Anfänge des Pietismus*, Tübingen 1970, 330f. See for the causes of Serrarius' hesitation the preface of his *Assertion du Regne de Mille Ans ou de la Prospérité de l'Eglise de Christ en la Terre . . .*, Amsterdam 1657; by the various devout and pious persons who were seeking the kingdom of God within themselves and who might be hurt by his exposition of an external kingdom on earth, 'comme si on vouloit les amuser à des choses de dehors pour les empescher en la poursuite des choses internes et purement spirituelles' could be meant the English Seekers, but also the Quakers with whom Serrarius had come into contact in 1656 or 1657 (pp. *3ro, vo).

mystical eschatology of 1654 with the later chiliastic utterances, but however this may be, from 1657 onward we meet in Serrarius a staunch and consistent defender of the millenarian position. In 1659 he wrote a work, *The treading underfoot of the Holy City*, which appeared together with a translation of a work of the sixteenth-century mystic Christian Entfelder, *On the many Separations which have this year arisen in Belief* (1530).[59] Serrarius wrote this work – and added his translation of Entfelder's work – in order to defend his friend Galenus Abrahamsz against the attacks of an anti-Collegiant Mennonite.[60] The dominant motif with Serrarius is that of the decline of the present-day churches as compared with the apostolic church: all churches have deviated so far that we should not expect a restoration of the congregation of Christ unless God intervenes in a miraculous way. On this point his view of the church coincides with his chiliastic opinions: there will be no renewal of the church until the Jewish nation will be converted to Christ, who then will reign on earth together with his saints.[61]

We mention some other works in which his chiliasm becomes manifest. In 1661 Serrarius published his *Answer to the Book, published in the year 1659 . . . on the Apostasy of the Christians*,[62] in fact an enlargement of the argument of his former work, now used as a refutation of an anonymous work of a very unorthodox character, *Of the Apostasy of the Christians*.[63] This work of Serrarius is interesting not only because it contains a clear and succinct explanation of Revelation 20,[64] but because of its expositions on the doctrine of predestination and the

---

[59] Serarius, P., *De vertredinge des heyligen stadts*, ofte Een klaer bewijs van 't VERVAL der Eerste Apostolische Gemeente. . . . Mitsgaders Christiaen Entfelders Bedenckinge over de veelderley Scheuringen ende Dwalingen . . . , Amsterdam 1659. See for Entfelder: *The Mennonite Encyclopedia* II, 226f.; Jones, R. M., *Spiritual Reformers in the 16th and 17th centuries*, London 1914, 39ff.

[60] See for the background of this controversy: Meihuizen, op. cit., 61ff.

[61] See esp. pp. 10–16 and the questions, put in the addendum to the work which follows the translation of Entfelder.

[62] *Antwoort op 't Boeck in 't Jaer 1659 uytgegeven Van de Apostasie ofte Afval der Christenen* . . . , Amsterdam 1661.

[63] The author afterwards appeared to be the former *assessor* of the Court of Holland, Lancelot van Brederode. See: Zilverberg, S. B. J., 'Lancelot van Brederode en zijn geschrift "Van de Apostasie dat is van den Afval der Christenen" ', *Nederlands Archief voor Kerkgeschiedenis*, NS L (1970), 230–43.

[64] Op. cit., 14.

authority of the creeds. With regard to the first point, Serrarius tries to steer a middle course between Arminianism and the doctrine of absolute predestination, and his view has some affinity with the ideas of the school of Saumur;[65] with regard to the second point he expresses his fear of all credal formulations which do not simply repeat the words of Scripture.[66] Still, in a letter which he sent to Maresius in 1662, he stated that he believed no doctrine among Christians was more in accordance with the Scriptures than reformed doctrine.[67] This letter was written in order to accompany the gift of a little book, *A Further Message on the occasion of the great Conjunction of all Planets, in the Sign of Heaven, called Sagittarius, to happen the 1/11 December Anno 1662.*[68] In this work – to which Maresius replied in his *Chiliasmus Enervatus* – Serrarius combined his chiliastic interpretation of the relevant Old and New Testament passages with a number of very elaborate astrological speculations. He expected the speedy arrival of the fifth monarchy, the time in which the stone cut without hands (Dan. 2:34, 35) would humiliate all earthly kingdoms and fill the earth with its presence. The work is also remarkable because of its very sympathetic attitude towards the Jews – a sympathy which manifested itself in various ways; it earned for Petrus Serrarius and his brothers Louis and Joseph the praise of their fellow chiliast Jean de Labadie.[69]

In his last published work,[70] *Responsio ad Exercitationem Paradoxam Anonymi cujusdam, Cartesianae Sectae Discipuli*[71] Serrarius attacked the rationalist propositions of the anony-

---

[65] Op. cit., 153f., 160ff.

[66] Op. cit., 150.

[67] Maresius, op. cit., p. 6; according to Maresius, whose favourable judgement of the person of Serrarius we mentioned above, he was 'Ἰδιογνώμων, ac creditus in Schwenckfeldianismum pronior'.

[68] *Naerder Bericht wegens die groote Conjunctie ofte 't samenkomste van allen Planeten in het Teecken des Hemels, ghenaemt de Schutter, te geschieden den*¹/₁₁ *December Anno 1662*, Amsterdam 1662. An English translation appeared in the same year under the title: *An Awakening Warning to the Wofull World;* also a Latin edition, entitled: *Brevis Dissertatio De fatali et admiranda ... Planetarum Conjunctione ...*

[69] de Labadie, J., *Oordeel der liefde en gerechtigheyt over den jegenwoordighen toestandt der Joden*, Amsterdam 1667, A2vo, 3ro. No doubt De Labadie was influenced by Serrarius in his chiliasm: see Wallmann, loc. cit.

[70] A commentary on the Apocalypse, at one time as a manuscript in the possession of Gottfried Arnold, was never published: Arnold, loc. cit.

[71] See note 40; a Dutch edition appeared in the same year.

mous author[72] of the work *Philosophia S. Scripturae Interpres* ('Eleutheropoli', 1666). Over against the rationalist approach, Serrarius defends the mystical and pietist tradition with regard to the interpretation of Scripture, which maintains *'interpretationem S. Scripturae non esse humanarum virium, sed gratiae divinae opus'*; the right interpretation of Scripture is a matter of *'interna revelatio'*, *'internus afflatus'*. He fully realized that because of this he would be accused of 'enthusiasm', but to this he replied: *'Quid enim est Enthusiasta proprie, nisi qui profitetur dari* ἐνθουσιασμούς, i.e. *Spiritus Divini afflationes'*. In this context, the Quakers are mentioned:

> *Non enim sani theologi eas ideo rejicient, quia de Lumine et Spiritu, internisque Illuminationibus loquuntur; sed tantum, quia de Spiritu quodam jactitant qui supra S. Scripturas, imo contra S. Scripturas sese effert, et plus arrogantiae et ostentationis quam humilitatis prae se fert.*[73]

The differences between Serrarius and the Quakers revealed themselves as early as 1657. In a pamphlet, which appeared in that year, Ames rejected the objections, brought up by Serrarius and by an unknown author 'F.D.' against twenty-three questions, put by Ames.[74] The main subject of this early discussion was the central question of the relation between Scripture and Spirit. Serrarius emphasized the indispensability of the work of the Spirit for the right understanding of 'the sense of God and of Jesus Christ', and in this, of course, Ames agreed with him, though with a proviso which, in the form of an *argumentum ad hominem,* is typical of what might be called Ames's 'existential' approach: 'If you own in your life, what you express in words, the spirit will not condemn you'. But the Quakers objected to the juxtaposition of Scripture and Spirit, external and internal knowledge: we know Christ first of all internally, through the Spirit, through the Light.[75] Here

---

[72] The Amsterdam medical doctor Ludovicus Meyer; *Nieuw Nederlandsch Biografisch Woordenboek* V, 342ff.

[73] Op. cit., C3ro; 49; 51f.

[74] *Een Wederlegginge van een Boeck, ghenaemt Antwoort op 23 Vragen, door F.D. als mede een Wederlegginge van een andere Antwoort, die door P.S. daer op gedaen was, waer in syne dwaesheyt ontdeckt is* . . ., 1657; though I have not been able to trace the work of Serrarius to which Ames refers, it is easy to reconstruct the argument from what Ames writes.

[75] Op. cit., 1ro, 2ro, vo.

we touch upon the point which, ten years later, Serrarius was to formulate as a 'boasting on the Spirit which raises itself above, yea even against the Scriptures'.

In his *The treading under foot of the Holy City*, Serrarius had implicitly criticized the views of the Quakers with regard to the restoration of primitive Christianity in its purity. He shared with the Quakers the view of church history as a history of apostasy from the apostolic ideal. At the same time, he agreed with Galenus, who in the 'XIX Articles' (which contained a succinct exposition of his views) had remarked that nowadays no church or congregation was in conformity with the situation of the first and unique church, 'to which alone is given in the New Testament the names of a congregation of God, Bride, Spouse, body of Christ'.[76] Furthermore, he held – on this point he was more explicit than Galenus – that this restoration could only come about through a dramatic, an apocalyptic intervention of God, which the Quakers arbitrarily anticipated in their activities. To this, Ames replied in his *The Light which shines in the darkness proved to be the Way to God*:

> Well Peter, what an outcry has there been amongst you against me because of the judging of others? And do you now judge all men as being outside the congregation of Christ? What, has Christ in these times no body which is separate from the world? . . . has there nothing been left in the whole wide world, on the ground of which some people could be called the Apostolic Congregation of Christ?

On this point, Ames brings in the subject of eschatology, which was so closely bound up with the ecclesiological question. According to Serrarius, the coming restoration of the church could only be expected in the time of the millennium; but over against this Ames argued that the day had arrived in which God would appear in his glorious light and would be appearing in many thousands of his saints. 'If you do not believe in the Light, the day of God will pass by

[76] Abrahamsz, G., and Spruyt, D., *Nader verklaringe van de XIX Artikelen,* Amsterdam 1659, a 3ro (art. XII).

you . . . God has a people, in which Christ lives, and which can truly say: here is Christ.'[77]

Here we meet with one of the most characteristic elements of early Quaker eschatology.[78] It was not undramatic; it even had millennial traits. George Fox wrote in 1654:

> The mighty day of the Lord is coming, that all things must be brought to light, and all your secrets brought to light . . . the candle is lighted, the day does appear that God will rule in his Saints above the heathen, above the wicked and the ungodly men . . . the eternall God will rule and reign in his Saints, and be admired, magnified and glorified in them above you all.[79]

It sounds like a Fifth Monarchy pamphlet, but the eschatological scheme is different: Fox believed that the prophecy of Daniel with regard to the fifth monarchy had been fulfilled with the coming of Christ on earth in order to establish his spiritual kingdom in the hearts of men:

> . . . and this fifth kingdom the Kingdom of the Messiah is spiritual, and doth subdue the power of darkness, and gather people up into unity, and is not to be understood literally, for it is everlasting. . . .[80]

This is the background of Ames's eschatology. As we saw above, with him, too, the 'dramatic' element was not lacking, but his ultimate interest lay elsewhere: in the struggle between light and darkness, between the Light and the anti-Christian powers, as it takes place in the heart of men. Serrarius was deeply interested in the *externa* of eschatology, in the unfolding of eschatological events in the course of history, in what would happen to the people of Israel in the time of the millennium, in the future glory of the earthly kingdom of Christ. In 1661

[77] Ames, *Het Ligt dat in de duisternisse schijnt/beweesen den Weg tot God te sijn . . .*, Amsterdam 1660, 6ff.

[78] See for early Quaker eschatology: Barbour, Hugh, *The Quakers in Puritan England*, New Haven and London 1964, esp. 181–90; Underwood, T. L., 'Early Quaker Eschatology', in Toon, P. (ed.), *Puritans, the Millennium and the Future of Israel*, Cambridge and London 1970, 91–103; Ball, B. W., *A Great Expectation*, Eschatological Thought in English Protestantism to 1660, Leiden 1975, esp. 192–211.

[79] Fox, G., *Newes Coming up out of the North Sounding towards the South*, London 1654, 6.

[80] Fox, G., *An Answer to the Arguments of the Jewes . . .* [1661], esp. 11.

he published his *Of the true Way to God,* in which he put the following questions to Ames and Higgins:

> Whether at one time all the blessings, Deut. 28, intended for the people of Israel, will receive their turn on earth, as all the curses will have had their time?
>
> Whether before the last Judgment the God of Heaven will establish a Kingdom on earth, in which justice will prevail and in which there will be a fullness of peace?[81]

Ames, however, was scarcely interested. In his *The true Light protected* – a reply to *Of the true Way to God* – he put over against the chiliastic expectations of Serrarius his Quaker views, which have recently been characterized as a form of 'realized eschatology'.[82] When Serrarius argued that the great time had not yet come because the nations did not yet walk in the light of Jerusalem (Rev. 21:24) – and he took this expression quite literally—Ames shortly replied that those who are saved already walk in the light.[83] And he would not deny that something would happen in the future – the Quakers did not abandon the traditional eschatological scheme as such[84] – but what in the eyes of Serrarius took a central place, to Ames was only of marginal importance: to the questions of a more eschatological nature, put by Serrarius, he devoted no more time and space than that of a monosyllabic 'yes'. Serrarius had maintained he knew 'all this and much more' (the eschatolocal scheme) through 'the flesh of Christ', *i.e.* on the grounds of his external word; to this, Ames retorted: 'Well, Peter, this is highly boasted, as if you know everything, and we nothing; I think you have it not through his spirit, but I am content with what I know.'[85]

Ames thought of Serrarius as a man who was proud of his carnal wisdom; conversely, Serrarius saw in the Quakers people who thought they already possessed that for which they ought to wait in patience and humility. On the 17

---

[81] *Van den Waere Wegh tot God,* op. cit., 120.

[82] See for the application of the term to Quaker eschatology the studies of T. L. Underwood and B. W. Ball, mentioned in note 78.

[83] Ames, *Het waere Licht beschermt,* op. cit., 20.

[84] See also Underwood, op. cit., 103.

[85] *Het waere Licht beschermt,* op. cit., 20; 33.

March 1660 (O.S.) Serrarius wrote to an English friend, the
Seeker John Jackson:

> Your sober word I have runn through with great delight my
> spiritt symbolizing with yours and glorifying God both for the
> clearness of the truth and of the expressions of it. Would to God
> this people might increase both in multitude and earnestness. . . .
> Are these your seekers in England? Then I'le rather joyne with
> them, than with such as presume they have found and possessed.
> Better is a poor man in his uprightness acknowledging his want
> than a rich man that perverteth his words (saith Solomon) and
> makes show to bee what hee is not. This controversy beginneth
> to bee much ventilated in these parts.[86]

In this letter, Serrarius refers to John Jackson's *A Sober
Word to a Serious People* (London 1651), an interesting exposition of the Seeker's point of view,[87] with which Serrarius
clearly was more in sympathy than with that of the Quakers,
who, of course, are meant by those who 'have found and
possessed'. Here he was perhaps less than fair to the Quaker
point of view, which was not that of the *beati possidentes*;
George Fox himself had used the word 'possessors', but with
him it stood in the context of a *theologia crucis*: 'Be not professors but possessors and take heed of getting above the
cross. . . .'[88] Still, Serrarius did not condemn the Quakers in
everything; he recognized the legitimacy of their speaking
about the Light, the Spirit and internal illumination. In
spite of all differences, of all their 'contrary thoughts',
Quaker and chiliast had a common background in their
deep reverence for the work of the Spirit in the heart of
man. In view of this background, I close this tribute to a
scholar, who has written such an inspiring work on the Holy
Spirit in the life and thought of Puritans and Quakers, by
quoting from a hymn, possibly written by the English

[86] A manuscript copy of this letter – which Dr Nuttall brought to my notice some
years ago – is found between two tracts of Jackson in the *Friends' Library*, London,
Tracts Vol. 309.

[87] See for the author and his book: Jones, R. M., *Studies in Mystical Religion*, op. cit.,
458ff.

[88] Nuttall, G. F., *Studies in Christian Enthusiasm, Illustrated from Early Quakerism*,
1948, 44.

archbishop Stephen Langton, but attributed by Serrarius to the early church:[89]

Veni sancte Spiritus
et emitte caelitus
lucis tuae radium.
Da tuis fidelibus
in te confidentibus
sacrum septenarium.
Da virtutis meritum
da salutis exitum
da perenne gaudium.[90]

---

[89] *Responsio*, op. cit., 58: 'Toto corde cum Primitivae Ecclesiae ad Deum sitientibus Animabus saepe repetamus Canticum illud . . .' Serrarius reads l. 3, 'verbi tui radium'.
[90] See: Raby, F. G. E. (ed.), *The Oxford Book of Medieval Latin Verse*, Oxford 1959, 375f.; Schulte Nordholt, J. W., *Hymnen en Liederen*, Hilversum, etc., 1964, 134f., 219.

X

Occasional Conformity

CHRISTOPHER HILL

MY SUBJECT is the much-maligned practice of occasional conformity – the dissenting habit of going to a service of the Church of England once or so a year. In the later seventeenth and eighteenth centuries nonconformists qualified themselves for state office this way. Occasional conformity has in consequence been denounced as a hypocritical practice, and so no doubt it often was. But it was advocated by the Independent Henry Jacob in 1616, long before there was anything to be gained by it: it has a very respectable intellectual ancestry. I want to try to put it into some sort of historical perspective.

We may find one clue in the fact that the fiercest opponents of occasional conformity came from the extremes of the political spectrum. Quakers denounced it as a cowardly compromise; a high Tory like William Bromley spoke of 'that abominable hypocrisy, that inexcusable immorality'.[1] Occasional conformists saw themselves as following a *via media*.

On Guy Fawkes Day, 1709, Henry Sacheverell preached a sermon before the Lord Mayor and the London City Fathers which was to become famous, or notorious. His main target was occasional conformity. He took for granted the wickedness of dissent, of separation from the national church. But he delivered a rather surprising backhand blow at one of Queen Elizabeth's Archbishops of Canterbury, whom Sacheverell even down-graded – 'that false son of the church,

---

[1] Holmes, G. (ed.), *Britain after the Glorious Revolution*, 1969, 167–8.

Bishop Grindal'.[2] Against Sacheverell's rejection of Archbishop Grindal we may set John Owen's claim that he and his fellow dissenters 'do sacredly adhere unto . . . the doctrine of the Church of England . . . as it is contained in the Articles of Religion, the Books of Homilies, and declared in the authenticated writings of all the learned prelates and others for sixty years after the Reformation'.[3] He was claiming that dissenters were the true Church of England, the successors of Archbishops Grindal and Abbot.

Sacheverell's hero would presumably have been Laud, an Archbishop of Canterbury whose concept of the church was very different from that of Grindal or John Owen. Two years after Laud's death the Presbyterian Francis Cheynell declared that it was the Archbishop who had been 'rather schismatical, imposing such burdens, than the people in separating from external communion'.[4] And – to round off my argument that the idea of continuity from the pre-Laudian church to dissent had a long history – Henry Jacie as early as 1633 was recalling nostalgically Grindal's stand for preaching;[5] Michael Sparke in 1652 looked back to the days of 'that learned, pious, painful preaching Bishop Abbot'.[6] The perspective in which I want to put the practice of occasional conformity goes back for 150 years before Sacheverell's sermon.

There were problems about a Protestant state church. Calvinists had a dual concept of the church – in one sense it was the whole community, in another it was the true believers only. In Geneva or Scotland the dualism could be resolved to the extent that church and state worked closely together: by excommunication and exclusion from the sacraments, and by stressing the authority of elders, the sovereignty of the godly within the church could be upheld. But in England, where discipline was imposed from above by bishops, the situation was less satisfactory: there were Calvinists (as well as Anabaptists) who advocated separation from the national

---

[2] Sacheverell, H., *The Perils of False Brethren*, 1709, 35.

[3] Owen, J., *Works*, Edinburgh 1850–3, VII, 74–6, 133, 249; cf. III, 243–5; V, 164, 174; XV, 184–5. Cf. A. Marvell. *The Rehearsal Transpros'd*. 1672 (Oxford 1971), p. 33.

[4] Cheynell, F., *The Rise, Growth and Danger of Socinianism*, 1648, 62–6.

[5] *Collections of the Massachusetts Historical Soc.*, 4th Series, 1863, 458.

[6] Sparke, M., *Crumms of Comfort* Part II, 1652, Sig ¶, pp. 7–8, quoted in J. S. McGee, *The Godly Man in Stuart England*, Yale, 1976, 76.

church *in order that* the congregation might be able to excommunicate the ungodly. Bishops were able to score many
valid debating points against the Puritan demand for the right
of congregations to elect their own ministers – a practice
recommended by Luther, Tyndale and Calvin. How absurd
to entrust the election of ministers to the ungodly dregs of
the population, said Whitgift.[7] The negative point was more
effective than the positive argument that in England the
patron 'represented' the congregation when he presented a
minister to a living; no bishop, said one of them in 1570,
would think of accepting a minister not presented by a nobleman or a rich gentleman.[8] Presbyterian Puritans were reduced
to protesting that by election they did not mean selection by
the people proper, but by the well-to-do and godly members
of the congregation, with all the difficulties which even they
recognized in equating these two categories. They at once
laid themselves open to attack from Brownists, though of
course the latter no more believed in the democracy of all
parishioners than prelatists or Presbyterians: theirs would
have been a democracy of the *separated godly,* not of the whole
people. This seems the logical conclusion to draw from the
two propositions that (i) ministers should be elected and (ii)
the mass of the people are unregenerate. But most Calvinists
managed to avoid this logic, so strong was the surviving ideal
of a national church.

If the visible church must consist of believers only, then the
godly should logically contract out of the state church, to
reunite as a voluntary congregation. But constructing models
like this is a way in which historians deceive themselves.
Looking through the wrong end of the telescope the distinction between national church (all inhabitants) and sect (the
separated godly) seems clear, simple and absolute. But history
was not like that. A missing term is millenarianism, the belief
that in the very near future *all* will be believers – either
forcibly under the rule of the saints, or convinced by Christ's
second coming. So separation from the national church is a
short-term operation, not an end in itself: withdrawal in order

[7] Whitgift, J., *Works,* Parker Soc., 1851–3, 308, 405–6.
[8] Cf. *The Writings of John Greenwood, 1587–90,* ed. Carlson, L. H., 1962, 247–50.

to return, just as those who went into exile in the Netherlands or New England hoped to come back to a better England in the very near future. Hankerings after a national church lurked in most of those to whom posterity looks back as the founders of separatist sects, to be shed gradually only as their millenarian hopes faded into the light of common day. Historians have a natural tendency to read back what later became self-evident truths (the millennium is not just round the corner) into the men of the sixteenth and seventeenth centuries, by whom these truths were discovered, if at all, only after long and painful search.

It seems obvious to us that an appeal to Scripture is an appeal to the anarchy of individual consciences: that men have an infinite capacity to read into Scripture what they want to find there. But our recognition of this fact is the result of much disillusioning experience. In the sixteenth century, with the long secret text of the Bible at last made available, it seemed crystal clear to its readers. Similarly in mid-seventeenth-century England many men believed that once episcopal hindrances had been abolished, it was only a matter of time before all good men agreed on what the Bible said. The spirit of Christ *must* be the same for all men; otherwise why should God allow the Scriptures to be translated, bishops to be overthrown? University-educated divines might try to confuse simple Bible-readers: but in the apocalyptic atmosphere of the sixteen-forties there was widespread confidence in the clarity of the text for honest mechanics, such as the Apostles themselves had been. The early Christian belief that the time was short reappeared: separation or exile would be only of brief duration. Our knowledge of the end of the story is an obstacle to understanding.

Let us remind ourselves of the historical sequence of events. Many of the sincerest English reformers were disappointed with the half-way and erastian nature of the English Reformation, which allowed the survival of bishops and patronage and failed to use church property for education or poor relief. The experience of the years 1547 to 1559 led them to hope for continuing reformation. After surviving the testing period of Mary's reign, convinced protestants, whether they had been exiles or had remained at home, soon felt that Elizabeth's settlement did not go far enough. Once it was clear that she would survive, inevitably alternative schemes for further reformation were put forward.

Grindal's elevation to the see of Canterbury in 1576 and his 'opening to the left' seemed to offer prospects of a Scottish type of episcopacy modified by presbyterian institutions – the social pretensions of the higher clergy reduced, the shire rather than the diocese the unit of church administration, weaker church courts working with the natural rulers of the countryside, the J.Ps., the Geneva Bible replacing the Bishops' Bible. Elizabeth's suspension of Grindal in 1577 was a parting of the ways. His successor, Whitgift, was soon accused of setting 'himself against the gentry'.[9]

Presbyterianism was predominantly a clerical movement. But its sponsors needed the magistrate's support, since otherwise there would be no coercive power behind the church's discipline once bishops lost their political power. Hence the hope for reform by Parliament. When, as in the classis movement, local groups tried to introduce a form of presbyterian discipline in advance of Parliamentary legislation, they soon found that their censures could be effective only if backed by the authority of a friendly J.P. or even a bishop.[10] But Presbyterians were never a sect: they hoped for the transformation of the English church into a presbyterian church. They were perfectly straightforward in their appeals to Queen and Parliament against bishops. They had no more wish to abolish the Church of England than had Henry VIII and Cranmer; like them, the Presbyterians wished to change its government, in a further (and final) instalment of national reformation.

In the nineties the bishops went over to the offensive. They broke up the classis movement, and drove some of its supporters into separatism, or into appealing for popular support. This in its turn lessened Parliamentary enthusiasm for the movement. By the end of the century the hierarchy's

[9] I have drawn heavily in this paragraph on P. Collinson, *The Elizabethan Puritan Movement* (1967), esp. 164–7, 185–9 and 334.

[10] Usher, R. G. (ed.), *The Presbyterian Movement in the Reign of Queen Elizabeth*, Camden Soc., 3rd Series, VIII, 1905, 53–7, 102, and *passim*.

counter-attack, backed up by Hooker's theoretical statement, had been very successful; and this produced a new situation. The Marprelate Tracts' mocking exposure of the defects of the bishops and their government was intended to bring the whole hierarchy into disrepute. They contributed to drive many to believe that the Church of England was so fundamentally corrupt that reform from within was hopeless: that the only correct solution was withdrawal. Browne was followed into sectarianism by John Penry, probably at least part author of the Marprelate Tracts. On the other hand the scurrility and popular appeal of the tracts shocked and frightened some clerical and gentlemen supporters of the Presbyterian movement (including Thomas Cartwright himself); together with the rise of separatism this helped to complete the rout of its defenders in Parliament. The appeal to the people failed to produce rapid reformation; the Presbyterian policy of reform by political coup had failed. Only two alternatives remained – separatism, which might mean exile and would certainly involve persecution; or conformity and a longer-term, slower policy of permeation from within by preaching, moral reform, self-discipline.

For those who clung on to reformation from within there were many possibilities, varying from inaction to what was later to be called non-separating congregationalism. A congregation could often *in fact* (though not in theory) control its own affairs in many ways. There were some urban livings (fourteen or so in London) where patronage lay in the parishioners or the town corporation. The patronage of a friendly gentleman could on occasion be used: advowsons could indeed be bought.[11] In a poor living (and there were many such) judicious granting and withholding of an augmentation to the minister's stipend made it easier to obtain a man with the right theological outlook. Where it was impossible to influence the incumbent of the living, members of the congregation could subscribe to bring in a lecturer who would meet their doctrinal wishes. As Professor Haller put it, 'every Puritan group which at any time joined together

[11] Cf. G. F. Nuttall, *Visible Saints,* 23–4; my *Economic Problems of the Church,* Oxford 1956, ch. IV.

to engage a lecturer tended to become a gathered church'.[12] This *de facto* Independency was expressed by Henry Jacob and William Bradshaw, insisting on the right of each congregation to control its own affairs under the King, who would be the head of the churches in England rather than of the Church of England.

So far we have been looking at the disintegration of what we may call 'official' Puritanism – the nonconformity of clergymen, gentlemen and merchants. But we must not forget – as contemporaries never forget – the much older stream of lower-class heresy, into contact with which the separating congregations inevitably came after the watershed of the nineties. In England we can trace, from Lollards through Marian martyrs to Elizabethan Familists and the radical sectaries of the sixteen-forties and fifties, a tradition of hostility to the state and its church, to clerical pretensions, to tithes, church courts and oaths, to military service. The state existed to maintain privileges. The radical sects were the organizations of the unprivileged. They were far more difficult to suppress than a national Presbyterian movement. The fact that they lacked the backing of a Walsingham or a Leicester was a help rather than a hindrance: they had to exist underground. As units the congregations might be broken up or driven into exile, but only as units. The movement could not be utterly stamped out, since it met deep spiritual and social needs of the people.

Conformist Puritans differentiated themselves sharply from lower-class sectaries, and indeed claimed that their preaching, their discipline, would help to protect the English church and state from this threat no less than from that of papistry. Even a Commonwealth man like John Hales thought that Anabaptists and libertines, who 'would have all things in common', had helped to cause the English risings of 1549.[13] Anabaptism became a shorthand expression for traditional lower-class rejection of the state church, though rejection of tithes was no Anabaptist innovation, going back at least to

[12] Haller, W., *Liberty and Reformation in the Puritan Revolution*, N.Y. 1955, 119.
[13] White, H. C., *Social Criticism in Popular Religious Literature of the Sixteenth Century*, N.Y. 1944, 121.

the Lollards. But a man who believed in adult baptism would
naturally have scruples about paying tithes. This challenged
the economic stability of the state church at its most sensitive
point. In England the claim to collect tithes held by many
thousand impropriators made their rejection seem a threat to
lay as well as to clerical property. All commentators agree
that separatists were drawn from and attempted to appeal to
the poorer classes. Henry VIII spoke sharply of those who
'whilst their hands were busied about their manufactures had
their heads also beating about points of divinity'.[14] A rare
point of agreement between Archbishop Laud and Roger
Williams was that 'most of the separation' were 'of the lower
sort of people'. John Lilburne described Brownists as 'the
base and obscure fellows of the world'.[15] An early Baptist
like Leonard Busher, writing in 1614, was concerned with
social reform for the benefit of the poor – the abolition of
hanging for theft and of whipping, and putting an end to
begging and to the exploitation of the poor by usury and low
wages.[16] Walwyn and Winstanley, the most radical reformers,
and the men of greatest social compassion who wrote during
the interregnum, came from Baptist circles.

For many years the bishops and their supporters had been
arguing that 'if you had once made an equality . . . among the
clergy, it would not be long or you attempted the same among
the laity'.[17] Bishop Cooper and the Earl of Hertford, long
before James I, argued that no bishop would mean no king,
no nobility.[18] Richard Hooker pointed out that the titles of
bishops to their estates were as good as any lay title to
property. When in the Long Parliament Oliver Cromwell
attacked the great livings of bishops, he was at once told that
parity in the church would lead to parity in the state.[19] It was
perhaps an unfair argument for Elizabethan bishops to use
against those who wanted to establish a presbyterian disci-

[14] Quoted in Jones, R. M., *Studies in Mystical Religion*, 1909, 402.
[15] Williams, Roger, *The Bloudy Tenent of Persecution*, 1644, Hanserd Knollys Soc.,
1848, 425; Lilburne, J., *Come out of her my people*, 1639, 19.
[16] Busher, L., *Religious Peace*, 1614, 70–1.
[17] Whitgift, op. cit., II, 398.
[18] Cooper, T., *An Admonition to the People of England*, 1589, ed. 1895, 168–9.
[19] See my *Economic Problems of the Church* 46–7; Laud, W., *Works*, Oxford 1847–60,
I, 82–3.

pline; but the events of the sixteen-forties were to show that opponents of religious toleration had a case. Even Lord Brooke, in 1641, distinguished between those Anabaptists who 'hold free will; community of all things; deny magistracy; and refuse to baptize their children' on the one hand, and the other sort 'who only deny baptism to their children till they come to years of discretion, and then they baptize them; but in other things they agree with the Church of England'. The former type should be cut down by the sword as heretics or atheists: the latter were to be pitied. Brooke was quite clear about the 'twofold' nature of the sect.[20] Unlike Oliver Cromwell later he felt that no mercy should be shown to its seditious lower-class wing.

It is worth emphasizing the deep historical roots of the Puritan *via media,* of the call for further reformation *in order* (among other things) to avoid the threat from socially subversive sectaries. Calvin himself began his chapter 'Of Civil Government' by observing that he wrote at a time when 'on the one hand, frantic and barbarous men are furiously endeavouring to overturn the order established by God', whilst on the other hand 'the flatterers of princes, extolling their power without measure, hesitate not to oppose it to the government of God'. He thought it his duty to 'meet both extremes'. But he first demonstrated the necessity for a coercive state machine, against 'those who would have men to live pell-mell like rats among straw'.[21] Calvin's object was to show that true religion is completely consistent with the maintenance of private property, and yet does not necessitate an entirely uncritical acceptance of the existing state.

So when the bishops' campaign of the fifteen-eighties and nineties forced Puritans to choose between submission and separation, most educated, middle-class responsible Puritan laymen chose the former and so avoided being forced into the company of seditious sectaries. It was a preview of the dilemma of 1662, and on both occasions there was much disagreement among those who were faced with it. We must

---

[20] Brooke, *A Discourse . . . of . . . Episcopacie,* 1641, in *Traces on Liberty in the Puritan Revolution,* ed. Haller, W., N.Y. 1933, II, 140.

[21] Calvin, J., *The Institutes of the Christian Religion* (trans. H. Beveridge 1949), II, 651–4.

understand the position of 'non-separating congregationalists' in this light. They wanted to preserve links with the state church, for social as well as for theological reasons. Even though tarrying for the magistrate had failed, and some with Robert Browne argued for reformation without tarrying for any, the ultimate hope of most of those whom we call Congregationalists was still to take over and modify the state church. Browne himself – Lord Burleigh's cousin – returned to the fold. Others went to New England, where they made it clear that they wished to maintain a state church and that they had no use for religious toleration. The settlement of New England was at first envisaged as a sort of revolution by evasion: many New Englanders did in fact return to England in the sixteen-forties and fifties.

Attitudes towards conformity among the respectable separatists varied. Henry Jacob and his church allowed occasional conformity. John Robinson and his followers could hear preaching in the Church of England, but would communicate only privately with godly members of that church. Thomas Hooker also thought it lawful to hear preaching in the state church, but not to communicate either with that church or with Brownists. Henry Ainsworth and Francis Johnson were against any form of occasional conformity.[22] Helwys criticized refusal to break away from the national church.[23]

In 1610 James I appointed an Archbishop of Canterbury in the Grindal tradition, George Abbot; and for nearly two decades life was relatively easy for those who still hoped for further reformation of the national church. But the advent of Laud changed all that. He suppressed the Feoffees for Impropriations who were buying in patronage and augmenting livings; he forced subscriptions of conformity on ministers who were anxious only to have a blind eye turned on them; he suppressed lecturers, driving many of them into exile; his effective control of King and government made it clear that a loose federation of fairly self-governing congregations under

[22] Burrage, C. E., *Early English Dissenters*, Cambridge 1912, I, 171, 293, 305; II, 163, 301–2.

[23] Helwys, T., *The Mistery of Inquity*, 1612, 86–94, 101–23. I quote from the Baptist Historical Soc's reprint, 1935.

the royal supremacy was no longer practical politics. Laud seemed to Puritans the true schismatic, not only because of his attempt to enforce new doctrines and ceremonies, but also because he ended intercommunion with the Dutch and Huguenot churches. This isolated England from the Calvinist international at a time when the threatened advance of Catholicism in the Thirty Years War seemed to make unity among Protestants politically as well as theologically essential. Oliver Cromwell thought of emigrating; in fact he stayed on and led the policy of co-operating with lower-class sectaries to rescue England from the threatened return of popery.

It is in this perspective that we must see the conflict between those whom we too loosely call Presbyterians and Independents in the sixteen-forties. Both groups wanted to shift the centre of government of the Church of England so as to incorporate Calvinist Puritans. But the experience of the Dedham Classis[24] – and of Scotland – had shown that the full Presbyterian discipline could be established and maintained only with the aid of the civil magistrate. The 'Presbyterians' were those who feared the social consequences of religious toleration most of all: the 'Independents' would ideally have favoured a system of congregational Presbyterianism such as existed in New England, but when they were forced into accepting more radical allies they had sufficient social confidence to believe that they could ride the storm. They had no wish to replace the tyranny of old priest by that of new presbyter: there was never much support for Presbyterian discipline from lay members of congregations. By temporarily withdrawing from the state church, and either going into exile or risking persecution at home, the congregations ensured – however unintentionally – that they were composed exclusively of picked and devoted men and women; they acquired confidence, determination, experience in self-government and an ability to manoeuvre and compromise without fear of being swamped. When the Revolution came the 'Independents' led its radical wing with assurance: 'Presbyterians' on the contrary always had one eye looking backwards to the church and state machine within which they had flourished, and which

[24] Usher, op. cit., *passim*.

they had only wished to modify to their own advantage. They could, in fact, regain the position they had held from 1640 to 1644 only by restoring monarchy and bishops to check the lower orders.

So both 'Presbyterians' and 'Independents' proved right, the former in believing that religious toleration would threaten the existence of a state church subordinated to the natural rulers, the 'Independents' in believing that in the long run they could contain the radicals and win through to a state church which would neither be clerically dominated nor wield a strict coercive discipline. That is why so many 'Independent' M.P.s became elders when a Presbyterian state church was set up after 1646. They had wanted a greater share for laymen in running the episcopal Church of England, and certainly did not want to abolish a national church. If a Presbyterian establishment was the best that could be had, it was their duty to help to run it in the hope of continuing reformation.[25]

But these experiments were not carried out in a vacuum, and here 'Presbyterian' fears proved more justified than 'Independent' confidence. The *de facto* religious toleration of the sixteen-forties allowed the really radical sects to emerge from underground, to meet and discuss in public, to organize themselves under their own mechanic preachers, free from all control, either of the state church or of their social superiors. Liberty of the press, and the cheapness of publishing, allowed their views to be printed: the New Model Army spread these views across the country as it advanced to victory. Separatism ceased to be what it had been for the respectable godly, a regrettable necessity forced on them by the bishops; it became a principle, as it long had been for the radical sectaries. In the liberty of the forties and fifties the latter were able to work out a much more sophisticated theology and theory of church organization.

So the real dividing question was nakedly revealed: a state church or none? 'Presbyterians' and 'Independents' came from social groups which could hope to control a state church,

[25] Cf. Hexter, J., 'The Problem of the Presbyterian Independents', in *Reappraisals in History*, 1961, 163–84.

either from on top through Parliament, or by infiltration from below, through patronage and local influence. Those who whole-heartedly believed in religious toleration came initially from social groups which had no such aspirations – at least not until there had been a radical reform in the state as well as in the church, such as Levellers and others came to advocate.

I express this in what some may consider excessively sociological terms, in deliberate reaction against those denominational historians who are apt to push the origins of their own sect *in an organized form* too far back. A group of Dissenting Brethren in the Westminster Assembly in 1643, for instance, urged 'all ministers and people . . . to forbear, for a convenient time, the joining of themselves into church societies of any kind whatsoever, until they see whether the right rule will not be commended to them in this orderly way'.[26] They still envisaged a state church. The New Model Army's Heads of Proposals of 1647 shared the Dissenting Brethren's attitude to the church which they nevertheless wished to retain: there should be no coercive jurisdiction, no penalties for failure to attend parish churches, the Solemn League and Covenant should not be enforced. Liberty not to attend parish churches, legally established from 1650, was denounced by Presbyterians as schism, just as Whitgift had denounced their practice of electing ministers as schism.

The Barebones Parliament of 1653 contemplated abolishing tithes and patronage. But the moderates, in reaction against what they regarded as the 'excesses' of Ranters and Quakers, forced a change of attitude. Masson was quite right to say that 'the protectorate came into being in the interests of a conservative interest generally, and especially for the preservation of an established church and the universities'.[27] Cromwell's state church reunited moderate episcopalians, Presbyterians and many Congregationalists, together with some Baptists, in a loose federation of fairly independent congregations; it preserved tithes (until some better form of maintenance could be devised) and patronage. It would have perpetuated a more

---

[26] Waddington, J., *Congregational History, 1567–1700*, 1874, 426.
[27] Masson, D., *Life of Milton*, 1859–80, IV, 566–8.

liberal form of the *de facto* independency which many congregations had enjoyed in the pre-Laudian church. There was a great extension of election by parishes. Triers were not empowered to impose any doctrinal test. A Presbyterian who later became a bishop tells us that in 1656 Episcopalians, Presbyterians and Independents were in a fair way to be reconciled and 'upon a very calm temper'.[28] It has been estimated that nearly a quarter of the 1760 ministers ejected after 1660, were Congregationalists. Cromwell's church also contained Baptist ministers: six out of thirty-eight of the Triers of 1654 were Baptists.[29] But we should remember that Baptists and Congregationalists were still not precisely differentiated, and that inter-communion was frequent. John Bunyan described himself as a Congregationalist as late as 1672.[30] Many ministers who objected on principle to tithes were prepared to accept state stipends financed from confiscated church lands, as ministers in New England received stipends from towns, not tithes from parishioners.

Cromwell's was a last attempt at a broad-based national church, under lay control. It deserves more consideration from advocates of Protestant reunion. But Parliament repeatedly tried under the Protectorate to narrow the standards of orthodoxy to be imposed on ministers before they were eligible for public maintenance; and Quakers and the radicals among the Baptists fiercely attacked the whole conception of a state-endowed church and a professional ministry.

So the lines of division hardened. Any elected Parliament insisted on some ecclesiastical jurisdiction, on the maintenance of tithes, patronage and a professional clergy against the mechanic preachers of the radical sects. In 1656 the Nayler case was a turning point, convincing conservatives that a definition of orthodoxy enforced by persecution was the only alternative to anarchy and social unrest. It split the radicals, many of whom felt Nayler had gone too far. It finally destroyed the illusion that agreement could be reached among

[28] *Thurloe State Papers*, 1742, V, 598–601.
[29] Nuttall, op. cit., 22–6, 37–8, 135–41; Underwood, A. C., *A History of the English Baptists*, 1947, 80, 96, 103–5; Matthews, A. G. (ed.), *Calamy Revised*, Oxford 1934, xiii and xli.
[30] Waddington, op. cit., 606.

God's people. Presbyterians and Independents clung on to the idea of a state church; receipt of public maintenance was accepted in the Independent Savoy Declaration of 1658.[31]

Even the Levellers (in the 1649 Agreement of the People), Winstanley and Harrington had favoured some sort of national church whose ministers should be elected by parishioners (all of them, not only the godly). Those who rejected a national church were those who rejected a professional clergy, carrying the priesthood of all believers to the logical conclusion that a church can exist without a minister. If there were ministers, they should (in the words of the London Baptists in 1660), 'freely minister to others', and the congregation ought in return 'freely to communicate necessary things to the ministers (upon the account of their charge)'.[32]

In time the sects abandoned hope of recapturing the state church from which they had seceded. The unique freedom of the forties and fifties hastened acceptance of a more permanent sectarian status by enabling far more national organization than had ever before been possible. The Particular Baptists for instance had a confession by 1644. But in the fifties Baptists were still quarrelling among themselves about the lawfulness of taking tithes – which means about the lawfulness of a state church.[33] By the end of the fifties Quakers, General and Particular Baptists were organized as sects. The Westminster Assembly of Divines produced a Presbyterian confession which it had hoped would be accepted as that of the Church of England. The Congregationalists significantly adopted no separate confession till 1658, when they were rightly becoming nervous about the future of the state church to which they had hitherto accommodated themselves.

Who gained from the restoration? Sociologically it represented a reunion of the natural rulers against the radical lower orders. The royalist/Anglican position had always been clear and consistent. Edward Hyde in the early forties was unable

[31] Dale, R. W., *History of English Congregationalism*, 1907, 387–8; cf. Nuttall, op. cit., 64–8, 99–100.

[32] Nuttall, op. cit., 85–8; Barclay, R., *The Inner Life of the Religious Societies of the Commonwealth*, 1876, 338; Underhill, E. B. (ed.), *Confessions of Faith . . . of . . . the Baptist Churches of England in the Seventeenth Century*, Hanserd Knollys Soc., 1854, 115.

[33] Nuttall, op. cit., 135–41.

to conceive how religion could be preserved without bishops, who were necessary to control the lower clergy who control the people; nor could the law and government of the state subsist if the government of the church was altered.[34] This social argument for episcopacy was often used. Henry Oxinden in 1643 called on all gentlemen 'rather to maintain episcopal government . . . than to introduce I know not what Presbyterial government, which will . . . equalize men of mean conditions with the gentry'.[35]

In 1660 the lay descendants of the conformist Puritans got a national church purged of its dependence on a would-be absolutist monarchy and of divine-right bishops: a church subordinated to Parliament. The 'Presbyterians' were the real beneficiaries of the restoration, but they owed their victory to their own earlier defeat by 'Independents' and sectaries; and they accelerated their triumph by sacrificing those who had made that victory possible, together with the Presbyterian clergy. The latter, however, were relieved at the restoration of their fear of the radicals. That old anti-episcopalian Richard Baxter told the House of Commons in April 1660 that now 'the question is not whether bishops or no but whether discipline or none'.[36] The point was vividly put by Henry Newcome, looking back after his dispossession: 'Though soon after the settlement of the nation [note the phrase] we saw ourselves the despised and cheated party, . . . yet . . . I would not change conditions . . . to have it as it was then, as bad as it is'. For then 'we lay at the mercy and impulse of a giddy, hot-headed, bloody multitude' and faced 'a Munsterian anarchy. . . . far sadder than particular persecution'.[37]

The restoration purges, and especially the Corporation Acts, checked the spread of radical sectarianism in the towns; reassertion of the rule of parson and squire, plus the Act of Settlement, stopped the sects from spreading to the countryside. As a contemporary put it, 'conventicles can be suppressed in the country where the gentry live and the people have a dependence on them, . . . but in corporations it will

[34] Clarendon, *History of the Rebellion*, 1888, I, 406–7.
[35] Gardiner, D. (ed.), *The Oxinden and Peyton Letters, 1642–1670*, 1937, 36–7.
[36] Baxter, R., *A Sermon of Repentance*, 1660, 43.
[37] Newcome, H., *Autobiography*, Chetham Soc., XXVII, 1852, 118–19.

never be carried through by the magistrates or inhabitants, their livelihood consisting altogether in trade, and this depending one upon another, so that when any of these shall appear to act in the least measure, their trade shall decline, and . . . their credit with it'.[38] Tithes were preserved.

After 1660 Puritanism subsided into nonconformity: the sects were more concerned to disclaim responsibility for the execution of Charles I than with positive political ideals. Pacifism and withdrawal from politics became the order of the day, reinforced by the Clarendon Code's exclusion of dissenters from national and local politics, and from the universities. The Calvinist international no longer existed, and indeed religion had ceased to be a prime mover in international affairs. The French Huguenots were as anxious as English dissenters to proclaim that they were peace-loving, non-religious bodies. A further factor in the retreat of aggressive Puritanism was the fact that the state church quietly stole many of its clothes. Bishops no longer discouraged preaching and sabbatarianism, and the bourgeois virtues secured the patronage of men like Archbishop Tillotson, who thought that 'virtue promotes our outward temporal interests'.[39]

Clearly neither Presbyterians nor Independents could any longer hope to capture the state church. Yet neither took kindly to the status of sectary. Twelve days after St Bartholomew's Day, 1662, Henry Newcome and his Lancashire Presbyterian friends resolved 'to stick close to the public ordinances, and not to separate' from the national church.[40] In the same year the Presbyterian Philip Henry was 'loath . . . to encourage the people to separation', even though he himself felt constrained to resign his living. When Charles II issued his Declaration of Indulgence ten years later, Henry feared that 'the danger is lest the allowance of separate places help to overthrow our parish-order . . . and beget divisions and animosities amongst us which no honest heart but would rather should be healed'. He faced a 'trilemma' – 'either to turn flat Independents, or to strike in with the conformists,

[38] C.S.P.D., 1675–6, 1.
[39] Tillotson, J., *Sermons on Several Subjects and Occasions*, 1748, IX, 134–6.
[40] Newcome, H., *Diary*, ed. T. Heywood, 1849, 119.

or to sit down in former silence and sufferings till the Lord shall open a more effectual door'. The Independents in Henry's view 'unchurch the nation; . . . they pluck up the hedge of parish order'. Henry's choice of words is significant. He remained an occasional conformist.[41]

Attitudes towards the restored church among those 'who separate, or are rather driven from, the present worship'[42] varied even more dramatically than they had varied after the fifteen-nineties. Some ministers managed to retain their livings without conforming at all – e.g. Henry Swift at Peniston, Yorkshire, who had the support of the chief families in the parish. Richard Heyricke continued Warden of Manchester collegiate church. Bishop Wilkins of Chester, a Puritan who conformed in 1660, was very helpful to his old friends in such matters. Other clergymen, like John Ray, resigned their benefices and became lay conforming members of the Church of England. Presbyterians favoured occasional conformity more than others: there were no Presbyterian ordinations before 1672. Baxter, William Bates, Thomas Manton, Francis Chandler, Thomas Jolly and the members of his church, were all occasional conformists. Oliver Heywood attended his parish church from time to time.[43] John Humfrey, although pastor to a nonconformist congregation, was 'a conformist parishioner', who never received the sacrament elsewhere than at his parish church.[44]

In 1702 Calamy and other dissenters told Bishop Burnet that occasional conformity had been 'used by some of the most eminent of our ministers since 1662, with a design to show their charity towards the church'.[45] Norman Sykes observes that it is likely that acceptance of occasional conformity as a test for office took this practice into account. 'No man,' said John Howe sensibly, 'can allow himself to think that what he before accounted lawful is by this super-

---

[41] Lee, M. H. (ed.), *Diaries and Letters of Philip Henry*, 1882, 99, 250, 277, 328–9.
[42] Owen, J., *Works*, XV, 102.
[43] Whiting, C. E., *Studies in English Puritanism from the Restoration to the Revolution, 1660–1688*, 1931, 32–3, 60–1; Thirsk, Joan (ed.), *The Restoration*, 1976, 63.
[44] Matthews, op. cit., 284–5; Lacey, D. R., *Dissent and Parliamentary Politics in England, 1661–1689*, Rutgers U.P. 1969, 23.
[45] Calamy, E., *An Historical Account of My Own Life,* ed. J. T. Rutt, 1829, I, 473.

vening condition become unlawful.'[46] Occasional conformity no doubt increased when the laws were more strictly enforced between the mid-seventies and mid-eighties.[47] Pressure to accept a separatist position perhaps came from the Presbyterian laity rather than from the clergy. Congregations, wrote Joseph Williamson in 1671, 'are now come to ride their teachers and make them do what they will . . . All the Presbyterians are grown to Independents, and so must the teachers'.[48]

Among the Independents Thomas Goodwin thought that in most parishes, 'where ignorance and profaneness overwhelm the generality, scandalousness and simony the ministers themselves', occasional conformity was inadmissible. But in others there were godly members of congregations, under a godly minister whom they had chosen to cleave to. With such it was lawful to communicate, as with the reformed churches on the Continent. It was indeed a duty to 'break down this partition wall'; 'nothing provokes more than . . . to deny such churches to be true churches of Christ'.[49] John Owen, however, after arguing the case at length, came down against occasional conformity.[50] William Bridge threatened to excommunicate members of his flock who even went to hear an Anglican service. Philip Nye thought it was not only lawful but a duty to *hear* ministers of the state church, though not to join in common prayer or communion. His son Henry favoured occasional conformity.[51]

Some Baptists even were occasional conformists. John Tombes was doctrinally a Baptist. But he is not usually claimed by historians of the sect because, in addition to holding a living from 1630 to 1662, and apparently favouring a Presbyterian system of church organization, he said on his death-bed that he dared not separate from communion with the Church of England 'any farther than by going out of the church whilst that office [baptism] was performed, and

---

[46] Sykes, N., *From Sheldon to Secker*, Cambridge 1959, 96–7.
[47] Lacey, op. cit., 26.
[48] C.S.P.D., 1671, 496.
[49] Goodwin, T., *Works*, Edinburgh 1861–3, I, 557–8.
[50] Owen, J., *Works*, XV, 65–8, 345–58, 378–9; XVI, 241–53.
[51] Lacey, op. cit., 17.

returning in again when it was ended'. Thomas Grantham, who is accepted as a Baptist by Baptist historians, was buried in St Stephen's Church, Norwich, by the vicar of that church, who was later himself buried in the same grave.[52]

Patriotism came into it too. The breach with Rome had been a national act, or at least was so represented. Under Elizabeth and again in the sixteen-twenties and fifties Puritans had been the spearhead of English patriotism against Spain and the Pope. Under Laud patriotism and prelacy seemed to be diametrically opposed. But in the sixteen-seventies and eighties the Church of England revealed itself as firmly anti-Catholic, anti-French and therefore patriotic. The trial of the Seven Bishops probably did more to make occasional conformists than the mere desire for office.

After 1660 England again enjoyed a 'balanced constitution'. The existence of nonconformity checked effective reform of the Church of England; but the strength of urban dissent made the state church necessary to prevent any spread of radicalism to the countryside. The Tory/Anglican gentry bitterly resented the existence of dissent, which prevented the balance being tipped their way. In 1664 Elias Ashmole had told his Presbyterian brother-in-law Henry Newcome that 'nonconformity could be nothing but in expectation of a change'.[53] A change may have seemed likely to alarmed Tories in 1679–81, when the number of dissenting M.Ps. increased significantly.[54] They therefore had the less objection to governmental interference with borough charters, until James II actually began to flirt with Quakers and to re-open local government to real radicals.[55] The one constant factor from 1640 to 1689 is that any House of Commons elected on the traditional franchise favoured persecution, at least of radical sectaries.

Surveying the period from 1559 to 1689 we might say that the first century of the Church of England was also its last.

[52] Underwood, op. cit., 69–70, 111. The Presbyterian Philip Henry was also buried in his parish church (Lee, op. cit., 379–82).
[53] Newcome, *Autobiography*, I, 145.
[54] Lacey, op. cit., 119.
[55] For examples see Miller, J., *Popery and Politics in England, 1660–1688*, Cambridge 1973, 209, 219–22.

After 1660 the state church was no longer inclusive of the whole nation. Some of the most truly religious English men and women had chosen to withdraw from it, or had been driven out of it. The failure of the seventeenth-century revolutionaries to implement their ideals led to the exclusion of their successors from the main stream of national, political and intellectual life. Nonconformity was forced into a position in which it became provincial, 'sectarian' and 'Puritan' in the pejorative sense of those words.

One of the problems which Puritans failed to solve was the relation of the godly minority to the ungodly masses of the population. Puritans and sectaries had seemed to threaten the traditional rural way of life, its (pagan) festivals, its cakes and ale and cock-fighting. Presbyterians wanted the lower orders to be more severely disciplined; the sects would have offered them preaching, but would not have compelled them to come in. In the late forties and fifties we often find conservative Puritans like Baxter complaining that the ungodly rabble hankered after the old episcopal church. They had their revenge in 1660. The Church of England survived primarily because of its deep roots among the landed ruling class, whose interests it shared in so many ways; but also because 'the rabble' preferred its conservative laxity to an enforced Presbyterian discipline, or the voluntary self-discipline of the sects. In the last resort the main numerical support for the episcopal church may have come from those who least believed in its doctrines. The church and king mobs which bawled for Sacheverell in 1709 came from parts of London where there were fewest parish churches. Outside London, his strongest backing came from the Welsh border region.[56]

The sects, despite many attempts, never succeeded in re-uniting: they managed to survive insofar as they got respectable middle- or lower-middle-class support; and nearly died of it in the eighteenth century. Those which lacked such support – Muggletonians and the like – continued to exist only in a vestigial form. Wesley had to start from scratch in appealing to the lowest classes; and there was no room for Methodism in the state church either.

[56] Holmes, G., *The Trial of Dr Sacheverell*, 1973, ch. VII and X.

After 1660 the radical sectaries were driven out of politics, into which they had intruded during the revolutionary decades. They abandoned political aspirations, partly because of their own recognition that Christ's kingdom was not going to be realized on earth now, partly because three decades of fierce persecution weeded out all but the most convinced believers, at a time when belief was becoming more other-worldly. The final result was a disastrous split in English social and educational life, the consequences of which are still with us. The Church of England defined the privileged sector. Chamberlayne's *Angliae Notitia* of 1669 complained that 'it hath been observed even by strangers, that the iniquity of the present times in England is such that of all the Christian clergy of Europe . . . none are so little respected, beloved, obeyed or rewarded as the present . . . clergy of England'. But Isaac Barrow tells us that the Church of England enjoys 'the favour of the almost whole nobility and gentry'.[57] Both were right. The practice of occasional conformity was not only a way of qualifying insincere merchants for membership of town corporations; it was also a last symbolic attempt to bridge the gulf between the two cultures and proclaim the unity of the Protestant nation.

[57] Chamberlayne, Edward, *Angliae Notitia*, 1669, 401; Osmond, P. H., *Isaac Barrow: His Life and Times*, 1944, 77.

XI

Daniel Defoe and Scotland

BASIL HALL

DEFOE had been brought up in a devout Presbyterian home under the ministry of Dr Samuel Annesley, an ejected minister after 1662, and had been intended by his parents for the Presbyterian ministry. He wrote somewhat obscurely in 1709: 'I acknowledge the pulpit is none of my office. It was my disaster first to be set apart for, and then to be set apart from the honour of that sacred employ'.[1] A case can be made for showing that Defoe was a life-long loyal and thorough Protestant and also a religious man devoted to the cause of dissent, though eventually with personal variations; he especially admired the principles of the Presbyterians and he suffered in person and means for these causes. He remembered in later life that earlier he had been at a horse-race at Aylesbury where he saw the 'late Duke of Monmouth' amid a 'mighty confluence' of noblemen and gentlemen: to see the Protestant hero and note his following was a more likely motive than to seek a doubtful gain among the jockeys.[2] Defoe soon after that event followed the Protestant star in 1685, accompanied by old comrades from the Newington Academy, men 'who had they lived would have been extraordinary men of their kind, viz., Kitt, Battersby, young Jenkyns, Hewling', names lost to us but elegiacally remembered by him as having ridden with him to Bridgwater only to end their days with the Western Martyrs.[3] Defoe twice

[1] *A Review of the State of the British Nation*, 22 October 1709, vol. XV, 341.
[2] *A Tour Through the Whole Island of Great Britain*, Everyman ed., 1974, vol. 11, 26.
[3] Cited without reference in Morley, H., *The Earlier Life and Chief Earlier Works of Daniel Defoe*, 1889, 17.

gave a brief and vivid account of the final events of
Monmouth's venture, the skirmish near Bath, and the defeat
at Sedgemoor, and, when it was safe to do so, claimed proudly
his involvement as 'a Man that had been in Arms under the
Duke of Monmouth against the cruelty and Arbitrary
Government of his pretended Father'.[4] The Protestant flail
had failed at Sedgemoor but Defoe opposed Jacobitism in
word and deed in any of its forms throughout his life. It was
with the coming of the new Protestant star, William of
Orange, that he found escape from frustration, and in 1689
he rode, 'gallantly mounted and richly accoutred', to welcome
King William who had arrived in London to attend the Lord
Mayor's City feast. Enraged by the pamphleteer Tutchin, who
in *The Foreigners* had attacked the King and the Dutch, Defoe
wrote the poem *The True-Born Englishman,* 1701, which brought
him to the King's notice, approval and employment. He
always kept King William's memory with gratitude. Had the
King lived he wrote later he 'would never have suffered me
to be treated as I have been in the world'.[5] For his most
famous pamphlet, *The Shortest Way with Dissenters,* 1702,
brought him humiliation by his mockery of the extreme High-
Flying Churchmen, for him Jacobites by implication. But his
timing was wrong since he issued the pamphlet a few month's
after King William's death, and the High Court party were
now in a position to destroy Defoe. His humiliation lay in his
condemnation to the pillory and Newgate by a hostile Bench
consisting of High Church Tories some of whom he had
bitterly attacked previously for their political subservience
and vicious manners, and also of some Whig dissenters whom
he attacked for their practice of Occasional Conformity
which he regarded as the betrayal of dissenting principles for
the sake of holding office.[6] A brief triumph came when the
mob surrounded the pillory to protect him from attack and
praised his courage. This triumph which he marked by his

---

[4] Defoe believed in Monmouth's legitimacy; see his *The Succession to the Crown of England Considered,* 1701. The reference to being in arms is in *An Appeal to Honour and Justice Tho' it be of his Worst Enemies,* 1715, 195, 198.

[5] *An Appeal,* 195.

[6] See J. R. Moore, *Defoe in the Pillory and other Studies,* N.Y. 1973, for Defoe's trial and its consequences.

Hymn to the Pillory was short, for bankruptcy and Newgate held him fast. These events left their mark on him and did him psychological damage. He withdrew more into himself, his tendency to ambiguity and secretiveness increased. He was rescued by the Tory minister Harley; his family had already been given financial aid by Queen Anne who had written sympathetically to him when he was in prison. From now on he served the Queen and the government which had delivered him from ruin and probably from an ignominious death in gaol. His ambivalent sympathy for the rogue who had to fight a dangerous world for survival was to emerge with him from his observations of life in Newgate and appear in his later fiction. He wrote once: 'This is an age of Plot and Deceit and of Contradiction and Paradox. . . . It is very hard under all these Masks to see the true countenance of any Man.'[7] Again, he wrote he had learned to live dangerously like 'a Grenadier on the Counterscarp'.[8] All his life after William's death he lived as an outsider who had learned to use his masks and write in paradoxes, a career which prepared him for the life of a secret agent.

His experience and career as a Presbyterian, his Protestant zeal, his talent for persuasion, for example in his *Review,* his admiration for the Church of Scotland were all to be used in dangerous and fruitful activities insufficiently recognized in the making of the Union of England and Scotland. After his trial and its consequences when he had become more secretive, the years which followed showed him following a devious course as a secret agent of the government, though he claimed later he had been allowed to write according to his own judgement as a freelance while not opposing the Queen or her ministers in person, using this as an opportunity to maintain a Whig-like viewpoint while writing at times in the Tory interest.[9] He became a leading, if not the leading,

[7] *A Letter to Mr Bisset*, 1709, 6, 10.

[8] *An Appeal,* 203; the phrase is also used in a letter to Robert Harley, 11 September 1707, Healey, G. H., *The Letters of Daniel Defoe,* 1955, 242.

[9] This occasioned the view held of Defoe at the time, and since, that he was unscrupulous and time-serving. His most notorious activity was his writing for Nathaniel Mist's *Weekly Journal,* devoted to the Pretender. He undertook with some relish the dangerous work of 'disabling and enervating it' and other Tory journals, so that 'they could do no mischief to the government'. The role of double-agent appealed to his

figure in Harley's intelligence network in England. He wrote to Harley twice in July 1704 urging on him a system of private intelligence, '. . . a Correspondence may be Efficiently Settled with Every Part of England, and all the World beside, and yet the Very Clarkes Employ'd Not kno' what They are a doeing.' He referred to Sir Francis Walsingham, secretary of state to Elizabeth I, as the 'Greatest Master of Intelligence of the Age' and advised Harley to 'keep a Sett of Faithfull Emissary's Selected by your Own Judgement. Let them be your Constant Intelligencers of Private affaires in the Court. . . . Intelligence is the Soul of all Publick business.'[10]

This secretiveness and the clear apprehension of the theory and experience of the practice of intelligence work on behalf of the Queen's devious, subtle and able minister Harley must have brought Harley and then his successor Godolphin to see how important an agent Defoe could be in Scotland. Defoe had himself pointed out to Harley in his letter of July 1704:

A Settl'd Intelligence in Scotland, a Thing Strangely Neglected there, is without doubt the Principall Occasion of the present Misunderstandings between the Two kingdoms. In the last Reign it Caus'd the king to have Many ill things Put upon him, and worse are very likely to follow. I beg Leave to give a Longer Scheme of thoughts on that head, than is Proper here, and a Method how the Scotts may be brought to Reason.[11]

Harley could see him as uniquely matched for a unique service. Defoe had feared for the security of Protestantism in England (and in Scotland), and he had welcomed Monmouth and William to ensure it; he saw that the union of the kingdoms, by securing the establishment of the Church of Scotland in its Presbyterian form, would be a bulwark for a Protestant succession in England. He saw that through this union and its religious settlement the Pretender and Jacobitism would receive the severest political defeat, and all that would be

temperament, but it seems to be at least inconsistent with his assertions of his own honesty.
[10] *Letters*, 28, 30, 32.
[11] Ibid., 38.

left to them would be the double gamble of rebellion and the uncertain prospects of French military aid. He had welcomed Marlborough's bold conduct of the war since he hoped its successful conclusion would gravely weaken the military power of the French and their willingness to support Jacobite ventures. He was a Presbyterian, which would commend him to the Scots whose Church Assembly was a major political force: an Anglican agent from England to Scotland would have been defeated before he began. Yet he was not committed to the traditional dogmatic systems which still held their ground in Scotland; he could speak to various parties with a tolerant mind on theological issues, and even to Scottish Episcopalians, though it would have been difficult to find Episcopalians who were not, by force of political circumstances, Jacobite in sympathy. 'Prelatism' he had no use for and Protestant extreme sectarianism bored him. Other opinions which he held he knew he should keep to himself for fear of being thought lacking in zeal. A minister of the Church of Scotland could hardly accept unchallenged Defoe's view, in his *Advice to all Parties*, of 1705:

> The Church of England and the Dissenters have but one interest, one foundation and but one end. The moderate churchmen and the charitable Dissenters are the same denomination of Christians, and all the difference which now, looked at near the eye, shows large, if viewed at the distance of Heaven, shows not itself.[12]

This minister, and much more so a fierce Cameronian, or indeed a plain Scottish Protestant, would have considered Defoe's view of Popery in the same pamphlet to be an intolerable example of English frivolity.

> I believe there are a hundred thousand plain country fellows in England, who could spend their blood against Popery, that do not know whether it be a man or a horse.[13]

The theologically minded Scots knew better on that subject. But if challenged on this he could reply it was indignant

---

[12] *Advice to All Parties, By the Author of the True-Born Englishman*, 1705, 21.
[13] Ibid., 23.

irony. Further, Defoe was obviously a master of propaganda; his irony and sarcasm were well-tried and well-sharpened weapons which he could use with pungent force during the preparation of the union, and in defence of it after it was made. His ambiguous temperament allowed him to be open and direct in a coffee-house or merchant's home, showing himself as a no-nonsense businessman who knew about trade-figures and could be as ready as an accountant with estimates of tax-ratios between the two uniting countries, impressive in Edinburgh and the trading towns he would visit in Scotland.[14] On the other hand that ambiguity could show him as the solitary observer, by his isolation capable of seeing what another would not have noticed since he would allow himself no partisan emotions in this service, and would be able coolly to calculate where the centre of an issue lay amid the confusions created by conflicting Scottish passions. He possessed something of the temperament and talents which the English sometimes admire in, or concede to, the Scots; for example, hard-headed shrewdness, and, as one writer said of him, 'he could have founded a colony'; successful colonizing in the former English territories was going to be a Scottish export enterprise after the union.[15]

That Harley saw all these elements in Defoe as a potentially successful agent in Scotland where such a man could be so useful is a matter of reasonable conjecture: he knew Defoe well, he had used him already as an agent, he knew Defoe's powers, and, to Defoe's uneasy surprise, in September 1706, he ordered Defoe to go to Scotland. That Defoe did well to be uneasy and write to Harley saying that he would go like Abraham not knowing whither he went, could be seen from his writing in the letter of July 1704 that Richelieu's success in part was due to the fact that he 'Sacrifyz'd Many a faithfull Agent after he had Done his Duty, that he might be sure he should Not be betraid'.[16] The modern vogue for spy-stories has made us familiar with such a state of mind. Defoe could

[14] *Letters*, 155 ff.
[15] *The Gentleman's Magazine*, vol. LV, 882. 'Swift is superficial when compared with the details in Robinson Crusoe; Defoe might have founded a colony' – Scott, W., *Miscellaneous Prose Works*, Edinburgh 1847, I. 401.
[16] *Letters*, 39.

foresee what exposure on the counterscarp might involve. The dangers of the Edinburgh mob would be familiar to him. In his reply to Harley's order he asked, 'Under these Anxious Thoughts', for the terms of the treaty and the characters of those who had taken part at the meetings in London, and then he set down what he conceived to be duties: to inform himself of those parties and persons who were opposing the proposed union, and find ways to undermine their activities; in conversation to persuade people of influence on the virtues of the union; to write rejoinders to pamphlets attacking the union, the English and the Court; to remove apprehensions about the future status of the Church of Scotland.[17] Harley knew that the strongest opposition would come from Scotland, and had decided that the proposed treaty should be put to the Scottish Parliament first.

The commissioners from both kingdoms had begun to meet in London to prepare the treaty in April 1706, and Defoe was in print by May 1706 with two pamphlets aimed at removing prejudices against it; he continued the series (with four more under the same title) into the following January after he had arrived in Scotland.[18] But it was in his *Review* that he hammered at the theme of the necessity of Union, exposing the absurdities of the arguments against it, and pushing everything that could be said for it. From 26 September 1706, onwards, the main line of his *Review* papers was mockery and cool indignation at the views of opponents of the union. His readers who may not have realized at first that he was in Scotland grumbled that he overworked the subject.[19] In the issue of 26 September he wrote of enemies of the Union in England who were trying to persuade the dissenters to reject it and then would put the blame on them if the Union failed. Also he noted that English groups were intending to dissuade the Scots from accepting the treaty and then blame the Scots for the breakdown, while others were arguing that the English Church and English trade would be

[17] Ibid., 126.
[18] *An Essay at Removing National Prejudices against a Union with Scotland,* Part I, 1706, Parts II–IV, 1706, Part V, 1707.
[19] 'The fellow could talk of nothing but the Union, and had grown mighty dull of late' – cited by T. Wright, *The Life of Daniel Defoe,* 1894, 140.

ruined by a Union. He already was juxtaposing the contradictory positions of his opponents, namely, that it would destroy the dissenters and at the same time be hazardous to the established Church; that it would be fatal to unite and yet an army should be sent to Scotland to enforce it.[20] In the same year he wrote a fanfare for his efforts to persuade the Scots to union in his full length poem *Caledonia* in honour of Scotland and the Scots nation.[21]

Scotland was not unknown territory to him: it will be remembered that Crusoe after visiting the north of his island was greatly attracted by it and Defoe as is well known said *Robinson Crusoe* was an allegory of his own life; from 1684 onward Defoe visited Scotland more than once, and had at one stage thought of removing his wife and family there either to avoid pressures from his creditors, or because he intended to set up in business and live there.[22] On 8 October he asserted that those who wanted a war with Scotland would, if it were ever to happen, be the foremost among those to stay at home, and he presented them with what he called paradoxes, statements based on his knowledge of former wars between the two countries and the futility of hoping to achieve anything by war in 1706.[23] He pointed to the real possibility of war if efforts for union failed and 'it will be bloody enough . . . every Victory you gain over them in the Field, you are beaten; the Scots are Conquerors by it and you Losers. . . . At the End of every War, they shall have the better of you, it shall cost you more to hold them, than to gain them, and more to lose them, than both.'[24] He appears to suggest that those in favour of a war are a section of the High Flying Tories who hold no hatred to the Scots as a nation but as a Presbyterian nation they detest them. He concluded with further telling paradoxes which by their irony and cogency must have been galling:

---

[20] *Review,* 6 October 1706, vol. III, 477, 478.
[21] *Caledonia,* 1706, a folio of 60 pages dedicated to the Duke of Queensbery.
[22] *Letters,* 188. Burch, C. E., 'Benjamin Defoe at Edinburgh University, 1710–11', *The Philological Quarterly,* vol. XIX, October 1940, 347, 348.
[23] *Review,* 8 October 1706, vol. III, 478.
[24] Ibid., 478.

How is it possible, they can propose a conquest of Scotland as the shortest Way to Peace and Union?

Secondly, How a Union with England can endanger the Church of England; and the Kirk of Scotland both at the same time?

Thirdly, How a Union of Scotland will endanger the Succession of the House of Hannover, and the House of Perkin, etc., both together? [presumably a mocking reference to the Pretender by inferring a status no higher for him than that of Perkin Warbeck].[25]

In the next issue on 10 October he stated that the advantages of union 'are infinite unaccountable, and as Times go, incredible on both sides', and showed who would be the losers by it, essentially the French who would no longer be able by bribes and guile to weaken both kingdoms and turn 'the Swords of two valiant People into the Bowels of one another'.[26] On 12 October he mocked at a pamphlet by what he called an 'English Jacobite', since only so stupid a person could entertain such a notion; who was apparently worried by the Act of Security in Scotland being a contrivance for recalling the Stuarts when the Act intended the very opposite and as to 'Religion and Liberty, no Man can suppose so meanly of the Scots, as to imagine they could seek the safety of those two in a Frenchified Papist'.[27] Again and again he repeated in the *Review* in his period in Scotland that Scotland would increase in wealth, England in strength, both in tranquillity. He referred as frequently to the attitude of both the Churches, each suspicious of the consequences of union, and demonstrated that it meant the establishing of the constitution and church-government of both Churches; that English Churchmen were foolish to fear a Presbyterian-izing movement from Scotland since they outnumbered Presbyterians and dissenters by eight to one; that as things were the Church of Scotland was far from safe, and that nothing but miracle or union could make it so; and he urged that dissenters of both nations would be more secure. On this point if he meant they need not fear the return of Popery he was right, but in the event, in Scotland, one consequence of

25 Ibid., 479.
26 Ibid., 481.
27 Ibid., 486.

the union was Presbyterian anger at the proposed English folly of toleration since for them Episcopalians were a dangerous sect for whom toleration meant increase, insolence and challenge.[28] He noted such oddities of emotion as the assertion in Scotland that the English dissenters were inclined to episcopacy and therefore not to be trusted by the kirk; or the Scots nobleman who told dismal stories of Scots merchants with no trade, the poor with no salt, and the ladies no husbands; and also he bantered those who claimed he had been sent to Scotland in the pay of the English Presbyterians to bring about the union.[29] He cited a vigorous critic of his presence in Scotland and his writings there: he was accused of 'Lyes, Forgeries and Counterfeit', the intention being to ruin the Church of God. He mocked at these criticisms, for he had to suppress the questioning and obey Harley's construction.[30]

On 24 October 1706, he wrote to Harley of the meeting of the Commission of Assembly and of his concern about some members claiming *jure divino* principles, but the more moderate majority had overruled them:

> I work incessantly with (the Commission). They go from me seemingly satisfyed . . . but are the Same Men when they Come Among Their parties . . . in Generall They are the Wisest weak men, the Falsest honest men, and the steadyest Unsettled people Ever I met with. . . .[31]

Defoe's paradox is typical both of his style and of his anxieties over the Presbyterian ministers; these men were important, their decisions in the Church courts were more significant politically than activities in the Scots Parliament. Defoe added a vivid brief account of rioting in the streets; 'a Scots Rabble is the worst of its kind'. He told of how the mob sought him as 'One of the English dogs', and of his fear of being 'De Witted'; this reads like a passage from Scott's description of the Porteous riots, but with crisper force.[32] In his next letter

---

[28] *Letters*, 302, 303; *Review*, vol. III, 539.
[29] *Review*, 18 March 1707, vol. IV, 61; *Letters*, 196.
[30] *Review*, 2 September 1707, vol. IV, 347.
[31] *Letters*, 133.
[32] Ibid., 135. Jan de Witt, Grand Pensionary, was killed by a Dutch mob, 1672.

he wrote of a country minister preaching before the Commission on the text, 'Let no man take thy Crown', pretending an allegory but reminding the impatient Defoe, who endured its length, of the mob's fury at the threatened loss of the Scots Crown.[33] Defoe used his skills as a casuist in trying to ease the conscience of those who consulted him on the problem of uniting with so sinful a nation as England. Addresses were coming in from all parts written in what he called the 'Cant of the Old Times' about a further Reformation, and of the Lord's covenanted people.[34] He also noted the presence of a number of Highlanders in Edinburgh: 'Formidable Fellows', fully armed, who 'are all Gentlemen, will take affront from No Man, and Insolent to the Last Degree.'[35] He was worried that if a rising took place the army was not to be relied upon save for many of its officers; and there was real danger from the west where if the weather had not been excessively wet 15,000 Cameronians might apparently have marched on Edinburgh.[36] Harley seems to have been stirred enough to send some English regiments up to the Border to encourage the troops in Edinburgh who felt their weakness in numbers, since Defoe, anxiously excusing his presumption of offering advice, feared that 'if there is the least Violence here all will be in blood'.[37]

Defoe was not only working to alleviate ecclesiastical and party problems but also energetically advising the committee of Scots lords which dealt with the complex issues of how Scottish taxation and excise duties could be related to the English fiscal pattern, and of the 'equivalents' to be paid to Scotland, and 'drawbacks' paid to England.[38] He talked to merchants of conditions of trade, allaying their fears on the price of oatmeal, salt, and corn, which on one matter at least

[33] Ibid., 137.
[34] Ibid., 142. Defoe added in the *Review*, 26 November 1706, that these addresses were invented by Episcopalian Jacobites to confuse the people. This was denied by the Jacobite, George Lockhart, in *Memoirs concerning the Affairs of Scotland*, 1714, 229.
[35] *Letters*, 146.
[36] Ibid., 150. The Rev. John Hepburn, the Cameronian leader, was opposing the Union publicly but privately betraying Cameronian proposals to the government: possibly he wanted to save his people from bloodshed.
[37] Ibid., 150 and fn. 7.
[38] Ibid., 143 and fn. 2.

were justified; this was to cause trouble later, as he had foreseen and sought to forestall.[39] This he did in Edinburgh and
through his agents elsewhere. He wrote complacently to
Harley that he was all things to all men; to merchants he talked
trade; to lawyers he said he would purchase land, though 'God
knows where the Money is to pay for it', a hint ignored by
Harley; to men from Aberdeen, Glasgow, Perth and the rest
he talked of identifying with their concerns as though he
were a fish merchant, or woollen or linen trader. 'I think I do
my Country good service, and this Country no Injury', was,
in the event, a reasonable comment.[40] But he described himself to Harley with blunt bravado as a spy with sums of money
at his disposal. This must have been an attempt to quieten the
embarrassment shown in the self-justifying passages in the
Serious Reflections of Robinson Crusoe; he was the outsider free
from other men's passions triumphing a little in his aloofness
and yet uneasily aware that he was manipulating, for example,
some of the ministers whom he regarded as honest men. Scots
wrote of him with furious contempt, suspecting him at the
time; and two hundred years later Scots, after the publication
of his letters to Harley, have expressed as great a loathing –
though perhaps they should take more note of how some
Scots could be bought then.[41]

In my Mannagemt here I am a perfect Emissary. I act the Old part
of Cardinal Richlieu. I have my spyes and my Pensioners In Every
place, and I Confess tis the Easyest thing in the World to hire
people here to betray their friends. I have spies in the Commission,
in the parliament, and in the assembly and Undr pretence of
writeing my history I have Every thing told me.[42]

The Duke of Hamilton, one of the powerful opponents of
the Union, who was cheered by the mob when he appeared

[39] Ibid., 165, 166. In 1725 riots broke out on the Malt Tax at Glasgow and Edinburgh;
see Brown, P. H., *History of Scotland*, 1911, vol. III, 207–9.

[40] Ibid., 159, 163.

[41] Lockhart, op. cit., and *Memoirs of the Life of Sir John Clerk of Penicuick (1676–1755)*,
Scot. Hist. Soc., 1892, 64. For a more recent view see J. D. Cockburn, 'Daniel Defoe
in Scotland', *Scottish Review* 1900, 'a cool rascal . . . a liar . . . greedy . . . moral myopia
. . . sordid qualities', 268, 269.

[42] *Letters*, 211.

DANIEL DEFOE AND SCOTLAND

in the streets of Edinburgh, and who was a constant cause of anxiety to Defoe and his Scottish associates, was present at a private meeting where a bitter protest was made, with some point, saying that the Scots Parliament was imposed upon by English bribes, that Scotland was betrayed, bought and sold. Defoe learned of this and wrote to Harley that he had been promised a view of the document.

> In This Little scheme of their Affaires I have Acted a True Spy to you, for by an Unexpected success I have Obtained a Converse with Some Gentlemen belonging to the D of Gordon [a leading Jacobite] who are Very Frank, and I Dare say the particulars Above are Unknown to the Commissioner himself.[43]

His spying was, among other matters, seriously concerned to forestall risings by Jacobites or by Cameronians or by urban armed mobs, which could have escalated into serious bloodshed.

Defoe was accused at the time and since of making money out of his activities; therefore what he did with the money Harley had originally entrusted to him for use in Scotland requires a comment. Defoe was an enthusiastic if not always successful business man, though he blamed his losses on the malice of others or on his political misfortunes; but that he misappropriated money to his own use is at least unproven, to use the Scots law term, if not simply erroneous.

> I am lookt on as an English man that Designs to settle here and I think am perfectly Unsuspected and hope on that foot I do some service – Onely I spend you a great Deal of Money at which I am Concern'd but see no Remedy if I will go thro' with the work . . . tis the most Expensive place I was Ever in. But Indeed Sir that has not been my Expence. . . . I have had £75 and a Horse of Mr Bell [of Newcastle upon Tyne, Harley's man for keeping himself in touch with the North of England and Scotland] and I have just 13 guineas left, about 6 of which I propose to lay Out for the Effectual spreading this letter at Glasgow [*A Letter to the Glasgow Men*] and over all the West, and therefore propose to print about 2500 of them . . . the press Dreins me . . . I cannot relieve My Own

[43] Ibid., 189.

Affairs Tho' My Wife wrott me last week she had been 10 dayes without Money. . . .[44]

There is no explicit reference in Defoe's letters to the passing on of money from Harley through Defoe and his agents to Scots in positions of influence, unless his words referring to the Assembly represent bribery: 'I have some Engines at work among the Ministers. In short, Money will do anything here'.[45] Much of the money went, as the passages quoted above show, in paying his agents, in printing his replies to attacks on the proposed union and less in providing for his daily living and that of his family. He had been made bankrupt in the summer of 1705 and his pleas for help from Harley mount anxiously: 'If you were to See Me Now . . . without Subsistence, allmost grown shabby in Cloths . . . you would be Mov'd to hasten My Relief.'[46] In the event Defoe obtained neither an adequate government post, nor an adequate livelihood from his work on behalf of Harley and Godolphin during his periods of residence in Scotland. Except for the occasionally bantering tone about Scottish affairs to suit Harley's taste there is nothing to indicate that he was other than strongly committed to the Union, for religious and politically Protestant reasons. He genuinely admired the Scots, he told Harley: 'This people are a Sober, Religious and Gallant Nation, the country good, the Soil in most places capable of vast improvements and nothing wanting but English Stocks, English Art [agricultural and other skills] and English Trade to make us all one great people'. His powerful influence in the making of the Union can be seen in Godolphin's letter to Harley: 'Defoe's letter is serious and deserves reflection. I believe it is true and it ought to guide us very much in what we are doing here. . . .'[47]

After the Union was accomplished he stayed in Scotland again at least twice, the first time on government service. In 1708 he went at three days notice: 'My errand was such as

[44] Ibid., 143, 159, 169, 170 ('The grenadier on the counterscarp' again appears, 242).
[45] Ibid., 214.
[46] Ibid., 242.
[47] Ibid., 187, for Defoe on Scotland. Godolphin's letter is in Hist. Mss. Commission Report, Appendix, vol. IV, 382.

was far from being unfit for a sovereign to direct or an honest man to perform.' His visit was caused by the threat of a Jacobite rising, the French had attempted to put ashore the Pretender with 5,000 men in the hope of rousing Jacobite support and wrecking the Union.[48] Defoe was disturbed to find that there were a number of Scots now saying leave matters to the English and the French and 'let them fight it out'. What his activities were is apparently not now known. In 1709 his full and careful account of the *History of the Union* was published in which he used the records which he ironically described as being trustingly given to him by the Scots at the time of the Union – but the book shows no hint of irony or disparagement, on the contrary it is fair to the Scots and still valuable for its historical content. From September 1710 to February 1711 he was again in Scotland but it is not clear that this time he was on government service. He had seriously thought of bringing his family to Scotland and setting up in business: his talking of trade to the Scots whom he had hoped to influence earlier was not merely a feigned political game. He entered his son Benjamin at the University of Edinburgh, and Defoe strongly promoted the view that English and Irish dissenters should study there since they were excluded from other universities by tests and oaths imposed on them. He wrote a memorial to Principal Carstares on this subject, the man who had been especially helpful to him in the Assembly in winning support for the Union: 'Mr Carstares in particular Merits Great Consideration' he had told Harley at the time.[49] Defoe had joined the Edinburgh Society for the Reformation of Manners in March 1707 from which he withdrew with indignation in February 1709 because the Society had failed to reprove one of its members, a barrister accused of adultery before the Edinburgh Presbytery: 'While you punish the poor, and the rich go free . . . you must expect to find no reformation in Scotland, any more than they have in England' – he had accused the English Society of the same weakness.[50] With

[48] Ibid., 257, fn. 1.
[49] Ibid., 193 and fn. 3. Also see Burch, C. E., 'Benjamin Defoe at Edinburgh University 1710–11', *The Philological Quarterly,* vol. XIX, October 1940, 347, 348.
[50] *Review*, 7 April 1709, vol. VI, no. 4. See also Burch, C. E., 'Defoe and the Edinburgh Society for the Reformation of Manners', *Review of English Studies*, vol. XVI, 1940, 306ff.

journalistic enterprise he gained control of *The Edinburgh Courant* and *The Scots Postman*; further, he worked with the publisher John Moncur.[51] Defoe even began to use Scots words in his pamphlets of this period.

His concern for Scotland's economic strength and the sound establishment of the Church of Scotland can be seen in his memorandum of improvements for Scotland which contained a long description of the need for a naval base and dockyards in the Forth, anticipating by two hundred years the building of Rosyth, which would bring money, employment and increase of trade and provide against French naval attacks.[52] Again with real and urgent seriousness he insisted to Harley in 1710 that the Church of Scotland should be maintained in its just Rights and Established privilege', and that 'Intrusions', 'the placing of ministers in parishes without the consent of the people, should be discouraged and discontinued: Defoe foresaw what was coming. In 1712 the Toleration Act was passed allowing toleration to Scots Episcopalian dissenters which also restored the rights of patrons in appointing ministers to parishes. Defoe was justified in his anxiety: patronage was to be a continuing source of trouble and was a major cause of the Disruption of 1843.[53] In his *Memoirs of the Church of Scotland* of 1717 he wrote that since no full account of the glories and sufferings of the Church of Scotland was yet given he, 'an officious stranger', set seriously about the work 'of ransoming things of such Consequence from the grave of forgetfulness' out of 'disinterested Zeal to do Justice and Service to the People of Scotland and to a Cause which he had too much at Heart to let lie neglected any longer . . .'. He opposed the idea that the Superintendents of the sixteenth century had anything to do with episcopacy since they were subject to the Assembly of the Church, and he burst into capitals in stating that that Church was 'PRESBYTERIAN' in its origin. It is a highly partisan account; for example, the

[51] In 1710. For Moncur see Chalmers, G., Collection on Scottish Printing, Laing Mss., 11, 452, Edinburgh University Library.

[52] *The Proposall*, in *Letters*, 280-4.

[53] Defoe described Scottish indignation at the proposed Act in the *Review*, 26 January, 2 and 5 February 1711-12. He wrote to Harley urgently opposing it 24 January, 1711-12, *Letters* 367.

murder of Archbishop Sharp is glossed over, which is strange in view of Defoe's dislike of fanaticism. With dialogue and anecdotes which give colour and energy to his story he praises those who suffered persecution after 1689 including indiscriminately those whom Scott gently mocked in *Old Mortality*. His real goal was no doubt both to oppose Episcopalianism tarnished by its Jacobitism, and to protest against the 'Depradation' upon the Church through the restoration of lay patronage: he cites in full a memorandum sent to him earlier by three ministers of whom his friend Carstares was one, seeking his aid to try and prevent the passing of the Act.[54]

His dedication of his *History of the Union* to Queen Anne contains the following words which sum up his rejoicing at the Union:

> The humble Author of these sheets, Madam, having, amidst a throng of disasters and sorrows, been honoured by your Majesty, in being rendered serviceable to this great transaction, and having pass'd thro' all the hazards tumults, and disorders of that critical time thinks himself doubly rewarded in having the honour to lay this account of these things at your Majesty's feet. . . . It ought to be the comfort as it is the honour of the Church of Scotland, that her safety and your Majesty's authority, have the same establishment, are linked together by the indissolvable bonds of the same Union, have the same enemies, and the same friends, and in all probability must have the same duration.[55]

He had been pilloried for supporting the principles of dissent through which he believed that the liberty of the people could be secured, for opposing the Anglican High Church *jure divino* position and Jacobitism, and for seeking to ensure the Protestant succession. His humiliation was not entirely overcome by his having to become a government agent – though he spoke of this proudly as the service of the Queen – but the aspirations for which he had suffered were achieved

---

[54] *Memoirs of the Church of Scotland*, 8, 90. *The Memorandum*, which is a very able analysis of the historical background to and disadvantages of patronage was written by William Carstares, Thomas Blackwell and Robert Baillie. Defoe wrote to Harley 14 February 1711–12, 'I sincerely Lament the Case of Scotland' when the Act was before the Lords, *Letters*, 370.

[55] *History*, 1786, Dedication, XXVIII, XXVI.

as the words in his Dedication to Anne show. His later years formed his great period of creative power in the novels which express his own paradoxical view of human nature combined with an intense realism hardly achieved by other writers. He died where he began in the parish of St Giles, Cripplegate, described in the parish register as 'gentleman', another aspiration won.[56] He was obscurely in hiding from the threat of a debtor's prison, away from his family, a solitary, an outsider and enigmatic to the last, having achieved a life of remarkable variety, danger, obloquy, downfall and triumph. His last words might have been those of his favourite utterance, *Te Deum Laudamus,* showing as they did his buoyant trust in the Providence which had given him a Daemon like that of Socrates to drive him onward.[57]

[56] Wright, 383ff.
[57] Wright, 40, 83, 150, 163, 181.

XII

Jonathan Edwards's Notebooks for 'A History of the Work of Redemption'[1]

```
————◁◦◉◦▷————
```

JOHN F. WILSON

WHEN, in 1757, Jonathan Edwards received the invitation to succeed his son-in-law, Aaron Burr, as president of the recently founded College of New Jersey, he expressed considerable reluctance not only because he thought himself unsuited for the job by temperament and training, but also because he foresaw that undertaking the leadership of the struggling institution would deflect him from several projects that were much on his mind. The years from 1751 to 1757 were a time of relative isolation at Stockbridge, an Indian mission between the Connecticut and Hudson River valleys, and they had been difficult years for Edwards. His removal from the Northampton parish, situated on the Connecticut River, was, effectively, a kind of banishment from the chief inland settlement of the Massachusetts colony to a frontier outpost. His life there proved to be the more uncertain since Stockbridge was an exposed location as the Seven Years War broke out. Once at the mission, moreover, Edwards had to struggle to protect the interests of the colony and the native Indians against agents who sought to aggrandize themselves at the expense of both. Finally, the

[1] I am deeply indebted to Professor Wilson Kimnach for several discussions of these notebooks and the questions raised in analysis of them. His doctoral dissertation on 'The Literary Techniques of Jonathan Edwards', University of Pennsylvania, 1971 (published on demand by University Microfilms, Ann Arbor, Michigan) is basic to understanding how Edwards worked as an author. In addition, I have depended on Professor Kimnach's familiarity with the attempts at analysis of the inks Edwards used in different periods. Of course I bear responsibility for judgements, errors, and oversights. The notebooks are located in the collection of Edwards's manuscripts at Yale University Library as Folder 37.

move from Northampton seems to have initially placed Edwards deeply in debt.

In spite of these unfavourable circumstances – made the more difficult by prolonged poor health – Edwards turned the years of residence at Stockbridge into an extraordinarily productive period. His stature as the foremost theologian of the Reformed tradition to arise in the English-speaking world in the period from the sixteenth through to the eighteenth centuries is based on the treatises written while he was at the Indian mission at the edge of civilization.[2]

First among the projects which Edwards had on his mind and heart to complete as he pondered the invitation from the Trustees of the institution at Princeton was 'a great work, which I call a *History of the Work of Redemption*'.[3] In the spring and summer months of 1739, which fell between the periods of intense revivals under his ministry at Northampton (in the years 1734 through 1735 and 1740 through 1742), Edwards had preached a series of sermons on Isaiah 51:8. The doctrine he framed in plain-style fashion was that 'The Work of Redemption is a work that God carries on from the fall of man to the end of the world'. He conceived of the series along cosmic lines as 'A History of the Work of Redemption'. Sermon series were conventional within his tradition and he had previously made use of the device. He had preached a series in the preceding year, for example, posthumously published as *Charity and Its Fruits* (1852).[4] Another series became reworked and published in the 1740s as *A Treatise Concerning Religious Affections* (1746).[5] Several other series also remain in

---

[2] The major treatises which derive from the Stockbridge period are: *A Careful and Strict Enquiry into the Modern Prevailing Notion, of that Freedom of Will which is supposed to be Essential to Moral Agency, Vertue and Vice, Reward and Punishment, Praise and Blame*, Boston, New England 1754, republished in a critical edition, by Paul Ramsey, as *The Works of Jonathan Edwards*, Volume I, New Haven, Connecticut 1957. *The Great Christian Doctrine of Original Sin Defended*, Boston, New England 1758, republished in a critical edition, by Clyde A. Holbrook, as *The Works of Jonathan Edwards*, Volume 3, New Haven, Connecticut 1970. 'Concerning the End for which God Created the World' and 'The Nature of True Virtue' were published together as *Two Dissertations*, Boston, New England 1765, not yet issued in *The Works of Jonathan Edwards*.

[3] For the letter see Sereno E. Dwight, *The Life of President Edwards*, New York 1830, pp. 568–71.

[4] Edited from the original manuscripts by Tryon Edwards (New York, 1852).

[5] Boston, New England 1746, republished in a critical edition, by John E. Smith, as *The Works of Jonathan Edwards*, Volume 2, New Haven, Connecticut 1959.

manuscript form and seem not to have been intended for print.

Although Edwards had not turned to rework the text of this particular series, the booklets in which he originally wrote out the sermons in 1739 and from which he delivered them do exist. At his death the series (whether in the form of the original booklets or transcribed we do not know) made its way into the hands of the Reverend John Erskine. Erskine, who had frequently corresponded with Edwards and was at that point located in Edinburgh, edited the sermons but little touched their substance, apart from removing transitional material between the individual sermons and adding the biblical texts where citations had been given. In this way *A History of the Work of Redemption* was first published in Edinburgh and London (1774). Subsequently it appeared in Utrecht (1776) and finally went through an American press (New York, 1786).[6]

At least two of the three notebooks in question were made by Edwards for his own use. Each is distinctive physically as well as in terms of content. The most substantial (in terms both of the number of separate entries and the importance of the whole) has a title on the front sheet given to it by Edwards (in part in shorthand): 'History—Work of Redemption. B. I.' Sewn together out of an extraordinary assortment of paper scraps (which are not regular in size or shape), it consists of the front cover and one hundred and twenty-three consecutively numbered pages, beginning with the reverse side of the cover (the back cover is missing). On close inspection, the original notebook seems to have consisted of the initial ninety-one pages, undoubtedly with a back cover. Three separate sections augmented that booklet. Pages 92 through 107 consist of a series of extremely small leaves otherwise largely unused. Pages 108–19 is a bundle of materials, added as a unit, which were a single series of letters. The final four pages conclude the notebook. It is a reasonable conjecture that the addition of the sections weakened the original back cover, resulting in its loss.

[6] Johnson, Thomas H., *The Printed Writings of Jonathan Edwards, 1703–1758; A Bibliography*, Princeton, N.J. 1940, is invaluable for tracing the publication of Edwards's works.

The materials are extremely diverse. Early sheets appear to be printer's proofs from Joseph Bellamy's *True Religion Delineated* (1750)[7] to which Edwards had contributed a preface. Another large number of irregularly shaped pages seem to be trimmings from the legendary fan-papers, a project the women in the Edwards household undertook in the course of the difficult Stockbridge years (by tradition the fans were sold in Boston).[8] Various 'envelopes' and letters were used, as also outdated lists (page 47 is a list of male citizens, conceivably concerned with a church controversy or other public question). The draft of a prayer for Deacon Clark whose health was failing became page 62, and proclamations of marriage intentions were utilized (pages 64 and 71). The most human interest may attach to the second, a certificate executed by Joseph Hawley, the Mayor of Northampton, to the effect that Elihu Parsons and Sarah Edwards had indicated their intentions in 1750. A title page from the 'farewel-Sermon' (1751) (preached at Northampton on 22 June 1750) was appropriated for use.[9]

The bundle consisting of pages 108–19 is constructed from a letter to 'the honourable Andrew Oliver, Esq.' who was the treasurer of the Commissioners for Indian Affairs in Boston and from related correspondence. By means of Captain Timothy Woodbridge, who seems to have been engaged to make the trip to Boston, Edwards requested payment of the 'half-years salary due on the 17 day of this month' (December 1754, page 116). These materials (and the above are a selection only) hold sufficient interest for serious students of Edwards's later life to warrant close inspection. Our attention will return to particular items; for the present it is simply important to establish the physical characteristics of the notebook which shall be identified as Notebook A. (In the course of an inventory of the Edwards material, perhaps the Partridge list, it received the designation 10– on the front cover and the last page.)

The second notebook is rather different. It has a cover with

---

[7] Boston, New England 1750.
[8] See reference in Dwight, op. cit., p. 487.
[9] *A Farewel-Sermon, Preached . . . On June 22, 1750*, Boston, New England, 1751.

title, apparently in Edwards's hand, on both front and rear: 'History of the Work Redemption vol. II' (all in shorthand). The inside covers are left blank. The thirty-two inner pages (numbered by Edwards) are, without exception, taken from a copy of Arnauld's *De la fréquente Communion* (to be precise, pages 449–80). Edwards turned them upside down and made his notations in the original bottom margin, occasionally carrying his writing down the sides of those pages which did not have printed notes there. This we will identify as Notebook B. (A pencilled inventory number 25 is entered on the front and rear covers.)

A third and final notebook, probably also constructed by Edwards, has an outside front and rear cover which seems to be a scrap of wallpaper. An inside cover is blank except for a notation 'Book – 2 – ' (which appears to be in the same hand which numbers the other notebooks 10 and 25 respectively). Otherwise both inside and outside of this second cover, front and back, are blank so that there is no indication in Edwards's hand that it was a part of the 'History of the Work of Redemption' project. There are twenty-one numbered regular pages not previously used, followed by sixteen blank ones. This we will identify as Notebook C.

The contents of the three notebooks are as different as the booklets are in physical characteristics. C is the most coherent and consistent and appears to be one of numerous notebooks Edwards created as reference works, on the basis of his reading and study, to which he might turn as occasion required. On pages neatly divided down the middle, and with lines carefully separating each entry, Edwards compiled notes on the popes, beginning with Victor, the thirteenth Bishop of Rome. The entries concern innovations in ceremonies and practices, and events in the development of the papal office. The last entry is devoted to King Pepin and Pope Stephen II (1775). References make it clear that these are consecutive reading notes from Bower's *History Of Popery*: Volume one (beginning on page 1), Volume two (beginning on page 3), and Volume three (beginning on page 12).[10] A section on

---

[10] Undoubtedly Archibald Bower. The *History* was apparently published in 7 volumes, 1748ff.

pages 16 and following is titled 'of the Worship of Images', which theme underlies the entries on the five concluding pages. Nothing in the text explicitly connects these notes with the *History of Redemption* project. The relevance of the subject matter suggests at least a collateral association with it, however, even if it was compiled without direct reference to that undertaking.

Notebook B is much the shortest, being approximately one-third the content length of C and one-fifth the content length of A. Its entries are jottings, notes an author writes to ensure he will recall a point or a line along which an argument should be developed. There are very few references to other authors: among them one to Stapferus and one to a sermon by Bellamy on Galations 3:24. A few additional references, possibly added later, concern Edwards's own 'Miscellanies', and a sermon he had composed on Luke 9:51.

Notebook A is not only the most extensive, it is also by far the most internally diverse. Many entries are broadly typological – concerned with the clarification of particular Old Testament types and their antitypes. Others are notes on arguments for the approaching end of history; Isaac Newton's philosophy, for example, is proposed as a means for the setting up of Christ's kingdom. Some entries detail particular points to be made in the discussion of incidents from the Old Testament. Still others concern specifically theological arguments, for example, on the nature of the death of Christ. These are all broadly theological materials, that is, they are elaborations of biblical and historical points from the perspective of the theological programme which underlies the project.

Other entries are sets of biblical texts which Edwards marshals under topical headings. There is, for example, a set which 'intimate[s] that the saints in heaven have communion with the church on earth in all that belongs to its prosperity'. The references are largely to the New Testament writings, especially Hebrews, Revelation, and John, but some Old Testament passages are included, mostly from the Psalms. Other entries are short expositions of Scripture texts; for example, Edwards argues that Genesis 5:29 is the 'second prophecy we have in scripture of the salvation of the messiah'.

Sections of varying lengths are also pertinent reading notes from a variety of books. A good example is a series of entries which seems to reflect Edwards's working through Dr Winder's *History of Knowledge,* Volume 2.[11] In this respect parts of Notebook A resemble Notebook C. Other references note sections of Edwards's own works which are relevant to *The Work of Redemption.* Numerous particular entries, for example, refer to the 'Miscellanies', scriptural comments in his great interleaved Bible, and to particular sermons.

Then, there are entries which come under the general heading, 'method'. In these he reflects upon the approach he will take to a particular issue: 'perhaps in the beginning have an introduction in a discourse to prove the Redemption to be the greatest of God's works and the end of all other works of God.' Elsewhere he outlines parts of the proposed work in broad-brush strokes. These reflections extend to themes which will run throughout the whole as well as to controlling images which appear suitable as he reflects on the project. Finally, the title of the treatise concerns him. One version he proposes with different variations at separate points is 'The Scheme and Progress of the Work of Redemption'.

It will be clear from this summary that the three notebooks, especially the one here identified as A, are extremely interesting and valuable for the light they shed on Edwards's reflection about his project. Before entertaining a series of more conjectural questions, there is an issue which can be addressed with some certitude in light of the existence of these booklets. This is the question when and for how long Edwards gave his attention to this project of revising the 1739 sermon series. To be more precise, there is in the aforementioned letter to the Trustees of the College of New Jersey the expression of Edwards's concern that to accept the proffered appointment would deflect him from completing his reworking of the *History of the Work of Redemption.* But is that to be read as a relatively conventional indication of the unexpectedness of the invitation and how disrupting the prospect of accepting it was – or as an indication that Edwards

[11] Apparently an edition of Henry Winder, *A . . . History of the Rise, Progress, Declension, and Revival of Knowledge, Chiefly Religious,* 2nd edition, London 1756.

was in fact deeply committed to a new project and had recently in fact turned to work on it with his customary zeal? The outline of the projected study which he gives to the Trustees will be read in different ways depending upon the answer returned to this question.

The notebooks permit us to establish, in conjunction with certain other material, and with considerable precision, the period of time within which Edwards must have been at work producing these notes. That in turn puts us in a better position to interpret the place of this work in the broader Edwardsian corpus as it took shape in the Stockbridge years.

Different kinds of evidence provide means for us to attempt to date the development of the notebooks. There is strictly internal evidence, namely the limitations inherent in the materials out of which Edwards constructed the booklets. This approach is especially promising with respect to A because it incorporates such a diverse group of materials. It does not help with respect to C, made of otherwise unused paper, or B which utilizes pages from one printed book, a matter which will concern us later. Another approach is to seek to correlate references in the notebooks with other information we have about Edwards. Here his isolation in Stockbridge proves helpful because some correspondence survives, particularly with John Erskine in Scotland, which enables us to determine when he first had particular books available to which reference is made in the notebooks. Finally, analysis of the ink Edwards used, compared with already dated inks, provides another framework.

First we may assume that the consistency of materials and the uniformity of their size in the case of both B and C establish that they were sewn together as booklets prior to his writings on the pages. As a project took definite shape in his plans, Edwards's habits seem to have included this practice. Notebook A represents a rather different matter. One hypothesis would be that he wrote on separate scraps of paper, gathering them into one notebook only after a considerable number had been accumulated. On this hypothesis some of the entries could be placed in the Northampton period. As an example, page 47 appears to be a list of males, headed by Colonel (Timothy) Dwight, which probably was occasioned by some event in the town or the church. Page 62, the petition for prayer for Deacon Clark, also seems to come from that period. The certificate of marriage intention between Simeon Clark of Hadley and Rebeckah Strong of Northampton (page 64) is dated in 1749, and that proclaiming the intentions declared by Elihu Parsons and Sarah Edwards (page 71) was from the next year. Some few pages do directly reflect the Stockbridge years, especially the bundle inserted as pages 108–19. Strictly speaking, then, in terms of this hypothesis, on the basis of the materials out of which Notebook A is made, the *terminus a quo* for beginning notetaking would have to be the late 1740s in Northampton. This would entail the assumption that Notebook A was constructed by Edwards towards the end of the Stockbridge period from incidental notes written over a six or seven-year period.

The other hypothesis, namely that Edwards constructed Notebook A (initially forty-five leaves with covers) before notetaking began, seems the more likely in terms of its physical characteristics. In its present augmented form Notebook A cannot have been constructed before early 1755 (new style). This follows from the bundle of scraps which became pages 108–19. It includes the letter to Andrew Oliver, Esq. This carries the date 20 December 1754. It was presumably taken to Boston and returned, and another scrap addressed to Edwards seems to have come back with it. Page 118, a private letter to Captain Woodbridge, concerns related matters and is dated 4 January 1755. Thus the materials used for construction of Notebook A in its augmented form, indicate that Edwards gave sustained attention to his projected *History of the Work of Redemption* at least as late as the spring months of 1755.

There is quite another means of approach to this issue. Edwards began correspondence with a group of Scottish divines in the early 1740s on the basis of their common interests in the evangelical awakenings on both sides of the Atlantic, interests which eventuated in the 'Concert of Prayer'. John McLaurin of Glasgow seems to have been the first of these correspondents with Edwards, but soon the group widened to include several others. As part of this exchange of letters, Edwards developed a special affinity for one of the younger of the Scotsmen, John Erskine, who first settled near Glasgow, then moved to Culross in 1753 and finally to Edinburgh in 1758.[12] From Edwards's point of view, this was a most worthwhile correspondence, and, indeed, the contact was continued into the third generation, first as Edwards, Jr., took it up and then as it fell to Timothy Dwight (Erskine died at eighty-two in 1803).

After Edwards's death, Erskine was instrumental in publishing some of his works in Britain, including *A History of the Work of Redemption* which he edited from the text of the sermons.[13] But during Edwards's lifetime Erskine's service to him was of a rather different kind. He seems to have made it deliberate policy, one for which Edwards expressed warm appreciation, to send him a steady stream of books. Edwards requested at least some of the particular titles, others Erskine may have thought worthy of his interest. In the study of his great-grandfather Sereno Dwight published the letters Edwards wrote to Erskine (in so far as he possessed them). These letters enable us to approach the question of dating the booklets from another vantage point, namely the content of the references Edwards makes in the notebooks.

In a letter to Erskine dated 7 July 1752, for example, Edwards thanked him for sending Arnauld's *De la fréquente Communion* as part of a packet (apparently dated 11 February 1752) which had arrived that spring. 'Arnauld on frequent communion will not be very profitable to me [Edwards remarked], by reason of my not understanding the French'.[14] This makes it immediately apparent why Edwards was prepared to sacrifice that book for purposes of constructing his notebooks. Another notebook in the Yale collection of Edwards materials was also constructed from Arnauld.[15]

[12] See *Account of the Life and Writings of John Erskine, D.D.* by Sir Henry Moncreiff Wellwood, Edinburgh 1818.

[13] 'The manuscript being entrusted to my care, I have not presumed to make any change in the sentiments or composition. I have, however, taken the liberty to reduce it from the form of sermons, which it originally bore, to that of a continued treatise; . . .' Preface signed by John Erskine, Edinburgh, 29 April 1774.

[14] Dwight, op. cit., p. 496.

[15] Identified as Folder 38 in the Collection of Edwards manuscripts at Yale University Library.

That one was used, it appears, in drafting the treatise on *Original Sin,* and Edwards excised the pages which no longer served his purposes. In any case, this establishes that it would have been impossible for Edwards to have begun Booklet B before the late spring of 1752.

Another letter to Erskine (dated 15 April 1755) makes reference to Edwards's having received, in the spring of 1754, a copy of Merrick's *On Christ the True Vine.*[16] This appears as the first work noted in the course of many references in Notebook A, and relatively near its beginning. References occur on later pages to John McLaurin's posthumous volume – perhaps also sent to Edwards by their mutual friend Erskine.[17] Since this was published in 1755, it seems to require us to conclude that the bulk of Edwards's attention to the *Work of Redemption* project did not come until late in the Stockbridge period. A reference to Thomas Salmon's *Geographical Grammar* in its third edition (1754) argues to a similar conclusion.[18] Thus even if Notebook A, and this seems most unlikely, was sewn together only *after* entries had been made on loose sheets (some of which might have been available in the Northampton years), the inference to be drawn from the *content* of many of the references is that serious work on the notebook could not have been undertaken before the late winter of 1755.

From various references to the Stockbridge period it seems that Edwards's extraordinary literary productivity while there resulted from the intensity with which he concentrated on particular projects at certain periods. *Freedom of the Will* (1754) was drafted, apparently, between the end of November 1752 and mid-April 1753, an accomplishment to which Dwight did not fail to call attention.[19]

The months from July 1754 through January 1755 were a time of severe illness which left Edwards too weak to carry on correspondence; one may plausibly argue that serious writing was certainly out of the question and that extensive reading

---

[16] Dwight, op. cit., p. 545.
[17] See Edwards's reference to his death in Dwight, ibid., p. 546.
[18] Probably an edition of Thomas Salmon, *A New Geographical and Historical Grammar*.
[19] Dwight, op. cit., p. 533. See also, Ramsey, editor, op. cit., p. 7.

and notetaking would have been difficult.[20] Sereno Dwight believed that Edwards used the spring months of 1755 to compose 'The End for which God Created the World' and 'The Nature of True Virtue' (published together post-humously as *Two Dissertations* 1765). In these spring and summer months (1755) Stockbridge was exposed to the threat of raids as warfare proceeded in the interior lands. Dwight believed that Edwards wrote the *Great Christian Doctrine of Original Sin* (1758) in the summer, autumn and winter months of 1756, completing it for the press in May 1757.[21] Thus *possible* periods for beginning *sustained* work on this project might be the fall and winter of 1755, the spring and summer months of 1756, or the summer of 1757. Of course the nature of the notebooks does not require us to envisage that Edwards gave exclusive attention to this one project – although that seems to have been a mode in which he chose to work in this period.

A further consideration is provided by analysis of the ink Edwards used in the notebooks. Ink analysis of these note-books is difficult because such diverse materials were used to construct Notebook A. Working with other notebooks and papers, it appears that the ink used, especially for the later entries in Notebook B, resembles a high gloss type dated in 1757 in connection with the manuscript titled 'Images and Shadows'. The early pages in Notebook A may date from 1755; the later pages use inks which probably come from 1757. In particular the ink of page 111 seems identical to an August 1757 notation relating to a sermon on Nehemiah 1:3f.

The cumulative evidence, then, suggests that Edwards began serious and concerted work on notebooks for this project no earlier than the spring of 1755. It also is clear that he was very much at work on them through the summer of 1757, perhaps even as he received and pondered the invitation from the Trustees of the College of New Jersey. The inference seems warranted that a *History of the Work of Redemption* was the major treatise to which Edwards was directing his energies as the Stockbridge period ended.

[20] See Dwight, ibid., p. 546.
[21] Ibid., p. 556.

If these arguments are accepted certain additional conjectures follow. The powerful treatises composed during the Stockbridge period resemble each other as basically theological parts of Edwards's comprehensive rational scheme. But that scheme was preliminary to a systematic exposition of revealed religion such as was represented by *The Work of Redemption*. The notebooks seem to indicate that in 1757 Edwards was at a transitional point in his career as a theologian, preparing to return to exposition of strictly biblical themes but in a more rationalistic manner than had characterized his earlier sermon-based work. Had the project been completed, it seems likely that the *Work of Redemption* would have synthesized types of Edwardsian interests frequently viewed as antithetical. The transition to Princeton, then, appears to have coincided roughly with the beginnings of a new intellectual stage of his career.

Certain general conclusions seem to be warranted on the basis of these booklets. First, they establish very clearly the kinds of materials Edwards was seeking to use as he thought about reworking into a major treatise a series of sermons preached almost twenty years earlier. There was the attempt, through canvassing such writings as those of Bower, Thomas Salmon and Winder, to reach beyond the chiefly biblical materials which had provided so much of the content and dictated so much of the form of the initial series of sermons. It can only be a subject for speculation to question how much more broadly Edwards might have read for the project if, instead of completing it on the frontier, he had managed to continue its preparation after his removal to the College of New Jersey. At the same time it is clear that he was expending great energies on the strictly biblical questions, working over John Owen on Hebrews, using Synopses of the Old and New Testaments which he possessed, and developing his own great Harmony of the Bible. He was also welcoming and working with whatever recent theological materials were available to him; such as those obtained through the good offices of his Scottish correspondents. His use of Merrick, McLaurin, Doddridge and Bellamy suggests how he positioned himself within the complexion of trans-Atlantic theological discussions in the mid-eighteenth century. Also, not surprisingly, Edwards was thinking of this project in terms of his other writings. There are numerous references to his 'Miscellanies', that storehouse of nuggets which he squirrelled away against his future needs and in which the brilliance of his private intellectual life is displayed. His sermons are frequently referred to and also the 'blank bible'. Finally, there seems to be a reference to the text of *Original Sin,* a further very strong argument for a late dating (in the summer 1757). What this means is that *The Work of Redemption* as it developed synthesized interests, resources, and issues which were vital to him in that productive isolation as the years at Stockbridge drew to a close.

Second, the booklets, and reflection about them, put a context around the passage in the well-known letter to the Trustees of the College of New Jersey. This suggests that the letter should be read quite literally as indicating that Edwards's intellectual energies were becoming centred on *The Work of Redemption,* and that accepting the Trustees' invitation would require him to turn aside from that project in a far more immediate sense than has usually been thought to be the case. This context supports the conclusion that the references Edwards makes to this project are not to be read as part of a conventional disclaimer only. It also suggests that attention should be given to the passage as a summary outline of the proposed work, fuller and more systematically or comprehensively developed than any single comparable passage in the booklets:

> . . . I have had on my mind and heart, (which I long ago began, not with any view to publication), a great work, which I call a *History of the Work of Redemption,* a body of divinity in an entire new method, being thrown into the form of a history; considering the affair of Christian Theology, as the whole of it, in each part, stands in reference to the great work of redemption by Jesus Christ; which I suppose to be, of all others, the grand design of God, and the *summum* and *ultimum* of all the divine operations and decrees; particularly considering all parts of the grand scheme, in their historical order. — The order of their existence, or their being brought forth to view, in the course of divine dispensations, or the wonderful series of successive acts and events; beginning from

eternity, and descending from thence to the great work and successive dispensations of the infinitely wise God, in time, considering the chief events coming to pass in the church of God, and revolutions in the world of mankind, affecting the state of the church and the affair of redemption, which we have an account of in history or prophecy; till at last, we come to the general resurrection, last judgement and consummation of all things; when it shall be said, *It is done. I am Alpha and Omega, the Beginning and the End.* — Concluding my work, with the consideration of that perfect state of things, which shall be finally settled, to last for eternity. — This history will be carried on with respect to all three worlds, heaven, earth and hell; considering the connected, successive events and alterations in each, so far as the scriptures give any light; introducing all parts of divinity in that order which is most scriptural and most natural; a method which appears to me the most beautiful and entertaining, wherein every divine doctrine will appear to the greatest advantage, in the brightest light, in the most striking manner, shewing the admirable contexture and harmony of the whole.[22]

Third and most general, *The Work of Redemption*, whether Edwards would have titled it a 'History' or a 'Scheme of Progress', or given it some other name, was basically a theological programme. It would have been an elaboration of the doctrine of Redemption as the most fundamental definition of the divine relationship to the world, subordinating the doctrine of Creation within Divine Purposes, and setting the true context for the doctrine of Original Sin, which he had brilliantly plumbed. It promised to incorporate basic elements of the English Puritan tradition, such as the emphasis on deep personal piety and the collective construction of redemption, all set forth in an eschatological modality, and to recast them in a yet more universal framework. However isolated in the Indian mission at Stockbridge at the edge of the exposed English colonial frontier, Edwards must, in the last analysis, be appreciated as promising the fullest flowering of the English Reformed theological tradition. But while that promise locates Edwards against, so to speak, the sixteenth and seventeenth century background, no less was he transitional to a

[22] Ibid., pp. 569–70.

nineteenth-century American society which in diverse ways thought to realize his aspirations. By virtue of this location, in time as well as in space, he is a liminal figure standing between two worlds, fully a part of neither. That status is nowhere made more evident than in the modest notebooks he composed at the Indian Mission in Stockbridge as he began to undertake a revision of *A History of the Work of Redemption.*

XIII

The Nature of the Puritan Tradition

RICHARD L. GREAVES

THE major contribution which Geoffrey Nuttall has made to the extensive literature on Anglo-American Puritanism is to set forth with sympathy and understanding the elusive nature of that tradition. Writers of the preceding century tended to stress questions of polity when discussing Puritanism, for most adherents of that tradition proposed altering the established form of episcopalian government. Yet such eminent Puritans as Samuel Ward the diarist, Richard Baxter the theologian, and John Preston the chaplain were not Puritans because of any considerations of polity. Others have delineated the nature of Puritanism in theological terms, the most sophisticated analysis being that of John New.[1] Yet while most Puritans were Calvinists, there were significant exceptions, including the Arminians John Milton and John Goodwin. Simultaneously there were important Calvinists, such as Archbishops John Whitgift and James Ussher, who were not Puritans.

Attempts have also been made to find the key to Puritanism in its doctrine of soteriology, especially as manifested in covenant theology. Perry Miller and Leonard Trinterud, among others, have contributed key studies in this vein.[2] Nevertheless covenant theology is developed by certain Anglican writers, including Ussher, but not (in a meaningful

---

[1] New, J. F. H., *Anglican and Puritan: The Basis of their Opposition, 1558–1640*, 1964.

[2] Miller, P., *The New England Mind: The Seventeenth Century*, 1939; Trinterud, L. J., 'The Origins of Puritanism', in *Church History*, xx (March 1951), 37–57. See McGiffert, M., 'American Puritan Studies in the 1960s', in *William and Mary Quarterly*, 3rd ser., xxvii, January 1970, 36–67.

sense) by some of the Puritans. What the covenant means to a Puritan such as John Goodwin is altogether different from what it means to, and the role it is accorded by, John Owen and Thomas Goodwin.[3] Moreover the covenant is largely a schematic device used by the Puritans to assist them in better understanding the nature of their religious experience, which is accorded primacy of place. Those like Edward Dowden and Douglas Bush who view Puritanism essentially in terms of the doctrine of authority, i.e. the insistence on positive Scriptural precedents, and those like A. S. P. Woodhouse who concentrate on the fellowship of holiness for which those in the Puritan tradition strove, confuse the characteristics or manifestations of Puritanism with its fundamental nature.[4] Clearly something *compelled* them to seek purified congregations or (ultimately) fellowships of visible saints set apart from the world. They adduced Biblical support in this quest, but to regard their position on the necessity for explicit Scriptural sanction as the essence of Puritanism is to overlook the deep-seated spiritual experience which initially motivated them to develop religious societies in keeping with what they believed to be the dicta of the Spirit.

Following clues in seventeenth-century writings, astute attempts have additionally been undertaken to establish a class orientation for Puritanism. The most success here has been achieved by Christopher Hill, who has demonstrated a perceptible tendency for the 'middling sort' of persons, particularly merchants and artisans, to be attracted to Puritanism.[5] What must be ascertained, however, is *what* it was that drew these people to the Puritan way. Thrift, industry, and discipline are often cited as Puritan emphases which appealed to the 'middling sort', but these virtues were certainly preached by Anglican divines as well.[6] In some of his latest work Hill has substantially adopted Nuttall's view of the Puritan tradi-

[3] Greaves, R. L., *John Bunyan*, 1969, ch. 4.

[4] Dowden, E., *Puritan and Anglican: Studies in Literature*, 1900, ch. 1; Bush, D., *English Literature in the Earlier Seventeenth Century, 1600–1660*, Oxford 1945, 7–9; Woodhouse A. S. P., *Puritanism and Liberty*, Chicago 1945, 7–9.

[5] E.g., Hill, C., *Society and Puritanism in Pre-Revolutionary England*, 1964, ch. 4.

[6] Breen, T. H., 'The Non-Existent Controversy: Puritan and Anglican Attitudes to Work and Wealth, 1600–1640', in *Church History*, xxxv, September 1966, 273–87.

tion by calling attention to two significant trends of thought in radical Puritans, namely the conviction of continuous revelation and a reliance on the work of the Holy Spirit within the believer.[7]

A somewhat complementary approach to Hill's has been advocated by Michael Walzer, who argues for a gentry orientation for the Puritan tradition.[8] Based on such statistics as the heavy percentage of gentry among the Marian exiles in the formative period of Puritanism, and on the role accorded to the Puritan gentry in the outbreak of the Civil War by such diverse writers as R. H. Tawney and Hugh Trevor-Roper, there is apparent merit in Walzer's case. Yet Baxter himself reminds us that the majority of the gentry fought against the Roundheads, partly in defence of the Anglican establishment.[9] In any case we are still left with the enigma of what it was in Puritanism that appealed to a significant number of the gentry. Moreover it must also be remembered that Puritanism exerted a pull on such diverse persons as Robert Rich, Earl of Warwick, and William Fiennes, Viscount Saye and Sele, on the one hand, and those faceless persons at the lower end of the social scale whose names appear in the surviving records of Puritan congregations.

The essence of Puritanism is not to be found in matters of polity, theological dogma, principles of authority, or class orientation, but, as Geoffrey Nuttall has shown us,[10] in the deeply spiritual experience which Puritans and many sectaries shared and recognized in others. William Dell expresses this very well: 'The spirituall man judgeth all things, and yet he himself is judged of no man: and he being partaker of the power of God himself, can in some measure discern both the presence and want of it in others, both which he knowes in his own experience.'[11] What this means for the historian, however, is that the nature of Puritanism is elusive, impossible

[7] Hill, C., *The World Turned Upside Down: Radical Ideas during the English Revolution* 1972, 296–7.
[8] Walzer, M., *The Revolution of the Saints: A Study in the Origins of Radical Politics,* Harvard 1965.
[9] Baxter, R., *Reliquiae Baxterianae,* ed. M. Sylvester, 1696, Bk. I, pt. i, 30.
[10] Nuttall, G. F., *The Holy Spirit in Puritan Faith and Experience: The Puritan Spirit,* chs 1 and 10.
[11] Dell, W., *Power from on High, or, the Power of the Holy Ghost,* 1645, sig. A2v.

to define, label, or catalogue with crisp precision, quantitative data, or scientific accuracy. Certain fundamental characteristics may be delineated, but in the end there can be no substitute for a careful immersing in Puritan literature in a quest to grasp what is at root experiential in nature.

At the core of the Puritan experience is an evangelical piety dominated by an essentially emotional searching for a spiritual communion with God, made possible by the inner workings of the Holy Spirit, and achieved with an immediacy that sets it apart from traditional Anglican modes of worship, which are fundamentally sacerdotal in nature.[12] The search for this experience of direct communion is usually undertaken in the context of an understanding of God's relationship with his chosen as established in a covenantal bond. The covenant of grace provides the context within which the Spirit works, and thus a guide for the good thought and feeling which are characteristics of the disposition of a godly soul and mind. Simultaneously the covenant of works represents for the Puritan the rejection of the human element and the total reliance on divine intervention to establish the spiritual bond between man and God. The Puritan experience was not one achieved in unrestrained freedom, though the grace responsible for its nascency was freely bestowed, nor was it a pantheistic communion with nature. The spiritual encounter in fact occurred in such a clearly restricted manner that Robert Middlekauff has remarked that Puritans 'felt what their ideas instructed them to feel'.[13] No Puritan, of course, would have put it so baldly, though a comparison of spiritual diaries reveals such striking similarities that one suspects Middlekauff may be correct in many cases. The Puritans themselves, as Nuttall's work makes abundantly clear, attributed the initiative in establishing the communal experience to God and the unfolding of that encounter to the working of the Spirit. Similarities in experience would therefore be accounted for in the minds of the Puritans by the common author of that

[12] Cf. Maclear, J. F., ' "The Heart of the New England Rent": The Mystical Element in Early Puritan History', in *Mississippi Valley Historical Review*, xlii, March 1956, 623–4.

[13] Middlekauff, R., 'Piety and Intellect in Puritanism', in *William and Mary Quarterly*, 3rd ser., xxii, July 1965, 469; cf. 459. His remark would apply to other faiths also, as, e.g., Catholic communicants at Mass.

experience rather than by a predisposition to conform to certain established norms of piety and conduct.

To posit a spiritual experience as the core of Puritanism is immediately to raise the problem of continuity with other religious movements. This is particularly acute in assessing the relationship between Puritanism and sectarianism, or what has been called the 'underworld of Puritanism'. In many respects the immediacy and character of the Puritan communal experience is shared with the sectaries. The Puritan William Lyford wrote of 'the savour of Christ's knowledge [which] doth import a sensitive experimentall feeling knowledge: such as we have of fire, that it is hot, of honie, that it is sweet, &c.'[14] Likewise the Puritan divine Thomas Goodwin underscored the divine initiative in establishing the personal relationship with God which is the source of religious truth: 'Take your understanding, will, and affections, you shall find all these cannot help your faith in the truth; all that is in us is against this, all that is in us will still under-work all its workings, unless the power of God come with it.'[15] It is precisely this divine initiative in the establishment of the personal, almost mystical encounter which the Quaker Richard Farnworth posits as the basis of his conversion: 'I was made to deny the priests and their way of worship, and deny all that which I had gathered together under them, and wait upon God for teaching, counsel, and direction in all things. . . .'[16] There is, of course, a subtle difference between the encounters of Goodwin and Farnworth for whereas the Quakers rejected the human endeavours and experiences which preceded the advent of the Spirit, Goodwin expected the Spirit to enlighten and make efficacious his understanding, will, and affections. Yet they both shared a deeply personal experience, characterized by an immediacy and favour that left them convinced of the reality of their spiritual communion with God.

The continuity of religious experience which exists between a Richard Baxter on the one hand and a George Fox on the

[14] Lyford, W., *Three Sermons Preached at Sherborne in Dorsetshire*, 1654, pt. ii, 17–18.
[15] *The Works of Thomas Goodwin, D.D.*, ed. J. Nichol, 1861–66, II, 344.
[16] Cited in Nuttall, *Studies in Christian Enthusiasm Illustrated from Early Quakerism*, 42.

other has been appropriately recognized by Nuttall, who views the Quakers as the 'fag end' of Puritanism. The Quakers and the other sectaries are in fact depicted in Nuttall's writings as *radical* Puritans, the very men whom Christopher Hill has shown were striving to establish a new social order. What distinguishes these radical Puritans from their more conservative brethren in Nuttall's mind is not initially the radical nature of their social ideology but their perception of the correct relationship between faith and reason (or Spirit and reason). The extent to which this relationship is bound up with the experience that provides the core of their Puritanism is evident, for example, in this statement of the sectary John Everard:

> But now (saith the Soul) I hear and see, as David saith: The Lord spake it once, and I heard it twice, that God alone doth all; that is I heard it throughly, experimentally, I saw it ratified to my Experience, to me, within me; I heard it first by the Hearing of the Ear, I heard it in my Understanding, but my second Hearing, was my Experience, and seeing by the Eye, Job. 42, 5. believing it and knowing it in my self. . . .[17]

It was the sectarian tendency, as will be shown, to reject the Puritan attempt to establish a close relationship between fiducial and rational experience. It is their tendency to deprecate reason that makes the sectaries more *radical* than other Puritans, but it does not therefore make them 'more' Puritan.

The Puritan juxtaposition of Spirit and reason stopped short of rationalism, for reason without divine assistance was, as Baxter put it, 'dark and asleep'.[18] The intuitive element was clearly essential if the experiential core of his faith was not to be subjected to a negative rationalism that by its nature would have barred elements of trust and personal communion. Simultaneously the Puritan attempt to conjoin the fiducial and the rational provided a basis to refute the more extreme claims of the sectaries, which could and ultimately did lead to radical social formulations. Thus the Puritan Joseph Sedgwick warned:

[17] Everard, J., *Some Gospel Treasures*, 1653, ed. Christopher Sower, 1757, pt. i, 19.
[18] Cited in Nuttall, *Holy Spirit*, 47.

A confident boasting of dictates from above is not sufficient warrant that the doctrine is heavenly. Without better evidence then their bare word, we may modestly suspect that they are nothing but the distempers of a disaffected brain.[19]

There were actually several attempts to examine the sectarian claims from what is essentially a psychological standpoint.[20] The Puritans had to be careful, however, to establish the premise that their rationalism was Biblically oriented, or what Immanuel Bourne called 'Scripture-Reason'.[21] Both theological and epistemological reasons were used to defend this position, but there is a strong likelihood that psychological factors also played a role, at least in some cases. That type of personality which craves rational order could hardly be comfortable with the freer sectarian epistemology, which accounts in part for the frequent conservative charges against libertinism and antinomianism. Sedgwick is a case in point: 'I should be very ill satisfied in an irrational Gospel, and in an opposition betwixt the discovery of God in naturall light and post-revealed truth; for the first is a Divine Revelation.'[22]

Nuttall has demonstrated that the sectaries or 'radical Puritans ... through their reaction alike against dead "notions" and an over strict morality, sought to associate the Holy Spirit less with reason or conscience and more with a spiritual perception analogous to the physical perception of the senses and given in "experience" as a whole'.[23] Here, however, one must tread with care, for not all sectaries were willing to assume the posture of anti-rationalism. John Robotham identified reason with Christ and the Spirit, and the Quakers were concerned with condemning the misuse of reason in religious matters rather than rejecting its use entirely.[24]

[19] Sedgwick, J., A Sermon, Preached at St Marie's in the University of Cambridge May 1st, 1653, 1653, 6.

[20] Casaubon, M., A Treatise Concerning Enthusiasme 1655; (More, H.), Enthusiasmus Triumphatus 1656.

[21] Bourne, I., A Defence and Justification of Ministers Maintenance by Tythes 1659, pt. i, 8.

[22] Sedgwick, Sermon, 20. Puritans tended to be more socially conservative than the sectaries, perhaps because they had a greater stake in the established order.

[23] Nuttall, Holy Spirit, 38.

[24] Ibid., 36; Underwood, T. L., 'The controversy between the Baptists and the Quakers in England 1650–1689: A Theological Elucidation', Ph.D. thesis, University of London 1965, 102ff.

'Reason, like the sun,' suggested William Penn, 'is common to all, and 'tis for want of examining all by the same light and measure that we are not all of the same mind, for all have it to that end, though all do not use it so. . . .'[25] The general thrust of sectarian epistemology, however, stressed that religious truth was specially revealed through grace and faith. In effect it was a mystical, infused knowledge. It gave John Bunyan an intuitive contemporaneity with the events he proclaimed from the pulpit, and that was possible because 'there is put into the soul an understanding enlightened on purpose to know the things of god. . . '.[26]

Whereas the Puritans maintained reason and Spirit in a cognitive tension that was preserved only by recourse to 'Scripture-Reason', the sectaries developed a cognitive dualism in which reason was strictly subordinated but not placed in diametrical opposition to Spirit. Reason was not deprecated but assigned a more restricted sphere of operations than that accorded to it by the Puritans. In effect the respective spheres are the kingdoms which appear so often in sectarian writings, as in this example from a work of John Saltmarsh:

> I may dispute in Christs School, though refused in the School of Tyrannus. And if you will chalenge me in any point of Philosophie, I shall not refuse you there in Logick or Forms of Art. They are forms onely for the wisedom of men, not the wisedom of God. Nor dare I take my discoveries of Christ from Reason, nor seek the glory of him in forms so much belowe him, and fashion the Creator like to the Creature. . . . I allow Learning its place anywhere in the kingdoms of the world, but not in the Kingdom of God.[27]

Walter Cradock, whose character Nuttall has done so much to illumine, makes precisely the same point when he likens human learning to a fire which fulfils its purpose on the hearth but not in the house; 'the use that men make of it, to dress the simpli-

---

[25] *The Witness of William Penn,* ed. F. B. Tolles and E. G. Alderfer, 1957, 191.
[26] Bunyan, J., *Grace Abounding to the Chief of Sinners,* ed. R. Sharrock, Oxford 1962, paragraph 120; *The Doctrine of the Law and Grace Unfolded,* II; *The Miscellaneous Works of John Bunyan,* ed. R. L. Greaves, Oxford 1976, 149.
[27] Saltmarsh, J., *An End of One Controversie,* 1646, 6.

city of the Gospel with it, makes it abominable.'[28] The more
extreme sectaries, such as John Everard and James Parnel,
advocate an almost kenotic experience in which one must
empty oneself of all human reasoning if one is to become a
receptacle of spiritual truth.[29] Most sectaries, however, do not
establish such a blatant antithesis between the spiritual and
the rational.

The elements of continuity and discontinuity between
Puritans and sectaries which Nuttall has demonstrated by
examining the experiential nature of the Puritan tradition and
the epistemological differences which exist within it, can be
further illustrated by studying the increasing radicalization of
the lay spirit. Catholic theologians were substantially correct
in predicting what would happen if the laity were provided
with vernacular versions of the Bible. Men who could read
Scripture could presumably share in the government of the
church, something which was actually put into practice at
Zurich in the 1520s. By the 1540s Englishmen could observe
the results in the congregation of aliens whose minister was
John à Lasco. What some saw encouraged them to propose,
in the *Reformatio Legum Ecclesiasticarum* (1552), the involvement of laymen in ecclesiastical government, both at the
congregational and at the diocesan and provincial levels.[30] The
failure of the Church of England to adopt the proposals paved
the way for the subsequent assertion, in the Elizabethan era
and in the context of a growing Puritan movement, of
presbyterian demands by Thomas Cartwright, Walter Travers,
and their colleagues. Quashed rather effectively by Archbishop
Whitgift and the Court of High Commission, the classical movement lost its organization, but the quest for lay participation
remained unsated. By the time it re-emerged with any strength
in the 1640s, its character was dramatically altered by the
infusion of an Erastian spirit which the more traditional Presbyterians of London did not have the strength to withstand.

[28] Cradock, W., *Divine Drops Distilled from the Fountain of Holy Scripture*, 1650, 225.
Cf. Nuttall, *The Welsh Saints 1640–1660*, ch. 2.
[29] Everard, *Some Gospel Treasures*, pt. i, 133; Parnel, J., *A Tryal of Faith*, 1654, 5; *A
Collection of the Several Writings (of) . . . James Parnel*, 1675, 67.
[30] Spalding, J., 'The Reformatio Legum Ecclesiasticarum of 1552 and the Furthering
of Discipline in England', in *Church History*, xxxix, June 1970, 162–71.

By this point another movement in English religion was making its impact felt. Perhaps most significantly this movement was more conducive to the fundamental religious experience which was the heart of Puritanism, but it was also a movement in which the more radical ideas of the sectaries had a greater opportunity to flourish. This movement was, of course, the congregational way, comprising those whom Nuttall has so aptly called 'visible saints'. Their communal encounter with the divine required them to be separated from the world as a fellowship of believers which was gathered in freedom to live a holy life.[31] Admission to such a fellowship could be obtained only after its members had recognized that the applicant had in fact enjoyed a kindred spiritual encounter with the divine. '*Every one to be* ADMITTED, *gives out some* EXPERIMENTAL *Evidences of the work of* GRACE *upon his* SOUL (*for the* Church *to judge of*) *whereby he* (*or she*) *is* convinced *that he is* regenerate, *and* received *of God*. . . .'[32] John Bunyan allegorized this practice in *The Pilgrim's Progress*: When Christian arrived at the entrance of the stately palace and requested admission, a porter summoned one of the virgins, named Discretion, for a preliminary examination of the visiting traveller. If she approved, he would be introduced to the rest of the family and allowed to recount his spiritual experience.[33]

Puritans such as Thomas Goodwin and John Owen were in accord with the establishment of congregations of visible saints, in which membership required approval of the laity as well as the ministers. It was, however, but a relatively short step from ascertaining the validity of the Puritan experience in others to judging the contents of sermons, and then to proclaiming the message oneself. The same Spirit responsible for the initial personal encounter enabled one, as Dell said, to recognize the moving of the Paraclete in another. The Puritan could agree with this, but he could not take the last step with the sectary (or 'radical Puritan') and affirm the right of the layman to preach if, as the sectary believed, the Spirit had

[31] Nuttall, *Visible Saints*.

[32] Rogers, J., *Ohel or Beth-shemesh. A Tabernacle for the Sun*, 1653, 354.

[33] Bunyan, *The Pilgrim's Progress*, ed. J. B. Wharey and R. Sharrock, 2nd ed., Oxford 1960, 46–55.

called him to that task.[34] Juxtaposing rational and fiducial experience allowed the Puritan to accord an important role to the acquisition of theological training at Oxford or Cambridge preparatory to formal ordination and a subsequent clerical career. For the sectary, however, the immediacy of the spiritual encounter, because it was oft-repeated in time, became the fundamental source of knowledge about timeless truths. The noted sectarian educational reformer John Webster thus queries the Puritan and Anglican clergy:

> Dare you presume to aver that you are Christs Ambassadors, and know not the Message that you should deliver, but have it to frame, and hammer out by your study, cogitations, devices, and the working of your carnal wit, and corrupted Reason? or to scrape and gather up out of this and that Author, Father, Schoolmen, Modern Writers, this and that Expositor, Commentator, and the like? Is this to be made able Ministers . . . of the Spirit?[35]

The sectary did not need to study theology at one of the universities, but at what Francis Rous called the Heavenly University, where the curriculum consisted of the proposal of a right goal, the denial of human wisdom, conformity to God, and conversation with God by diligently attending his school.[36]

Nuttall has traced the English origins of lay preaching to the prophesyings which Patrick Collinson has in turn traced to the 1560s in England. A prophesying centred around Biblical exegesis, but also included an opportunity for exhortation and personal testimony.[37] Because the laity were often allowed to participate, the prophesyings became virtual schools for prophets, for some laymen began to refuse to restrict their views on Scriptural issues to a forum controlled by ordained clergy. By the 1640s lay participation in prophesyings had broadened to include the proclamation of the Gospel,

---

[34] See Greaves, 'The Ordination Controversy and the Spirit of Reform in Puritan England', in JEH, xxi, July 1970, 225–41.

[35] Webster, J., *The Saints Guide*, 1654, Epistle to the Reader.

[36] Rous, F., *Academia Coelestis: The Heavenly University*, 3rd ed., 1702, chs. 6–9.

[37] Nuttall, *Holy Spirit*, 76–7; Collinson, P., *The Elizabethan Puritan Movement*, 1967, 171.

which was a matter of consternation to Anglicans and Puritans alike. Their opposition to lay preaching was likened by the Leveller William Walwyn to the hated economic practice of engrossing.[38] William Hartley borrowed a favourite weapon from the Puritan arsenal and labelled clerical restrictions on lay preaching Popish. Ordained clergy were called on to 'lay down that Prerogative Honour fetcht from Rome, and lay aside that Popish distinction of Clergy and Laity, . . . and rather preach by vertue of Gospel abilities, then humane Letters Pattents'.[39] William Dell suspected that the attempts to stop the lay preachers were undertaken in large measure out of a desire to protect the worldly advantages which the traditional ecclesiastical livings conveyed on the ordained clerics.[40] Ultimately the source of the controversy was the nature of the experience which lay at the core of the Puritan tradition, for the sectary, as Webster explained, believed that a true minister can 'evidence his Calling to be immediately from and by the Spirit of Christ, both by the same Spirit in his own Breast, the power, and authority of the speakings of God in him, and by the Seal of his Ministry, the Conversion, and Confirmation of Souls . . .'.[41]

Apart from the question of religious toleration, probably no other issue sundered the broad Puritan tradition more than the issue of mandatory ordination for preachers. John Fry, who sat in the House of Commons, sarcastically commented that the Presbyterians were in effect carpet-baggers, for it was by the imposition of hands in the ordination ceremony that 'the holy Ghost is conveyed unto them as it was brought out of Scotland in a Cloak-bagg some few years since . . .'.[42] Neither Assemblies of Divines nor universities, Dell argued, could legitimately 'try spirits' and commend ministers to the work of God. Because the Spirit was common to all those who shared the encounter experience, the power of ordination was vested equally in them.[43] Yet even more threatening to

[38] Walwyn, W., *The Compassionate Samaritane*, 1644, 31.
[39] Hartley, W., *The Prerogative Priests Passing-Bell*, 1651, 4.
[40] Dell, *The Tryal of Spirits* 1653, 35.
[41] Webster, *The Saints Guide*, 22.
[42] Fry, J., *The Clergy in Their Colours*, 1650, 47–8.
[43] Dell, *The Tryal of Spirits*, 10; Hartley, *The Prerogative Priests Passing-Bell*, 3.

the established powers was the demand for lay preaching, which the Long Parliament attempted to stop in April 1645. The problem had become acute in the New Model Army, where the Spiritual sword had become almost as mighty in wreaking havoc on the old order as the physical sword. The Parliament's problem was to curtail lay preaching without dampening the spiritual enthusiasm of that magnificent fighting force. An anonymous defender of the Parliament's position determined to find a *via media*: lay preaching was prohibited, but

> you may both pray and speak too in the head of your Companies, Regiments and Armies, you may deliver the piety of your souls, the wel-grounded confidence of your hearts, the valour of your minds, in such Orations, in such Liberties of speech, as may best enspirit the men that follow you, with such a religious and undaunted animation as may render them unconquerable before the proudest enemy. . . .[44]

More than the army was affected by the growing practice of lay preaching, for Thomas Edwards, the gossipy chronicler of sectarian misdeeds, was horrified that Cambridge undergraduates were preaching in their chambers and in the homes of townsfolk, and presumably intended to gather churches.[45] The Scottish Presbyterian Robert Baillie, already frustrated by the Erastianism of the Long Parliament, observed that lay preachers had 'run' to every shire in England.[46] For the conservatives this meant that discipline had broken down, but the sectaries could only have viewed the changing climate as a greater opportunity for the Spirit to expand the sphere of the Gospel.

Indeed, it is at this point that the real impact of the radical challenge to the more conservative Puritans is dramatically seen. The sectarian stress on revelatory experience was fundamentally incompatible with a state church, whether conceived by a Hooker, a Baxter, a Cartwright, or even a Sedgwick.

[44] *The Cleere Sense*, 1645, sig. A2r, 10.
[45] Edwards, T., *Gangraena*, 1646, pt. i, 167.
[46] Baillie, R., *Anabaptism, the Trve Fovntaine of Independency, Antinomy, Brownisme, Familisme*, 1647, sig. A1r.

The Spirit had to be free to work where and when it would, unbound by the fetters of the Erastianism which had characterized the first century of the English Protestant tradition. As long as the experiential core of Puritanism was closely associated with reason, claims for religious liberty could be rejected as pleas for faulty logic and personal fantasies, but when the sectary liberated experience from rational limitations, he became a natural advocate of religious liberty and anti-professionalism.

The attack on the professionals in religion was but one front in a campaign against professionals in all spheres – law, medicine, and education. In this campaign a class orientation of the sectarian message began to emerge, but even here the immediate impression sometimes belies the truth. Nuttall, for example, has shown that an examination of seventy early Quaker missionaries reveals at least thirty yeoman or husbandmen, five gentlemen, four schoolmasters, and two other professional men.[47] Richard Vann's meticulous research has likewise shown that the early Quakers drew their adherents from all classes of society except the two extremes, and that the core of support came from the yeomen and wholesale traders.[48] Unfortunately, similar studies have not, to my knowledge, been undertaken for the Baptists and the more radical element of the Independents. Regardless of the social orientation of the sectaries, their messages were replete with an ideology that, as Christopher Hill has shown, demanded extraordinary social reforms (as the New Testament itself does). At the heart of these proposals is a fundamental anti-professionalism, which in turn derives from the original encounter with the supernatural. Because, however, the Puritans shared this spiritual experience with the sectaries, the question immediately arises as to why one group became vehemently anti-professional and the other did not. The answer lies, as in the case of lay preaching, in the disparate epistemologies of the two groups.

The attack on university professors was almost always a selective one, aimed primarily at those who taught theology,

[47] Nuttall, *Studies in Christian Enthusiasm*, 18–19.
[48] Vann, R. T., *The Social Development of English Quakerism*, Harvard 1969, 71–3.

philosophy, and in some cases classics (because of the 'pagan' content).[49] The experiential basis of the attack is apparent in the Baptist Thomas Collier's confident assertion that many true believers 'who never knew what an Art or Science meant in its form or method in way of School Study, have more natural Philosophy, Logick, Retorick in their heads . . .' than the university-educated clergy.[50] Most sectaries, including William Dell, Walter Cradock, Samuel How, and John Webster, admitted that learning in its appropriate sphere was acceptable.[51] A handful of radicals, however, launched highly anti-intellectual broadsides, such as the Quaker Robert Barclay's proposition that in his natural state man can know nothing correctly.[52] Francis Rous asserted far more than the usual sectarian cognitive dualism when he claimed that new truth, contrary to that presently known, might be discovered in the Heavenly University.[53] In effect he held out the possibility of conflicting bodies of knowledge, or substantive dualism. This is clearly a radical extension of the sectarian belief in continuing revelation. Rarely, a conservative Puritan such as Richard Baxter acknowledged some truth in the sectarian position, thus underscoring the common experience which they shared. 'Experience hath constrained me against my will to know,' wrote Baxter, 'that Reverend Learned Men are imperfect, and know but little as well as I; . . . I perceive that we are all yet in the dark. . . .'[54] The Quakers kept trying to convince Baxter that they had the Light to bring man out of that darkness. The Digger Gerrard Winstanley likewise asserted that a knowledge of the arts enables one to speak methodically of the past and conjecture about the future, but one who has the Light within can truly know.[55]

[49] See Greaves, The Puritan Revolution and Educational Thought: Background for Reform, N. Jersey 1969.
[50] Collier, T., The Pulpit-Guard Routed, 1651, 38.
[51] The Works of William Dell, ed. E. Huntington, 1817, 224; Cradock, W., Glad Tidings from Heaven, 1648, 51, and Divine Drops, 211; How, S., The Sufficiencie of the Spirits Teaching without Humane Learning, 1644, 19–20; Webster, J., The Judgement Set, 1654, 286. Cf. Solt, L. F., 'Anti-Intellectualism in the Puritan Revolution', in Church History, xxiv, December 1956, 306–16.
[55] Barclay, R., Apology for the True Christian Divinity, 1678, 4th proposition.
[53] Rous, Academia Coelestis, 35.
[54] Baxter, op. cit., Bk. I, pt. i, 129.
[55] The Works of Gerrard Winstanley, ed. G. H. Sabine, Cornell, 1941, 224.

There are unmistakable social tones of a revolutionary character in the sectarian message on education. In a pungent passage the Leveller William Walwyn blasted the educated for living off the unlearned, and therefore bestirring their wits when the latter presumed to know as much as they.[56] Winstanley, a vociferous critic of most professionals, struck at the clerical monopoly on theological training because it was the key to ecclesiastical expropriation of landed wealth. The Scripture, he argued, had been written by shepherds, fishermen, and other commoners who shared the immediacy of the divine encounter, but now university-educated clerics were glossing over their plain language in order to deceive the simple and become 'a prey of the poore, and cosens them of the Earth, and of the tenth of their labors'.[57] This sectarian attack on the propertied interests of the clergy met with a counter-offensive, a part of which included satirical doggerel:

> Wee'l down with all the Versities,
>> Where Learning is profest,
> Because they practice and maintain
>> The language of the Beast;
> Wee'l drive the Doctors out of doors,
>> And parts what ere they be:
> Wee'l cry all Arts and Learning down
>> And hey then up go we.[58]

The stringency with which many conservatives retorted to the sectaries is witness to the sting of the latter's attack on the old social order.

The sectarian attack on the professionals (like that of earlier reformers) also embraced the lawyers as a target. John Lilburne believed that if only godliness and true religion could be increased by sound preaching and godly discipline, England would be freed from the necessity of so many lawyers. As the Bible is in English, so, said Lilburne, should all the laws be in English for every layman to read for himself.

---

[56] (Walwyn, W.), *The Power of Love*, 1643, 48.

[57] Winstanley, *Works*, 474–5.

[58] *Rump: Or an Exact Collection of the Choycest Poems and Songs Relating to the Late Times*, 1662, pt. i, 15.

All legal proceedings must likewise be in the vernacular.[59] George Fox urged that the Spirit within be used as the criterion of the laws; they must be 'righteous, just, and equal, according to that of God in the Conscience . . .'.[60] His fellow Quaker Edward Burrough, writing in the stormy days of the Protectorate, was more pessimistic and millenarian: 'The Kingdome of the Beast must [be put] down, and the Princely power of darknesse must be overthrowne, and Lawes, and times, and things, and powers of men shall be overturned, and overturned, till he come to reigne in the earth. . . .'[61] In the meantime, wrote Samuel Chidley (in a tract printed in red ink), any laws which are not in accord with divine law and right reason are void and not binding on English citizens.[62] Winstanley made a special effort to link the lawyers and the clergy as the twin agents of Norman suppression. England, moreover, he depicted as 'a Prison; the variety of subtilties in the Laws preserved by the Sword, are bolts, bars, and doors of the prison; the Lawyers are the Jaylors, and poor men are the prisoners . . .'.[63] Winstanley did not propose the abolition of all law, but wanted only those laws conformable to the principles established by the working of the Spirit, which brings us once again to the experiential basis of the Puritan tradition.

Some of the sectaries had a similar attitude toward medicine, which they wanted reformed but certainly not abolished. Here, more so than in other areas, the link between Spirit-oriented, experiential medicine and developments on the Continent are obvious. The Basle physician Paracelsus linked inner piety and experience as the sources of medical knowledge. In Brussels the nobleman Van Helmont specifically asserted the necessity of divine illumination in the practice of medicine.[64] Their disciple, the English sectarian George

[59] (Lilburne, J.), *Englands Birth-Right Justified*, 1645, 8 and 37.
[60] Fox, G., *A Collection of the Several Books and Writings*, 1657, 27.
[61] Burrough, E., *A Measure of the Times*, 1657, 27.
[62] Chidley S., *A Cry against a Crying Sinne*, 1652, 6.
[63] Winstanley, *Works*, 358, 361, 522. See also Prall, S. E., *The Agitation for Lax Reform during the Puritan Revolution 1640–1660*, Netherlands 1966.
[64] Pagel, W., 'Religious Motives [in the Medical Biology of the XVIIth Century', in *Bulletin of the Institute of the History of Medicine*, iii, February–April 1935, 97–128, 213–31, 265–312; also 'The Religious and Philosophical Aspects of Van Helmont's Science and Medicine', ibid, supplement no. 2 (1944).

Starkey, could say that 'what I write, I write from the Treasury of Experience . . .'. Medical knowledge comes, he averred, only to those who possess a special and divine infusion of knowledge, hence he described himself as 'a Physician created of God and not of the Schools . . .'. His anti-professionalism is evident in his belief that the science of medicine had degenerated into the formality of a profession.[65] The writings of men such as Starkey must have prompted conservatives to redouble their efforts to quash the sectaries and their Spirit-oriented revolutionary proposals.

Goaded on by what they perceived to be the inner working of the Spirit, the sectaries strove for a veritable second revolution in which, at one time or another, virtually every aspect of traditional society was questioned. As the sectaries perceived what the Spirit demanded, the 'movement' (a term which implies an organization which hardly, in fact, existed) radicalized – at least in appearance. Certainly the radical demands are openly expressed, but this appears to be more the result of the collapse of censorship and discipline than of the influx of new ideas. We can profitably borrow Geoffrey Nuttall's analogy of streams which, like the great questions which engage men, sometimes flow underground.[66] The new soil and fresh rain of the 1640s and 1650s altered the volume and colour of the river, but its basic continuity remained. The work of A. G. Dickens and Christopher Hill lends support to this idea. We know about the long river of Lollardy, sometimes apparently underground, extending from the fourteenth century until the days of Elizabeth when, Dickens suggests, it tended to merge with the Puritan tradition.[67] Lollardy represents, at least in part, an anti-clerical, sometimes anti-professional, and distinctly experiential faith, with marked overtones of social criticism. Hill argues that such ideas were present before the 1640s and after the 1650s, when, once again, 'the island of Great Bedlam became the island of Great Britain . . .'.[68]

[65] Starkey, G., *Pyrotechny Asserted and Illustrated*, 1658, 87, and *Natures Explication and Helmont's Vindication*, 1657, 19 and 200.

[66] Nuttall, *Holy Spirit*, 2.

[67] Dickens, A. G., *The English Reformation*, 1964, 36 and *passim*.

[68] Hill, *The World Turned Upside Down*, 21 and 306.

Yet neither the Spirit nor the hope for a new social order died. The river was once again contained, at least in external appearances. New dikes were built by the old order, and most of the Puritans and sectaries settled for a more quiescent manifestation of their faith. The holy war to reform man and his society became but a memory of the past. The new holy war, as John Bunyan's classic makes evident, was one concerned with the struggles of the human spirit, waged within both the individual and the Nonconformist congregations. Puritanism (in both its conservative and radical manifestations) was once again evident as what it had always been – a spiritual pilgrimage rooted in a divine encounter, and characterized by a compulsion 'towards freedom from the corruption in the world around'.[69] The attempts of the 1640s and 1650s had failed to re-order that world and banish corruption, hence the lot of the Nonconformist was once more to concentrate on the inner experience from which all else had sprung. The real dangers of the future came less from the new dikes which the *ancien régime* had constructed than from the growing tendency of traditionalism to harden Nonconformist ways and prompt them to foster a narrow conformity of their own. A movement whose strength derived from its experience-oriented assault on the traditions of England's *ancien régime* was sapped of its very strength as it established norms for that experience and increasingly was accorded social respectability. By the turn of the century most of those in the Puritan tradition had got their perspective 'right' by recognizing that their forbears had misunderstood the Spirit when they tried to turn the world 'upside down'.

---

[69] Nuttall, *The Puritan Spirit*, 11.

XIV

A Bibliography of the Writings of Geoffrey F. Nuttall

1977

———⊸∘⊙∘⊶———

Compiled by
PROFESSOR TAI LIU
NEWARK, DELAWARE, U.S.A.

This bibliography is designed to include Dr Nuttall's books, pamphlets, articles and major reviews. Articles marked with an asterisk are reprinted in *The Puritan Spirit: Essays and Addresses* (London: Epworth Press, 1967).

Dictionary of National Biography: Bartlet, James Vernon (1863–1940).
Dictionnaire d'Histoire et de Géographie Ecclésiastiques: Fox, George.
Encyclopaedia Britannica: Browne, Robert; Calamy, Edmund; Cartwright, Thomas; Charles, Thomas; Emlyn, Thomas; Fox, George; Marshall, Stephen; Owen, John; Powell, Vavasor; Rous, Francis; Simpson, John.
Evangelisches Kirchenlexicon: Independentismus; Kongregationalisten.

1931
*'The Puritan Spirit Through the Ages', *TCHS*, xi, 164–73.

1932
'Cromwell's Toleration', *TCHS*, xi, 280–5.

1933
'Letter written to J. M. Hodgson . . .' [transcribed], *TCHS*, xii, 20–30.
'Was Cromwell an Iconoclast?', *TCHS*, xii, 51–66.

1934
'German Criticism of English Cathedrals' (review of *Geschichte der Kunst* by R. Hamann), *Builder,* 4 May, p. 750.

1935
'Benson Free Church', *TCHS,* xii, 239–40.
'The Lollard Movement after 1384: its Characteristics and Continuity', *TCHS,* xii, 243–50.

1936
*'Towards an Appreciation of Erasmus', *CQ,* xiv, 339–43.
'Dr Johnson and the Nonconformists' (with R. G. Martin and A. G. Matthews), *TCHS,* xii, 330–6.
'The Literary Interests of Nonconformists in the 18th Century' (with A. G. Matthews), *TCHS,* xii, 336–8.

1937
*'Walter Cradock (1606?–1659): The Man and his Message', *TCHS,* xiii, 11–21.
REVIEW
Werdendes Quäkertum, by T. Sippell, *CQ,* xv, 510–11.

1938
Christian Prayer: the theological background (pamphlet).
*'Bishop Pecock and the Lollard Movement', *TCHS,* xiii, 82–6.
*'The Quakers and the Puritans', *CQ,* xvi, 315–20.

1939
Letters of John Pinney 1679–1699 (ed.), London: Oxford University Press.
*'Chartres in May', *CQ,* xvii, 360–2.

1940
'Lyon Turner's *Original Records*: Notes and Identifications (1)', *TCHS,* xiv, 14–24.
'Morgans Hill Congregational Church, Bradford-on-Avon' [transcribed], *TCHS,* xiv, 40–7.

REVIEW
Archbishop Laud, by H. R. Trevor-Roper, *CQ,* xviii, 224.

1941
'History and Church History', *CQ,* xix, 125–31.
'An Eighteenth Century Church Member's Statement of his Experience' [transcribed], *TCHS,* xiv, 94–7.
'Lyon Turner's *Original Records*: Notes and Identifications (2)', *TCHS,* xiv, 112–20.

1942
REVIEWS
Opus Epistolarum Des. Erasmi Roterodami, x, ed. by P. S. Allen, *JTS,* n.s., xliii, 242–3.
Lessons of the Prince of Peace, by C. E. Craven, *CQ,* xx, 181–2.
Rome and the Counter-Reformation in England, by P. Hughes, *CQ,* xx, 364–5.
The Works of Gerrard Winstanley, ed. by G. H. Sabine, *CQ,* xx, 262–3.

1943
'Congregational Commonwealth Incumbents', *TCHS,* xiv, 155–67.
'Lyon Turner's *Original Records*: Notes and Identifications (3)', *TCHS,* xiv, 181–7.
'Reconstruct to Hear the Word!', *CQ,* xxi, 253–6.
'Alexander Gordon's "Obiter Dicta"' [transcribed], *Transactions of Unitarian Historical Society,* viii, 35–8.

1944
'Towards a Theology of the Holy Spirit', *CQ,* xxii, 305–19.
'George Fox and the Rise of Quakerism in the Bishoprick', *Durham University Journal,* xxxvi, 94–7.
'The Early Congregational Conception of the Church', *TCHS,* xiv, 197–204.
'Welbeck Abbey MSS.' [transcribed], *TCHS,* xiv, 218–32.
'Woburn Abbey MSS.' [transcribed], *TCHS,* xiv, 233–4.

1945
The Personality of Richard Baxter (pamphlet), repr. from
Friends' Quarterly Examiner, no. 314, pp. 99–110.

1946
The Holy Spirit in Puritan Faith and Experience, Oxford:
Blackwell, 2nd edn. 1947.
The Early Congregational Conception of the Church (pamphlet),
repr. from *TCHS*, xiv, 197–204.
'Lyon Turner's *Original Records*: Notes and Identifications
(4)', *TCHS*, xv, 41–7.
'The Dating of George Fox's Journey from Launceston to
London in the Autumn of 1656', *Friends' Quarterly Examiner*,
no. 318, pp. 117–21.
'Neave Brayshaw and Quaker History', *JFHS*, xxxviii, 3–6.
'James Grahame's Diary, 1815–1824: Some Extracts about
Friends', *JFHS*, xxxviii, 51–4.

1947
The Holy Spirit and Ourselves, Oxford: Blackwell, 2nd edn.
Epworth Press 1966.
'The Apostolic Ministry' (review of *The Apostolic Ministry*,
ed. by K. E. Kirk), *CQ*, xxv, 109–16.
*' "Unity with the Creation": George Fox and the Hermetic
Philosophy', *Friends' Quarterly*, July, pp. 139–43.

1948
Studies in Christian Enthusiasm Illustrated from Early Quakerism
(pamphlet), Pendle Hill, Wallingford, Pa., U.S.A.
'The Early Congregational Conception of the Ministry and the
Place of Women Within It', *CQ*, xxvi, 153–61.
'The Genius of Congregationalism', *Free Church Chronicle*, n.s.,
iii, pp. 6–7.
*'The Letters of Erasmus' (review of *Opus Epistolarum Des.
Erasmi Roterodami*, xi, ed. by P. S. Allen), Times Literary
Supplement, 10 January.
REVIEWS
The English Clergy and their Organization in the Later Middle Ages,
by A. Hamilton Thomson, *CQ*, xxvi, 81.

The Correspondence of Sir Thomas More, ed. by E. F. Rogers, *CQ*, xxvi, 176.
The Social Structure in Caroline England, by D. Mathew, *Hibbert Journal*, xlvi, 380–1.

1949

*'The Understanding of History and its Application in Theology', Oxford Society for Historical Theology, *Abstract of Proceedings* for the Academic Year 1948–9, pp. 36–42.
'Richard Baxter and the Puritan Movement', in *Heroes of the Faith*, London: Livingstone Press, pp. 20–9.
'MS. Autobiographies at Dr Williams's Library', *TCHS*, xvi, 108–12.
*'Reflections on the Life of William Temple' (review of *William Temple Archbishop of Canterbury: his Life and Letters*, by F. A. Iremonger), *CQ*, xxvii, 37–43.

REVIEW
The Religious Orders in England, i, by D. Knowles, *Hibbert Journal*, xlvii, 196–7.

1950

*'University Sermon', *University of Leeds Review*.
'Spirit of Power and Love: the Biblical Doctrine of the Holy Spirit', *Interpretation*, iv, 24–35.
*'The Principles of Congregationalism in their Historical Setting', *CQ*, xxviii, 301–9; repr. in *Congregationalism: a Statement made to the Faith and Order Commission of the World Council of Churches*, 1951, 2nd impression 1956.
'Richard Baxter's Correspondence: a preliminary survey', *JEH*, i, 85–95.
'The Worcestershire Association: its membership', *JEH*, i, 197–206.
'A Short Account of Some of G.F.'s Sufferings and Imprisonments' [transcribed], *Bulletin of Friends Historical Association*, xxxix, 27–31.
*'John Bunyan through French Eyes' (review of *John Bunyan: l'homme et son oeuvre*, by H. A. Talon), *CQ*, xxviii, 51–4.
'Some Bibliographical Notes and Identifications', *TCHS*, xvi, 154–8.

'A Bibliographical Note', *JFHS*, xlii, 75–9.

REVIEW
Christianity and History, by H. Butterfield, *Reconciliation,* March, pp. 790–1.

1951

The Reality of Heaven, London: Independent Press.
Philip Doddridge 1702–1751: his Contribution to English Religion (ed.), London: Independent Press.
Richard Baxter and Philip Doddridge: a study in a tradition (pamphlet), Friends of Dr William's Library Lecture, London: Oxford University Press.
*'Law and Liberty in Puritanism', *CQ*, xxix, 18–28.
'Richard Baxter: a great divine's continuing influence', *Birmingham Post,* 15 June.
'A Transcript of Richard Baxter's Library Catalogue: a bibliographical note', *JEH*, ii, 207–21.
*'Doddridge's Life and Times', in *Philip Doddridge 1702–1751* pp. 11–31.
*'Philip Doddridge – a Personal Appreciation', in *Philip Doddridge 1702–1751,* pp. 154–63.
'Philip Doddridge's Letters to Samuel Clark' [calendared], *TCHS*, xvi, 204–7.

REVIEWS
The Reformation in England, i, by P. Hughes, *CQ*, xxix, 176–7.
Socinianism in Seventeenth-Century England, by H. J. McLachlan, *JTS*, n.s., ii, 220–3.

1952

Early Quaker Letters from the Swarthmore MSS. to 1660 (calendared, annotated and indexed; typescript, deposited in major libraries).
'Presbyterians and Independents: some movements for unity 300 years ago', *Journal of Presbyterian Historical Society of England,* x, 4–15.
'The Death of Lady Rous, 1656: Richard Baxter's Account' [transcript], *Transactions of Worcestershire Archaeological Society* n.s., xxviii, 4–13.

'A Transcript of Richard Baxter's Library Catalogue (continued)', *JEH*, iii, 74–100.

*'George Fox and his Journal', introduction to George Fox, *Journal* ed. by J. L. Nickalls, Cambridge University Press, 2nd edn. London: Society of Friends, 1976.

'Philip Doddridge's Library', *TCHS*, xvii, 29–31.

1953

'What Is Essential Christianity?' (review of *Essential Christianity*, by W. E. Wilson), *Wayfarer*, xxxii, 52–3.

*'St Bernard of Clairvaux and his Ideal', *CQ*, xxxi, 221–6.

'Richard Baxter's *Apology* (1654): its occasion and composition', *JEH*, iv, 69–76.

'Early Quakerism and Early Primitive Methodism', *Friends' Quarterly*, July, 179–87.

'Ordination Sermons, 1697–1849' [listed], *TCHS*, xvii, 63–8.

REVIEWS

Archbishop Pecham, by D. L. Douie, *CQ*, xxxi, 369–70.

La Pensée de la Réforme, by H. Strohl, *JTS*, n.s., iv, 117–18.

Thomas Becon and the Reformation of the Church of England, by D. S. Bailey, *CQ*, xxxi, 176–7.

Godfrey Goodman Bishop of Gloucester 1583–1656, by G. I. Soden, *JEH*, iv, 236–7.

William Lloyd 1627–1717: bishop, politician, author and prophet, by A. Tindal Hart, *CQ*, xxxi, 268–9.

1954

The Manuscript of the Reliquiae Baxterianae, London: Dr Williams's Library, Occasional Papers, 1.

James Nayler: a fresh approach, Presidential Address to Friends' Historical Society, London: Friends' Historical Society, Supplement 26.

'Christ's Saving Work and the Place of Healing Within It', *For Health and Healing*, November.

*'The Church's Ministry of Suffering', in *Studies in Christian Social Commitment* ed. by J. Ferguson, London: Independent Press.

'The Correspondence of John Lewis, Glasgrug, with Richard

Baxter and with Dr John Ellis, Dolgelley', *Cylchgrawn Cymdeithas Hanes Sir Feirionnydd,* ii, 120–34.

'John Durie's Sponsors' [listed], *TCHS,* xvii, 91.

REVIEWS

Die Amerbachkorrespondenz, iv, ed. by A. Hartmann, *JTS,* n.s., v, 118–21.

Michel Servet, by R. H. Bainton, *Archiv für Reformationsgeschichte,* xlv, 127–9.

The Reformation in England, ii, by P. Hughes, *CQ,* xxxii, 270–271.

The Writings of Robert Harrison and Robert Browne (Elizabethan Nonconformist Texts, ii), ed. by A. Peel and L. H. Carlson, *CQ,* xxxii, 172–3.

Studies in Stuart Wales, by A. H. Dodd, *CQ,* xxxii. 173.

Members of the Long Parliament, by D. Brunton and D. H. Pennington; *Cromwell's Generals,* by M. Ashley, *CQ,* xxxii, 271–2.

William Roby (1766–1830) and the Revival of Independency in the North, by W. G. Robinson, *JTS,* n.s., v. 290–1.

1955

Christ's Saving Work and the Place of Healing Within It (pamphlet), repr. from *For Health and Healing,* November 1954.

The General Body of the Three Denominations: a historical sketch (pamphlet), repr. 1962.

*'The Lord Protector: Reflections on Dr Paul's Life of Oliver Cromwell' (review of *The Lord Protector,* by R. S. Paul), *CQ,* xxxiii, 247–55.

'Early Quakerism in the Netherlands: its wider context', *Bulletin of Friends Historical Association,* xliv, 3–18.

'The MS. of *Reliquiae Baxterianae* (1696)', *JEH,* vi, 73–9.

'Squire Baker of Wattisfield', *TCHS,* xvii, 117–22.

REVIEWS

*A History of the Ecumenical Movement 1517–1948, ed. by R. Rouse and S. C. Neill, *JEH,* vi, 117–21.

The Reformation in England, iii, by P. Hughes; *University Representation in England 1604–1690,* by M. B. Rex; *The New England Mind: the seventeenth century,* by P. Miller, *CQ,* xxxiii, 80–2.

Puritanism and Richard Baxter, by H. Martin, *JEH*, vi, 240–1.
Mr Pepys and Nonconformity, by A. G. Matthews; *Tillotson: a study in seventeenth-century literature*, by L. G. Locke, *CQ*, xxxiii, 276.

1956
*'A Reading of the *Paradiso*', *CQ*, xxxiv, 47–52.
'Notes on Richard Farnworth', *JFHS*, xlviii, 79–84.
'Stepney Meeting: the Pioneers', *TCHS*, xviii, 17–22.

REVIEWS
The Religious Orders in England, ii, by D. Knowles, *CQ*, xxxiv, 79–80.
The Restoration of Charles II, by G. Davies, *CQ*, xxxiv, 273–4.
Old Priest and New Presbyter, by N. Sykes; *History of the Moravian Church*, by E. Langton, *CQ*, xxxiv, 365–7.

1957
Visible Saints: the Congregational Way, 1640–1660, Oxford: Blackwell.
The Welsh Saints 1640–1660: Walter Cradock, Vavasor Powell, Morgan Llwyd, Cardiff: University of Wales Press.
*'The Heirs of Heaven', Drew Lecture on Immortality, *CQ*, xxxv, 9–20.

REVIEWS
An Historian's Approach to Religion, by A. Toynbee, *Hibbert Journal*, lv, 295–7.
Free Church Unity: History of the Free Church Council Movement 1896–1941, by E. K. H. Jordan; *Free Churchmanship in England 1870–1941: with special reference to Congregationalism*, by J. W. Grant, *JEH*, viii, 120–2.

1958
Christian Pacifism in History, Oxford: Blackwell, 2nd edn. 1971.
'New Light on a Medieval Christian Pacifist' (review of *The Political and Social Doctrines of the Unity of Czech Brethren in the Fifteenth and Early Sixteenth Centuries*, by P. Brock), *Friend*, 28 March.

REVIEWS

The Holy Pretence: a study in Christianity and Reason of State from William Perkins to John Winthrop, by G. L. Mosse; *Puritanism in the Period of the Great Persecution, 1660–1688*, by G. R. Cragg, *JEH*, ix, 110–12.

White Kennett 1660–1728, Bishop of Peterborough: a study in political and ecclesiastical history of the early eighteenth century, by G. V. Bennett, *JEH*, ix, 132.

Prince Charles's Puritan Chaplain, by I. Morgan; *The Moral Revolution of 1688*, by D. W. R. Bahlman, *JEH*, ix, 273–5.

Light and Enlightenment: a study of the Cambridge Platonists and the Dutch Arminians, by R. L. Colie, *JTS*, n.s., ix, 189–90.

1959

'Luther's Doctrine of the Two Kingdoms', *Christus Victor*, no. 105, pp. 6–7.

REVIEWS

Die Amerbachkorrespondenz, v, ed. by A. Hartmann, *JTS*, n.s., x, 446–8.

The Answer to the Whole Set of Questions of the Celebrated Mr William Apollonius . . . By John Norton, trans. by D. Horton; *Science and Religion in Seventeenth-Century England*, by R. S. Westfall, *JEH*, x, 130–2.

The Baptist Union: a short history, by E. A. Payne, *JEH*, x, 268.

1960

*Christian Love Manifested in History (pamphlet), repr. from *Reconciliation Quarterly*, no. 108, 13–22; also in German in *Versöhnung und Friede* (Zeitschrift des Deutschen Versöhnungs-bund), January, pp. 11–18.

The Beginnings of Nonconformity 1660–1665: a checklist (ed.), London: Dr Williams's Library.

'The Baptist Western Association, 1653–1658', *JEH*, xi, 213–218.

'Unitarian Theology: a criticism' (review of *Essays in Unitarian Theology: a symposium*, ed. by K. Twinn), *Inquirer*, 16 April, pp. 512–13.

REVIEWS

Le Livre du Recteur de l'Académie de Genève (1559–1878), i, ed.
by S. Stelling-Michaud, *JEH*, xi, 136.
George Fox and the Quakers, by H. van Etten, *JEH*, xi, 271.

1961

'George Lewis at John Pye Smith, 1819' [transcribed],
Cofiadur, no. 31, p. 42.
'Rhai Cymry a danysgrifodd at gartref George Whitefield ar
gyfer plant amddifaid yn Georgia' [transcribed], *Cofiadur,* no.
31, pp. 43–4.

REVIEWS

Three Treatises concerning Wales, by John Penry, *JEH*, xii, 130–1.
*The Puritans and the Church Courts in the Diocese of York, 1560–
1642,* by R. A. Marchant; *Post-Reformation Catholicism in East
Yorkshire, 1538–1790,* by H. Aveling, *JEH*, xii, 249–50.

1962

Better Than Life: the Lovingkindness of God, London: Independent
Press.
From Uniformity to Unity 1662–1962 (ed., with Owen Chadwick),
London: S.P.C.K.
'The First Nonconformists', in *From Uniformity to Unity 1662–
1962,* pp. 151–87.
*'The Influence of Arminianism in England', in *Man's Faith
and Freedom: the theological influence of Jacob Arminius,* ed. by
G. O. McCulloh, New York and Nashville: Abingdon Press,
pp. 46–63.
'Lyon Turner's *Original Records*: Notes and Identifications
(5)', *TCHS*, xix, 160–4.

REVIEWS

Five Pastorals, abridged and ed. by T. Wood, *JTS,* n.s., xiii,
213.
The Spirit of Protestantism, by R. McA. Brown; *The Protestant
Mind of the English Reformation 1570–1640,* by C. H. George
and K. George, *JTS,* n.s., xiii, 476–8.
*Two Early Political Associations: the Quakers and the Dissenting
Deputies in the Age of Sir Robert Walpole,* by N. C. Hunt, *JEH,*
xiii, 109–11.

1963

'Our Freedom as Christians: its ground and limits', *Reconciliation Quarterly*, no. 122, pp. 367–73.

'Dissenting Churches in Kent before 1700', *JEH*, xiv, 175–89.

REVIEWS

Walter Travers: Paragon of Elizabethan Puritanism, by S. J. Knox; *George Abbot: the Unwanted Archbishop 1562–1633*, by P. A. Welsby; *Die linke Flügel der Reformation: Glaubenszeugnisse der Täufer, Spiritualisten, Schwärmer und Antitrinitarier*, ed. by H. Fast; *Der Protestantismus des 17. Jahrhunderts*, ed. by W. Zeller, *JTS*, n.s., xiv, 540–2.

The New England Company 1649–1776: missionary society to the Indians, by W. Kellaway; *Congregationalism in England 1662–1962*, by R. T. Jones, *JEH*, xiv, 108–11.

The Career of John Cotton: Puritanism and the American Experience, by Larzer Ziff; *Nonconformity in Exeter 1650–1875*, by A. Brockett, *JEH*, xiv, 236–41.

Christian Thought from Erasmus to Berdyaev, by M. Spinka, *JEH*, xiv, 269.

1964

Contributor to *A Declaration of Faith*, London: Congregational Church in England and Wales, 2nd edn. 1967.

**'The Justification of War – how the Church's teaching has changed', in *Choose Your Weapons* ed. by D. Walker, London: Fellowship of Reconciliation.

'The Emergence of Nonconformity', in *The Beginnings of Nonconformity*, by G. F. Nuttall and others, Hibbert Lectures, London: James Clarke.

'A Note on the Ejected Ministers in Wales', *TCHS*, xix, 280.

'Relations between Presbyterians and Congregationalists in England', in *Studies in the Puritan Tradition* (Congregational Historical Society and Presbyterian Historical Society of England Joint Supplement), pp. 1–7.

'The Lamb's War' (review of *The Quakers in Puritan England*, by H. Barbour), *Quaker History*, liii, 113–15.

**'A. G. Matthews', *TCHS*, xix, 176–8.

REVIEWS

The Layman in Christian History: a project of the Department on the Laity of the World Council of Churches, ed. by S. C. Neill and H.-R. Weber; *Heirs of the Reformation,* by J. de Senarclens, *JTS,* n.s., xv, 458–63.

The Radical Reformation, by G. H. Williams, *JEH,* xv, 113–116.

1965

Richard Baxter (Leaders of Religion), London: Nelson (later A. and C. Black).

Howel Harris 1714–1773: the Last Enthusiast, Cardiff: University of Wales Press.

'Dante and Hus', *London Quarterly and Holborn Review,* 6th ser., xxxiv, 291–5.

'MS. Sermons and Letters by John Owen and others in the Library of New College, London' [listed], *TCHS,* xx, 43–4.

'Handlist of the Works of John Owen, with locations', *TCHS,* xx, 45–6.

'Northamptonshire and *The Modern Question*; a turning-point in eighteenth-century Dissent', *JTS,* n.s., xvi, 101–23.

REVIEWS

An Apologeticall Narration, ed. by R. S. Paul, *JTS,* n.s., xvi, 253–4.

Voluntary Religious Societies 1520–1799, by F. W. B. Bullock, *JEH,* xvi, 107.

Society and Puritanism in Pre-Revolutionary England, by C. Hill, *JEH,* xvi, 247–8.

The Pentecostal Movement: its origin, development and distinctive character, by N. Bloch-Huell, *JEH,* xvi, 256–7.

1966

'Philip Doddridge and "the Care of all the Churches": a study in oversight', Presidential Address to Congregational Historical Society, *TCHS,* xx, 126–38.

'John Wesley Presides' (review of *History of the Methodist Church in Great Britain* i, ed. by R. Davies and G. Rupp), *London Quarterly and Holborn Review* 6th ser., xxxv, 200–4.

REVIEWS

The English Presbyterians and the Stuart Restoration, 1648–1663, by G. R. Abernathy, Jr., *JEH,* xvii, 276.
Pietismus-Studien, i, by H. Weigelt, *JTS,* n.s., xvii, 516–17.

1967
The Puritan Spirit: essays and addresses, London: Epworth Press.
Congregationalists and Creeds (pamphlet), W. M. Llewelyn Lecture, London: Epworth Press.
' "Queen Anne's Dead!": an unusual funeral sermon', *TCHS,* xx, 200–1.

REVIEWS

The Heart Prepared: grace and conversion in Puritan spirituality, by N. Pettit, *Church Quarterly Review,* clxviii, 373.
The Fifth Monarchy Men, by P. G. Rogers, *JEH,* xviii, 270.
A History of the Baptists, ed. by R. G. Torbet; *Cumulative Index of the Transactions of the Baptist Historical Society,* ed. by D. C. Sparkes, *JEH,* xviii, 281.
The Rise of Evangelical Pietism, by F. E. Stoeffler; *Essays in Modern English Church History in memory of Norman Sykes,* ed. by G. V. Bennett and J. D. Walsh, *JTS,* n.s., xviii, 277–9.
Milton and the Christian Tradition, by C. A. Patrides, *JTS,* n.s., xviii, 525–8.
Daniel Waterland 1683–1740: a study in eighteenth-century orthodoxy, by R. T. Holtby, *Theology,* lxx, 375–6.

1968
'The Concept of the Chosen People in Christianity', *Common Ground,* xxii, 6–13.
'Calvinism in Free Church History', *BQ,* xxii, 418–28.
'The Beginnings of Old Meeting, Bedworth', *TCHS,* xx, 255–64.
'John Ash and the Pershore Church', *BQ,* xxii, 271–6.
'The Students of Trevecca College, 1768–1791', *Transactions of the Honourable Society of Cymmrodorion,* Session 1967, pp. 249–77.
'Charles Gore and the Solidarity of the Faith', Charles Gore Memorial Lecture, Westminster Abbey, *Church Quarterly,* i, 52–64.

REVIEWS

Zwanzig Jahre Melanchthonstudium: Sechs Literaturberichte (1945–1965), by P. Fraenkel and M. Greschat, *JTS*, n.s., xix, 680.

The Elizabethan Puritan Movement, by P. Collinson, *Kingsman* (magazine of the Theological Department of King's College, London), 1967–8, pp. 52–5.

Newcastle upon Tyne and the Puritan Revolution: a study of the Civil War in North England, by R. Howell, *JEH,* xix, 129–130.

Conscience: Dictator or Guide? A study in seventeenth-century Protestant moral theology, by K. T. Kelly, *Ampleforth Journal,* lxxiii, 87–8.

The Church and Christian Union, by S. Neill, *Church Quarterly,* i, 174–7.

1969

To the Refreshing of the Children of Light (pamphlet), Pendle Hill, Wallingford, Pa., U.S.A.

The Faith of Dante Alighieri, Sir D. Owen Evans Memorial Lectures, Aberystwyth, London: S.P.C.K.

Doddridge Intercalation: Interim Intercalated List of the Correspondence of Rev. Philip Doddridge (with A. S. Bell), typescript: London, Historical MSS. Commission.

The Significance of Trevecca College, 1768–91 (pamphlet), Cheshunt College, Cambridge, Bicentenary Lecture, London: Epworth Press.

'The Logic of Discipleship' (review of *Gewaltlosigkeit im Täufertum,* by C. Bauman), *Friends' Quarterly,* xvi, 294–300.

'Two Italian Cities', *Friends' Quarterly,* xvi, 375–8.

REVIEWS

Ecumenism: Theology and History, by B. Lampert, trans. by L. C. Sheppard, *JEH,* xx, 164–5.

Colloqvivm Erasmiavm (Actes du Colloque International réuni à Mons du 26 au 29 Octobre 1969 à l'occasion du cinquième centenaire de la naissance d'Erasme), *JEH,* xx, 346–7.

The Spirit of the Counter-Reformation, by H. O. Evennett; *Le Livre du Recteur de l'Académie de Genève (1559–1878),* ii, ed. by S. Stelling-Michaud; *Reason and Authority: the thought of William Chillingworth,* by R. R. Orr, *JEH,* xx, 178–80.

The Antinomian Controversy, 1636–1638: a documentary history, ed. by D. D. Hall, *JEH,* xx, 357–9.

James Ussher Archbishop of Armagh, by R. B. Knox; *Skepsis und Naturrecht in der Theologie Jeremy Taylors 1613–1667,* by M. Greiffenhagen, *JTS,* n.s., xx, 352–3.

Isaac Backus on Church, State, and Calvinism: Pamphlets, 1754–1789, ed. by W. G. McLoughlin; *Der Pietismus als Frage an die Gegenwart,* by P. Schicketanz; *Erweckungsbewegung und konfessionelles Luthertum im 19. Jahrhundert untersucht an Karl v. Rahner,* by H. Weigelt, *JTS,* n.s., xx, 694–7.

1970
'Shod with the Gospel of Peace', Sermon preached at St Martin-in-the-Field, *Methodist Magazine,* n.s., no. 3.

'Faith, Theology and Training for the Ministry', *Theology,* no. 600, pp. 264–71.

'The First Quakers', *History of the English Speaking Peoples,* no. 51, pp. 1634–9.

'Nonconformists in Parliament 1661–1689' (review of *Dissent and Parliamentary Politics in England 1661–1689: a study in the perpetuation and tempering of Parliamentarianism,* by D. R. Lacey), *TCHS,* xx, 334–40.

'Dr R. T. Jenkins' Articles in the *Dictionary of Welsh Biography*' [listed], *Journal of Welsh Biography,* x, 178–93.

REVIEWS

Dutch Anabaptism: origin, spread, life and thought (1450–1600), by C. Krahn; *John Cotton on the Churches of New England,* ed. by L. Ziff, *JTS,* n.s., xxi, 246–8.

The Work of William Perkins, ed. by I. Breward, *Churchman,* lxxxiv, 296–7.

Christian Ethicks, by Thomas Traherne, ed. by C. L. Marks and G. R. Gaffey, *JEH,* xxi, 269–70.

Quakers and Politics: Pennsylvania, 1681–1726, by G. B. Nash, *JEH,* xxi, 87–8.

1971
'Violence: some perspectives', *Friend,* 19 February.

'Cross-reference Table between LB and Opus Epistolarum', *Erasmus in English,* no. 3, pp. 18–23.

'The English Martyrs 1535–1680: a statistical review', *JEH*, xxii, 191–7.

'Juan de Valdés: fresh light on "A Quaker Forerunner"', *Friends' Quarterly*, xvii, 116–22.

'Puritans and Nonconformists round Puttenham and Wanborough, 1640–90', *Papers read to the Puttenham and Wanborough History Society*, 1970–1 session, pp. 15–23.

'Assembly and Association in Dissent, 1689–1831', in *Studies in Church History*, vii: *Councils and Assemblies,* ed. by G. J. Cuming and D. Baker, Cambridge University Press, pp. 289–309.

'The Ancient Merchants' Lecture, the Bromley Charity, and the Hodgson Trust', *Free Church Chronicle,* xxvi, 3–5.

'The First Seventy Years: from the origins to Robert Robinson, 1721–1790', in *St Andrew's Street Baptist Church Cambridge: three historical lectures,* ed. by K. A. C. Parsons, Cambridge, pp. 1–18.

'The Letter-Book of John Davies (1731–1795)', *BQ,* xxiv, 58–64.

'Autograph Letters Collected by Thomas Raffles' [listed], *TCHS,* xxi, 21–5.

'Fairbairn, Mansfield and Peake' (review of *Arthur Samuel Peake: a biography,* by J. T. Wilkinson), *Mansfield College Magazine,* no. 174, pp. 3–5.

REVIEWS

The Holy Spirit in the Theology of Martin Bucer, by W. P. Stephens, *Theology,* no. 610, pp. 169–70.

The Puritan Lectureships: the politics of religious dissent 1560– 1662, by P. S. Seaver, *TCHS,* xxi, 25.

Godly Rule: politics and religion, 1603–60, by W. M. Lamont; *Pulpit in Parliament: Puritanism during the English Civil Wars, 1640–1648,* by J. F. Wilson, *JEH,* xxii, 81–2.

The Pauline Renaissance in England: Puritanism and the Bible, by J. S. Coolidge; *The Half-way Covenant: church-membership in Puritan New England,* by R. G. Pope; *John Wilkins 1614–1672: an intellectual biography,* by B. J. Shapiro; *La Tradition au XVIIe Siècle en France et en Angleterre,* by G. Tavard, *JTS,* n.s., xxii, 284–91.

Calvinism and the Amyraut Heresy: Protestant scholasticism and humanism in seventeenth-century France, by B. G. Armstrong, *JEH,* xxii, 153–4.

George Whitefield: the life and times of the great evangelist of the eighteenth-century revival, i, by A. A. Dallimore, *English Historical Review,* lxxxvi, 850–1.

1972

Christianity and Violence (pamphlet), Frederick Denison Maurice Lectures, King's College, London, Arrington, Herts: Priory Press.

Contributor to *Violence and Oppression: a Quaker response,* London: Friends Peace and International Relations Committee.

'The English Separatist Tradition' (review of *The English Separatist Tradition* by B. R. White), *BQ,* xxiv, 200–4.

'Rowland Hill and the Rodborough Connexion, 1771–1833', *TCHS,* xxi, 69–73.

REVIEWS

Geschichte des Konzils von Trient, iii, by H. Jedin, *JEH,* xxiii, 186–8.

The Geneva Bible: a facsimile of the 1560 edition, ed. by L. E. Berry, *Religious Studies,* viii, 190.

The Family Life of Ralph Josselin, a Seventeenth-century Clergyman: an essay in historical anthropology, by A. Macfarlane, *JEH,* xxiii, 376–7.

Atheismus und Orthodoxie: Analysen und Modelle christlicher Apologetik im 17. Jahrhundert, by H.-M. Barth, *JTS,* n.s., xxiii. 521–4.

An Inventory of the Records of the Particular (Congregational) Churches of Massachusetts Gathered 1620–1805, ed. by H. F. Wortley, *JTS,* n.s., xxiii, 292–3.

1973

'Love's Constraint', Sermon preached before University of Oxford, *Theology,* no. 636, pp. 291–7.

' "Overcoming the World": the early Quaker programme', Presidential Address to Ecclesiastical History Society, in *Studies in Church History,* x: *Sanctity and Secularity: the Church and the World,* ed. by D. Baker, Oxford: Blackwell, pp. 145–64.

'Chandler, Doddridge and the Archbishop: a study in eighteenth-century ecumenism', Presidential Address to United Reformed Church History Society, *Journal of United Reformed Church History Society*, i, 42–56.

'Tanysgrifwyr Cymreig i *Family Expositor* y Dr Philip Doddridge' [listed], *Cofiadur*, no. 38, pp. 61–3.

'Henry Cadbury: the man and the scholar', *Friends' Quarterly*, xviii, 147–50.

REVIEWS

Storia dell'Anabattismo dalle Origini a Münster (1525–1535), by U. Gastaldi, *JEH*, xxiv, 418–21.

Common Places of Martin Bucer, trans. and ed. by D. F. Wright, *Theology*, no. 639, pp. 490–1.

Mysticism and Dissent: religious ideology and social protest in the sixteenth century, by S. E. Ozment; *Benito Arias Montano (1527–1598)*, by B. Rekers, *JTS*, n.s., xxiv, 613–15.

Puritanism in Northwest England: a regional study of the diocese of Chester to 1642, by R. C. Richardson, *JEH*, xxiv, 86–8.

The Interregnum: the quest for settlement 1646–1660, ed. by G. E. Aylmer, *JEH*, xxiv, 328–9.

The Fifth Monarchy Men: a study in seventeenth-century English millenarianism, by B. S. Capp; *New England Dissent 1630–1833: the Baptists and the Separation of Church and State*, by W. G. McLoughlin, *JTS*, n.s., xxiv, 309–19.

Pacifism in Europe to 1914, by P. Brock, *Quaker History*, lxii, 53–5.

1974

'Paradise Shared', *Reform*, November, p. 18.

'Abbess Roding Church 1698–1790' [transcribed], *Journal of United Reformed Church History Society*, i, 112–18.

REVIEWS

The Learned Doctor William Ames: Dutch Background of English and American Puritanism, by K. L. Sprunger, *Heythrop Journal*, xv, 224–5.

Arminius: a study in the Dutch Reformation, by C. Bangs, *Religious Studies*, x, 253–5.

The Puritan Experience, by O. C. Watkins, *English Historical Review*, lxxxix, 176.

The Faithful Shepherd: a history of the New England ministry in the seventeenth century, by D. D. Hall, *JTS,* n.s., xxv, 217–20.
Bright Essence: studies in Milton's theology, by W. B. Hunter, C. A. Patrides and J. H. Adamson, *Religious Studies,* x, 127–128.
The Shattered Synthesis: New England Puritanism before the Great Awakening, by J. W. Jones; *Nicholaus Ludwig Count von Zinzendorf, Bishop of the Church of the Moravian Brethren: Nine Public Lectures,* trans. and ed. by G. W. Forell, *JTS,* n.s., xxv, 542–4.
Victorian Nonconformity ed. by J. Briggs and I. Sellers, *BQ* xxv, 334–5.

1975

'The Meaning of Messiahship', trans. from *Y Brenin Alltud* by P. Davies, *Expository Times,* lxxxvii, 85–7.
'Puritan and Quaker Mysticism', *Theology,* no. 664, pp. 518–31.
'A Puritan Prayer-Journal 1651–1663', in *Der Pietismus in Gestalten und Wirkungen: Martin Schmidt zum 65. Geburtstag,* ed. by H. Bornkamm, F. Heyer, A. Schindler, *Arbeiten zur Geschichte des Pietismus* xiv, Bielefeld: Luther-Verlag, pp. 343–54.
'John Horne of Lynn', in *Christian Spirituality: essays in honour of Gordon Rupp,* ed. by P. Brooks, London: S.C.M. Press, pp. 231–47.
'Association Records of the Particular Baptists' (review of *Association Records of the Particular Baptists of England, Wales and Ireland to 1660,* ed. by B. R. White), *BQ,* xxvi, 14–25.

REVIEWS
Y Brenin Alltud, by P. Davies, *Diwinyddiaeth,* xxvi, 56–7.
The Correspondence of Erasmus: Letters 1 to 141: 1484–1500, trans. by R. A. B. Mynors and D. F. S. Thomson, annotated by W. K. Ferguson, Collected Works of Erasmus, i, *JEH,* xxvi, 402–3.
L'Erasmianus sive Ciceronianus d'Etienne Dolet (1535), ed. by E. V. Telle; *Erasmus von Rotterdam und die Einleitungsschriften zum Neuen Testament: formale Struktuern und theologischer Sinn,* by G. B. Winkler, *JEH,* xxvi, 92–4.
Calvin und Basel in den Jahren 1552–1556, by U. Plath, *JEH,* xxvi, 185–7.

Ecclesiologia ed Etica Politica in Giovanni Calvino, by V. Vinay, *JEH,* xxvi, 201.

Cases of Conscience: alternatives open to Recusants and Puritans under Elizabeth I and James I, by E. Rose, *Reconciliation Quarterly,* n.s., v, 44.

The Covenant Sealed: the development of Puritan sacramental theology in Old and New England, by E. B. Holifield, *Theology,* no. 662, pp. 441–2.

The Rota Pamphlets (facsimile reprints), *Theology,* no. 657, pp. 153–4.

The Rump Parliament 1648–1653, by B. Worden, *Heythrop Journal,* xvi, 336–8.

Contrasting Communities: English villages in the Sixteenth and Seventeenth Centuries, by M. Spufford, *Journal of United Reformed Church History Society,* i, 154–5.

The Lives of Philip Henry and Matthew Henry (reprints), *Journal of United Reformed Church History Society,* i, 180–1.

1976

'Church Life in Bunyan's Bedfordshire', *BQ,* xxvi, 305–13.

'George Whitefield's "Curate": Gloucestershire Dissent and the Evangelical Revival', *JEH,* xxvii, 369–86.

REVIEWS

The Correspondence of Erasmus: Letters 142 to 297: 1501 to 1514, trans. by R. A. B. Mynors and D. F. S. Thomson, annotated by W. K. Ferguson, Collected Works of Erasmus, ii; *Inquisitio de Fide: a colloquy by Desiderus Erasmus Roterodamus 1524,* ed. by C. R. Thompson, *JEH,* xxvii, 198–200.

Welsh Baptist Studies, ed. M. John, *Seren Cymru,* 30 August, p. 4.

1977

New College, London, and its Library (pamphlet), London: Dr. Williams's Trust.

'Cambridge Nonconformity 1660–1710: from Holcroft to Hussey', *Journal of United Reformed Church History Society,* i, 241–58.

'Questions and Answers: an eighteenth-century correspondence', *BQ,* xxvii, 83–90.

BIBLIOGRAPHY

REVIEWS

Thomas Hooker: Writings in England and Holland, 1626–1633, ed. by G. H. Williams, N. Pettit, W. Herget, S. Bush, Jr., *JEH* xxviii, 85–6.
Worship and Theology in England from Andrewes to Baxter and Fox, 1603–1690 by H. Davies, *JTS* n.s., xxviii, 236–41.

INDEX

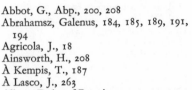